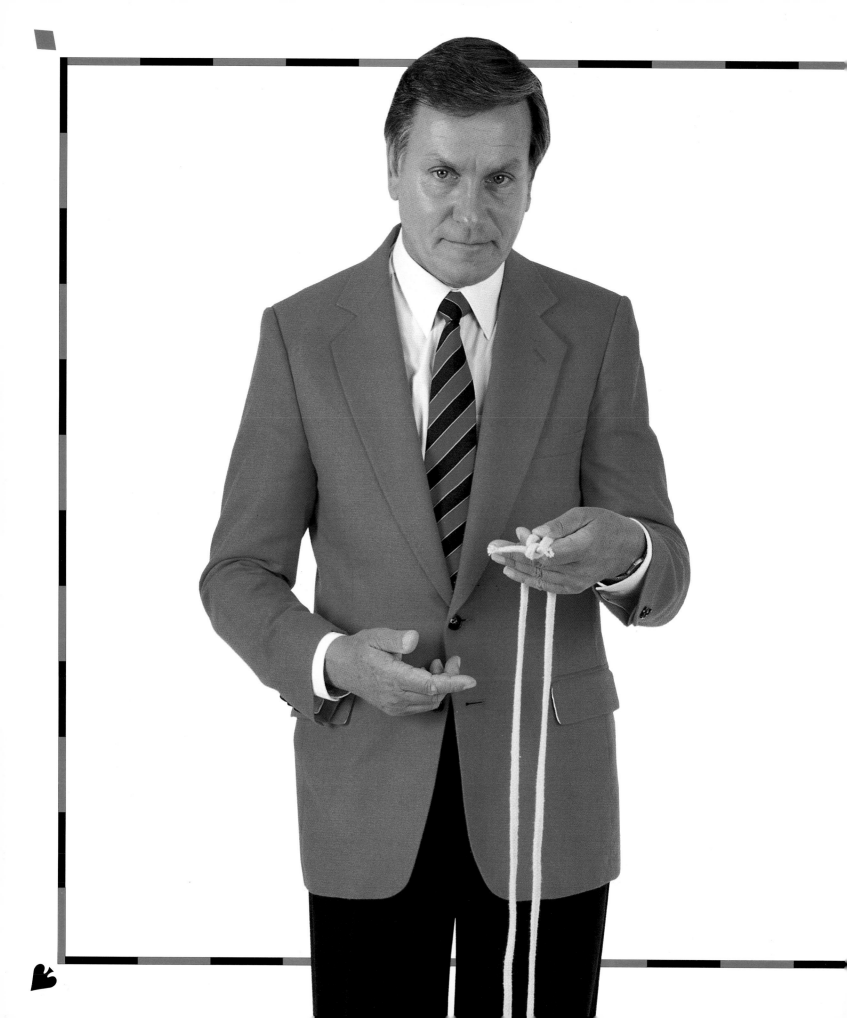

THE AMAZING BOOK OF
MAGIC & CARD
TRICKS

Jon Tremaine

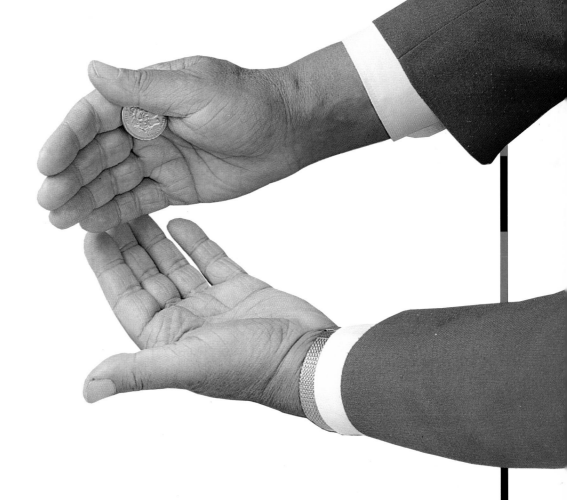

CLB

Dedicated to my wife
Suzy for making all my
impossible books possible

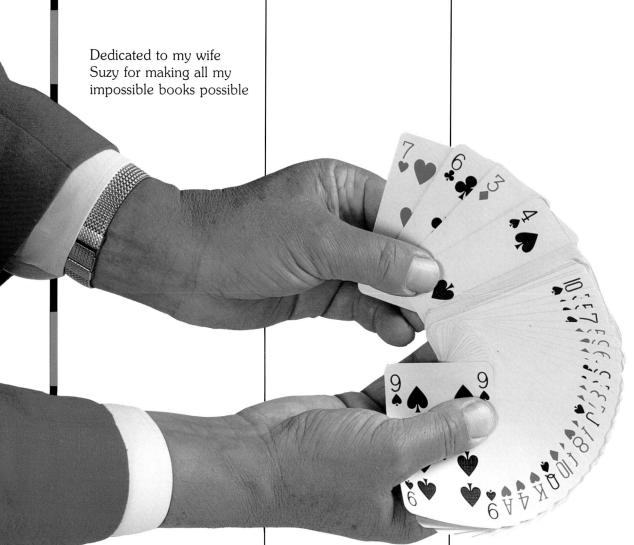

Amazing Book of Magic &
Card Tricks 3556
This edition published in 1998
by CLB, a division of
Quadrillion Publishing Ltd.
Godalming Business Centre
Woolsack Way, Godalming
Surrey, U.K.
Copyright © 1996 Quadrillion
Publishing Ltd.

Distributed in the USA by
Quadrillion Publishing, Inc.
230 Fifth Avenue, New York
NY 10001

ISBN 1-85833-398-9

Credits

Photography
Neil Sutherland

Editor
Philip de Ste. Croix

Designer
Stonecastle Graphics Ltd

Production
Ruth Arthur
Sally Connolly
Neil Randles
Karen Staff

Production Director
Gerald Hughes

Typesetting
SX Composing Ltd, Essex

Color Reproduction
Scantrans PTE Ltd,
Singapore

Printed in Singapore by
Star Standard Industries Pte. Ltd.

THE AUTHOR

Jon Tremaine has been a world class professional magi-
cian for nearly thirty years. He is a member of London's
Inner Magic Circle, and has been honored by them with a
Gold Star, the highest award that a magician can receive.
He has appeared on television, and traveled the world
entertaining in top night clubs, hotels, and cruise liners.
His particular specialty is close-up magic, the most difficult
branch of magic to perform; its exponents are few, and
Jon is undoubtedly one of the very best. He is the author
of a set of four books about performing magic specifically
for children – the series is entitled ''Let's Make Magic.'' He
is married and lives in Cuckfield, Sussex, England.

INTRODUCTION

I am going to show you how to do some outstanding magic tricks. You will learn to do some amazingly simple "sleight-of-hand" movements that will fool your audience completely. Some of the subtleties that you will learn are so outrageous that you will probably say to yourself:

"How on earth will I be able to get away with it without the audience realizing what I am doing?"

Don't worry! Take my word for it. If you are prepared to *practice*, there is no limit to the heights of skill that you will achieve or the degree of bewilderment that you will create by using the methods that I describe.

The secret of performing successful magic is to realize that 90 per cent of the effect of a trick is merely *presentation* or acting. There are even some tricks that are *100 per cent presentation*, requiring no manipulative skill at all! Successful *presentation* will make your tricks *entertaining* and *magical* – not simply novelty puzzles of limited interest to your audience. Your success will be due to a thorough knowledge of the workings of the trick and hours of dedicated practice before showing it to anyone.

I can give you the knowledge. No problem. However, only you can put in the *practice* that will lead you to a successful performance! The more practice you put in, the more you will get out of your magic, and the more your audience will be entertained by it. Secrecy is also import-

ant. The motto of The Magic Circle, the most famous and exclusive magic club in the world, is: *Indocilis Privata Loqui* (Not apt to disclose secrets) or, as we members more loosely translate it, "Keep your mouth shut!"

Do not pass your secrets on to others!

Why then am I writing this book and "spilling the beans"?

In buying this book, you have made a commitment. You have shown more than a passing interest in the world of magic and are obviously not just idly curious. If you want to perform tricks, you have got to start somewhere. Nobody is born a magician. Like all other skills, it must be learned.

I started by getting a book out of my local library. I was immediately "hooked." I soon discovered the joy in fooling other people. Four years later I gave up a promising career in architecture to become a magical entertainer. Maybe you will get hooked too!

I know that you will enjoy this book. You will learn a great deal. Just how far you go with this knowledge will be up to you. At best it could be the beginning of an exciting career for you. At the worst it will give you an insight into the fascinating world of magic and teach you a few tricks that you will delight in demonstrating to your friends. Your popularity will increase and so will your confidence.

Go for it!

Part One

Basic Handling Skills

CARD HANDLING

This first section starts by teaching you how to handle a deck of cards and how to perform sleight-of-hand feats and numerous subtleties with them. Then, your efforts in mastering basic handling skills will be rewarded by the disclosure of some two dozen super magical tricks that you will now be able to perform using the knowledge that you have gained from studying this section of the book. So, in no time at all, you will have a whole string of outstanding card tricks up your sleeve!

If you cannot find a deck of cards at home, go out and buy one. On second thought, buy three – two with *blue* backs and one with *red* backs. The spare blue deck will be used for making up "special" cards and supplying the duplicate cards that you may need for certain tricks.

Cards with a linen finish are best, although plastic coated cards are also nice to use. Cards that are just described as plastic are not easy to manipulate, because the material is too hard. It will make life easier, too, if you buy decks with white borders around the back designs. Why? Because occasionally a trick may require a card to be secretly reversed (i.e. turned over) in the deck. The white border of the back design will prevent it from being exposed prematurely.

The cards that we will be using for most of our tricks will have *blue* backs. It is a more positive color than red and is more easily seen.

Face-up card

Face-down card

Face-up deck

Face-down deck

Top of deck

Bottom of deck

THE LANGUAGE OF THE CARD MAGICIAN

There are many special words used by card magicians and you will need to remember them so that the explanations in the tricks section make sense.

♣ OVERHAND SHUFFLE ♣

A *shuffle* alters the order of all the cards in the deck. Your right hand grasps some of the cards from the back section of the deck (**1**) (assuming you are right-handed) and lifts them up and over the front part of the deck (**2**). Your left thumb now pulls off a card or bunch of cards (**3**) and keeps doing this until all the cards that were held in the right hand are now deposited on top of the original left hand group (**4**). This action is repeated a few times and a very good mix is thus obtained. Later on I will show you how to *false shuffle* the deck: apparently mixing all the cards up while actually keeping control of any card or cards that you choose to. Like the four Aces!

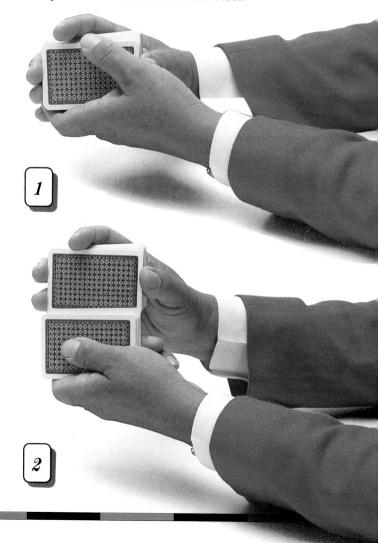

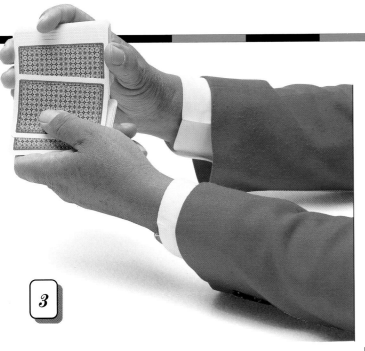

3

4

❧ CUTTING ❧

To "cut" the deck is to divide the cards by lifting off some of the cards and placing them to the side (**5**). To "complete the cut" is to put the remainder of the deck on top of the cards that you have just lifted off (**6**).

◆ CARD SPREAD ◆

A card spread can be executed across a table (**7**) or between your hands in the action of having a card chosen by a spectator (**8**).

5

7

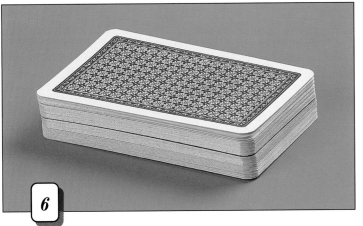

6

8

➤ OVERHAND FALSE SHUFFLE ◀

When you do a *false* overhand shuffle it must *look* exactly like the genuine one that you have already practiced. To practice the false shuffle put the four Aces on top of the deck (**1**).

Lift the bottom half of the deck upward as before (**2**). (This is called *undercutting*). Your left thumb now draws a card off the top of this half so that it lands on top of the four Aces. At the same time slide it *inward* so that it projects about ¼ inch over the edge (**3**). (This is called an *injog*). Shuffle off the rest of the cards unevenly on top of the *injogged* card so that the fact that it is sticking out a bit is less obvious (**4, 5**).

Your right hand now undercuts the deck again by pushing upward on the underside of the injogged card (**6, 7**), grasping all the cards below it and throwing them (still in one block) back on top (**8, 9**).

The four Aces are now back on top!

In magicians' language you have just undercut the deck, injogged one card, shuffled off, undercut at the injog and completed the cut! Aren't you clever! With practice, the injog can be very small indeed – just a fraction of an inch – hardly noticeable at all.

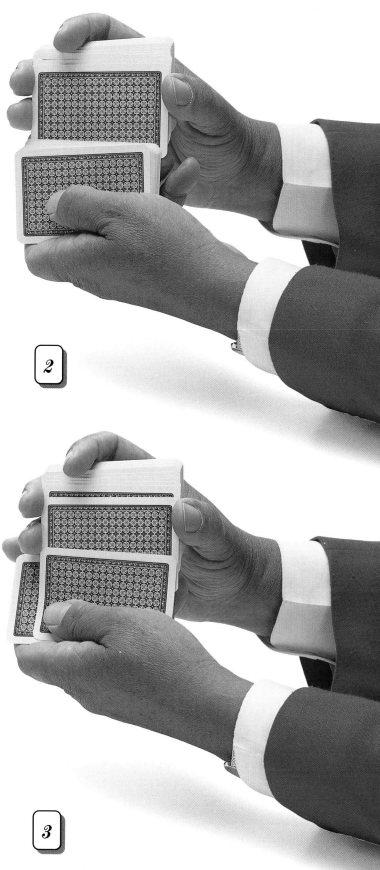

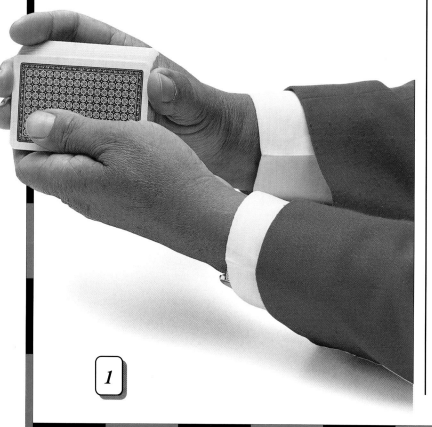

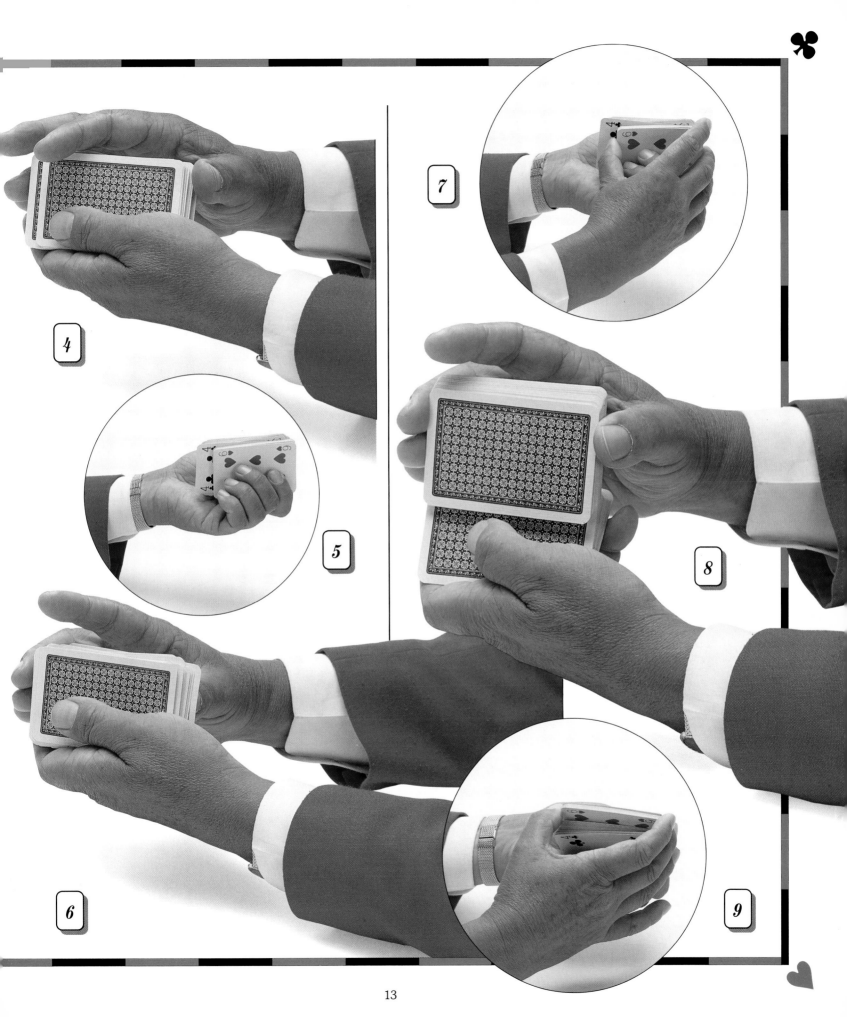

If a trick requires you *to shuffle the top card to the bottom*, proceed as follows:

Hold the complete deck in your right hand in the shuffling position. In this example, the eight of Spades is the top card (**1**). Draw off the top card *only* into your left hand by dragging it there with your left thumb (**2**). Now shuffle off the rest of the cards on top of this card (**3**). The card that was originally on top is now on the bottom (**4**).

To *shuffle the bottom card* (**5**) *to the top*:

Just start a normal shuffle (**6**) by undercutting the bottom half (**7**). Hang on to the original bottom card until last (**8**) and deposit it on top as you complete the shuffle (**9, 10**).

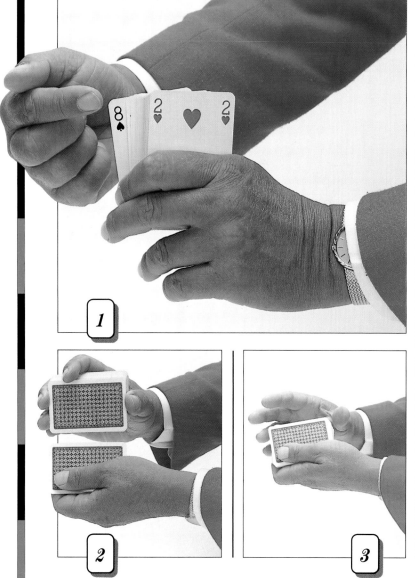

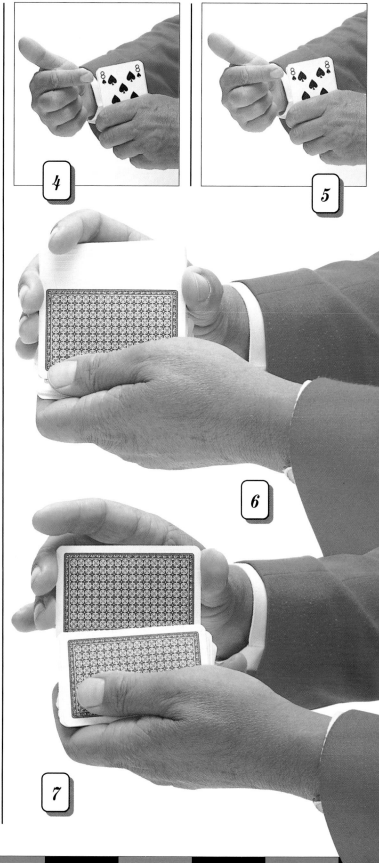

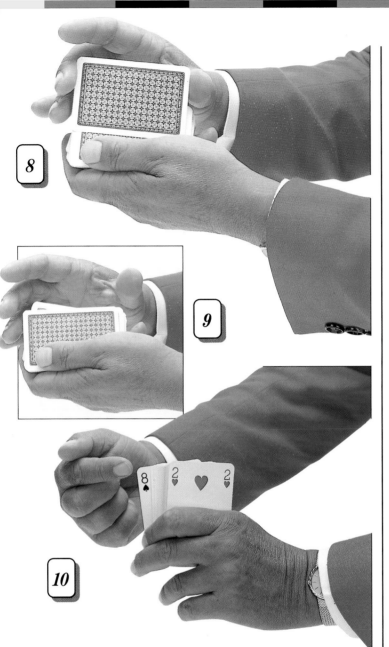

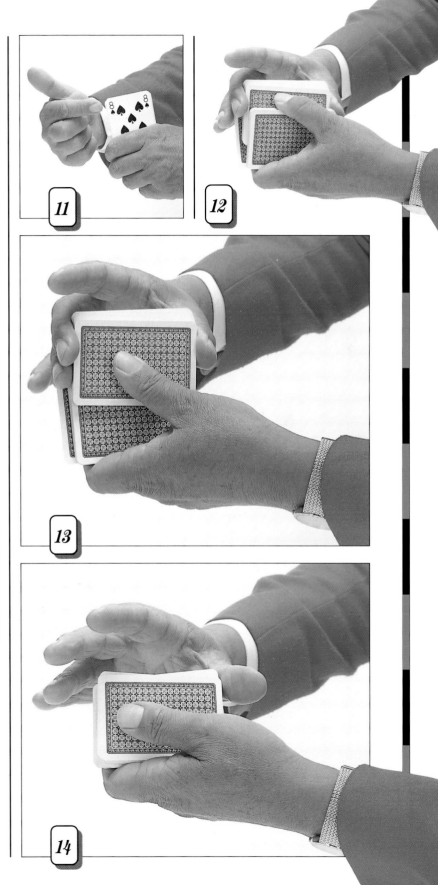

To *shuffle retaining the bottom card on the bottom* (**11**): Let the fingers of your left hand press on the face of the bottom card. As you undercut, let these fingers drag on the bottom card so that it is retained in your left hand (**12**). The original top half of the deck falls on it and the undercut bottom half of the deck in your right hand is now shuffled off in the normal way (**14**).

You are now executing *overhand shuffle control*. You must practice these actions until they become smooth and second nature to you. To avoid drawing attention to them, your shuffles should always appear to be casual. Not sloppy – just a little haphazard and natural looking.

OVERHAND SHUFFLE PRACTICE ROUTINE

This routine will help you practice the various card controls that I have just explained. Perform the complete routine over and over again until it becomes smooth and seamless in execution.

1 To help you keep track of what you are doing turn the top card face up!

2 False shuffle the deck to bring the top card back to the top by undercutting the deck, injogging one card, shuffling off, undercutting at the injog and throwing the block of cards on top. Your reversed card should now be on top again.

3 Shuffle the top card to the bottom and then back to the top again.

4 Shuffle the top card to the bottom. Shuffle again to keep it on the bottom. Now shuffle to bring it to the top again.

The simplest application of the overhand false shuffle is in controlling a spectator's chosen card once it has been returned to the deck. The deck is then apparently shuffled fairly and the chosen card lost forever! Or so the spectator thinks!

1 Shuffle the cards.

2 Spread the cards face downward between your hands and have the spectator remove the card.

3 Ask him to look at his card and remember it.

4 Undercut the deck and have the spectator replace his card on top of the pile in your left hand.

5 Carry on with the shuffle, injogging the first card, shuffling off, undercutting at the injog and throwing the block on top.

6 The chosen card will now be on top, although the spectator will think that it is lost somewhere in the middle of the deck.

7 You can now deal with his card as the particular trick that you are performing dictates.

♣ PALMING ♣

To palm a card means to hide a card or cards secretly in the palm of your hand. Palming is used when you wish secretly to remove a card (or cards) from the top of the deck. It can also be used secretly to add cards to the top of the deck.

Hold the deck face downward in your left hand. Let your thumb push the top card forward just a little (**1**), (an *outjog*). Bring the right hand over to the left and let your finger tips gently rest along the protrud-

ing edge (**2**). In this position, the palm of your right hand completely covers the deck.

Now, if you press down with your fingertips, the outjogged card will pivot upward into your palm (**3**). Arch your hand slightly so that you get a grip on the card using only your palm and finger tips. The card will follow the contours of your arched hand.

Move your right hand slightly to the right until your thumb is able to grip the nearside short end of the deck. You can now hold the complete deck between your thumb and fingers with the card still concealed in your palm (**4**). Move your left hand away. The whole action should look as if you have merely transferred the deck from one hand to the other.

When you first try to palm a card it will feel as if you are trying to conceal a sack of potatoes! Please do not worry about it. Keep practicing and it will suddenly all fall into place. Palming is always done on the "off beat" – the right psychological moment – when the spectator is distracted by your patter and least prepared to spot your sleight of hand.

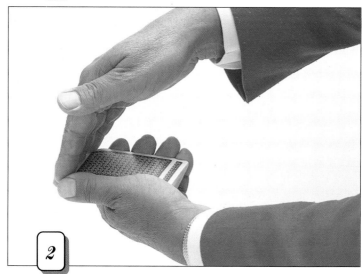

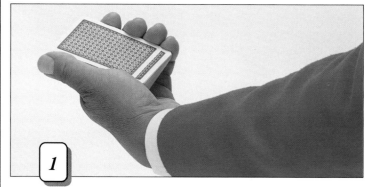

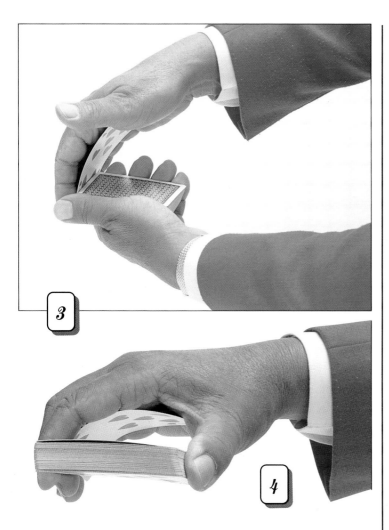

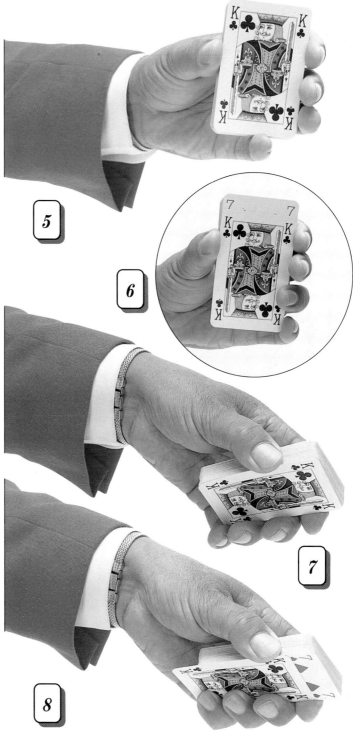

❧ THE GLIDE ❧

This extremely useful dodge enables us to achieve two things. If you show the bottom card of the deck and deal it onto the table, the *glide* enables you to change it for an entirely different one. We can also deal from the bottom of the deck and yet retain the bottom card where it is until we need it! For example, a chosen card can be secretly shuffled to the bottom. You could ask the spectator to call out a number under 20. Supposing he says "nine," if you started dealing cards from the bottom, the ninth one dealt will be his selected card! Very crafty!

Hold the deck, as shown, with your thumb on one long edge and your fingers curled under the other edge. Twist your wrist to show the bottom card (**5**). In our example, it is the King of Clubs which has the seven of Diamonds directly beneath it (**6**). Now return the deck to a face down position by twisting your

wrist the opposite way. As you do this, you pull back the bottom card with your left second and third finger tips (**7, 8**). This *small* action is disguised by the *larger* action of turning the hand over. By *gliding* back the bottom card in this way, you have exposed about a half-inch of the second from bottom card.

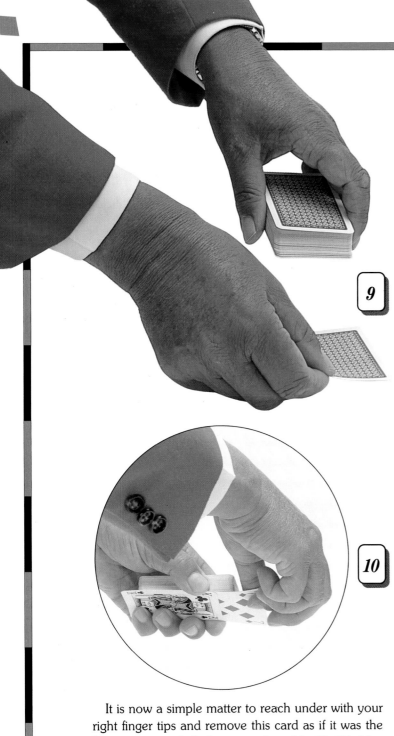

Lift Number One

Secretly get a little finger break under the top two cards (**1**). Push both cards forward about an inch with your right thumb (**2**). Grasp the two cards at the protruding end (**3**). Turn them both over and place them face up on top of the deck, still protruding a little (**4**). Be careful to keep the two cards exactly aligned so that they appear "as one" at all times. Now repeat the action, turning them face down again and this time squaring them up with the rest of the deck.

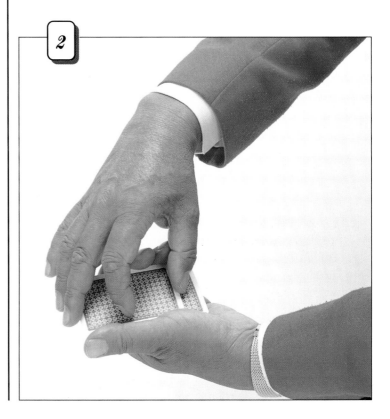

It is now a simple matter to reach under with your right finger tips and remove this card as if it was the bottom one and deal it upon the table (**9, 10**). You can now slide the bottom card back flush with the rest of the deck, and nobody will be any the wiser.

◆ THE DOUBLE LIFT ◆

The sleight we call a *double lift* is extremely useful. In simple terms it is the act of picking up *two* cards from the top of the deck and showing them as if you were only holding *one*. This way you can show that the real top card is not the top card at all!

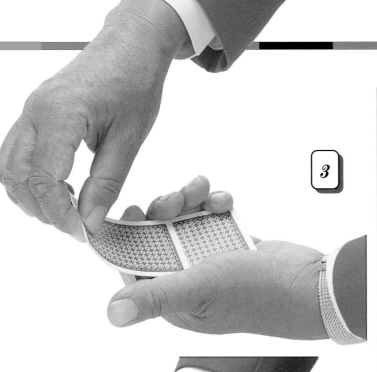

3

4

cards aligned. To complete the sequence, just reverse the movements and replace the "double lift" back on the top of the deck.

Simple Use
Control a spectator's card to second from top of the deck. Double lift to show that it is apparently the top card. Replace double lift. Remove the real top card and, without showing its face, bury it in the center of the deck. Make a "magic pass" and show that the chosen card has magically jumped back to the top of the deck again!

Practice the double lift until you can perform it smoothly and effortlessly. It is a valuable weapon and you will be asked to use it often.

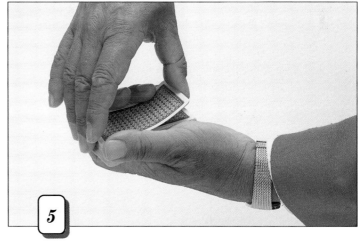

5

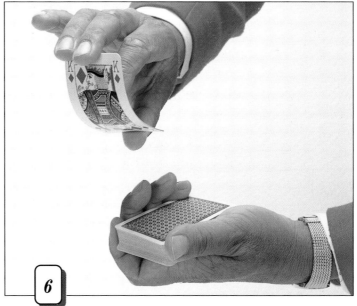

6

Lift Number Two
You may need to "double lift" without turning the cards face up. In this case, you secure a finger break under the top two cards as before. Now reach over with your right hand. Place your thumb at the near-side edge, your third and fourth fingers on the opposite edge (**5**) and your index finger pressing lightly on the center of the top card.

Lift the top two cards up (as one) and show the visible face to the spectator (**6**). Notice how the cards are *slightly* curved. This curvature helps keep the two

FORCING

For certain effects it is necessary to force the spectator to choose a specific card while apparently letting him have a completely free choice! Without this ability, the desired effects cannot be achieved. I will now teach you a few ways to do this. Practice them all and use the method with which you feel most comfortable.

The following forces all start with the card to be forced on top.

❤ FORCE 1: X-ING THE DECK ◀

False shuffle the deck and then ask the spectator to cut the deck in half (**1, 2**). Pick up the *bottom* half and rest it across the top half, like this (**3, 4**). Now you distract his attention by talking!

"You could have cut the cards anywhere, couldn't you?"

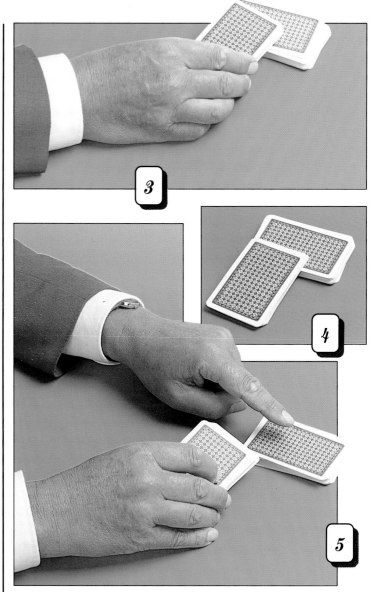

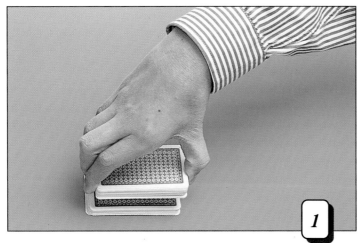

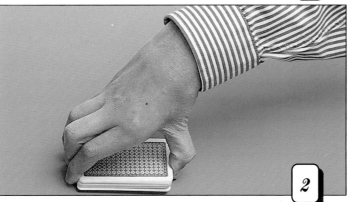

Point to the cards and say:

"And we have marked where you cut like this . . ."

Lift off the half that is resting on top and point to the top card of the half that remains on the table (**5**).

"Look at the card that you cut to, and remember it."

Of course it is your force card, the one that was originally the top one. When you talk to the spectator, it has the effect of distracting him. He will be unable to recall the exact sequence of events and will never question your bare-faced nerve!

♣ FORCE 2: SLIP CUT FORCE ♣

This is a simple yet very convincing force. Here, we shall use the nine of Hearts (**6**). False shuffle the deck and then hold it in your left hand as shown.

Your left thumb now riffles the deck at its upper left corner (**7**) and the spectator is invited to say *Stop* whenever he wishes. When he says "Stop," you stop riffling immediately and hold the gap. Your right hand now approaches your left and grasps the cards above this break between the thumb at the inner end and the second, third and fourth fingers at the outer end (**8**).

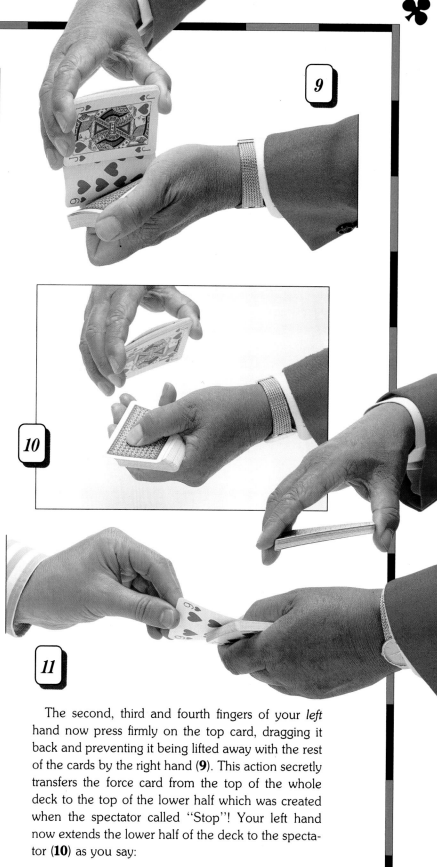

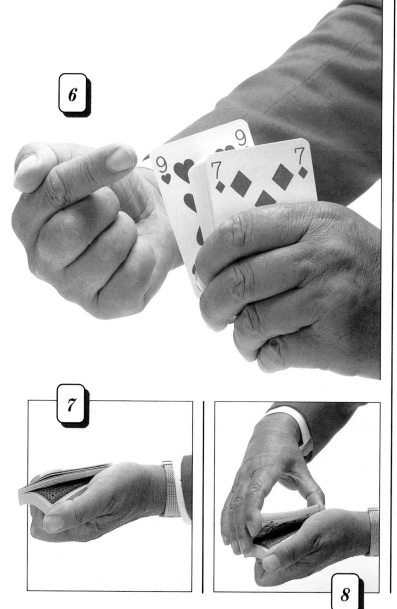

The second, third and fourth fingers of your *left* hand now press firmly on the top card, dragging it back and preventing it being lifted away with the rest of the cards by the right hand (**9**). This action secretly transfers the force card from the top of the whole deck to the top of the lower half which was created when the spectator called "Stop"! Your left hand now extends the lower half of the deck to the spectator (**10**) as you say:

"Please take the card that you cut to (11)."

◆ FORCE 3: HANKY PANKY FORCE ◆

You will need a good quality handkerchief or napkin to perform this highly effective force. False shuffle keeping the card to be forced (the ten of Clubs in this instance, **1**) on the top. Place the deck face downward on your right palm (**2**). Cover your hand and the cards with the handkerchief (**3**). *As you cover your hand, flip the deck over so that it is now face up (**4**)!* Practice until you can do it smoothly.

Ask the spectator to cut the deck *through* the handkerchief (**5**). As soon as he lifts his cards high enough, secretly flip the cards in your hand face down again (**6, 7, 8**) while still under cover of the handkerchief. Offer your right hand with your cards resting on the palm (**9**) and say,

"Take the card that you cut to."

Finally take away the handkerchief containing the other cards with your free hand. Simple but very effective! He has taken the ten of Clubs!

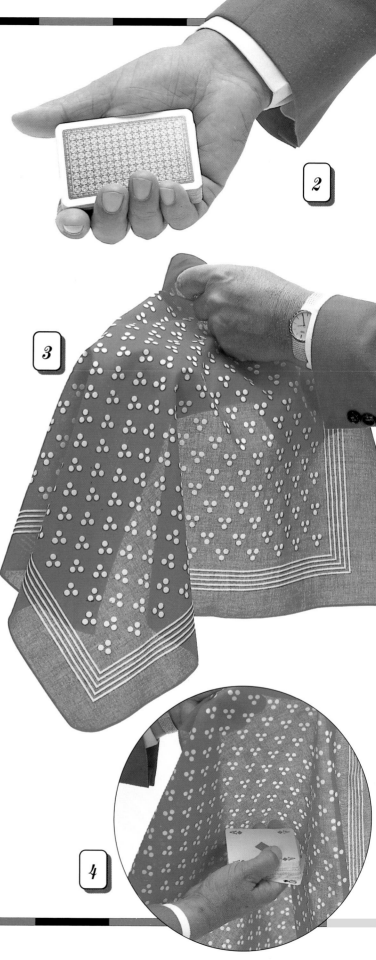

22

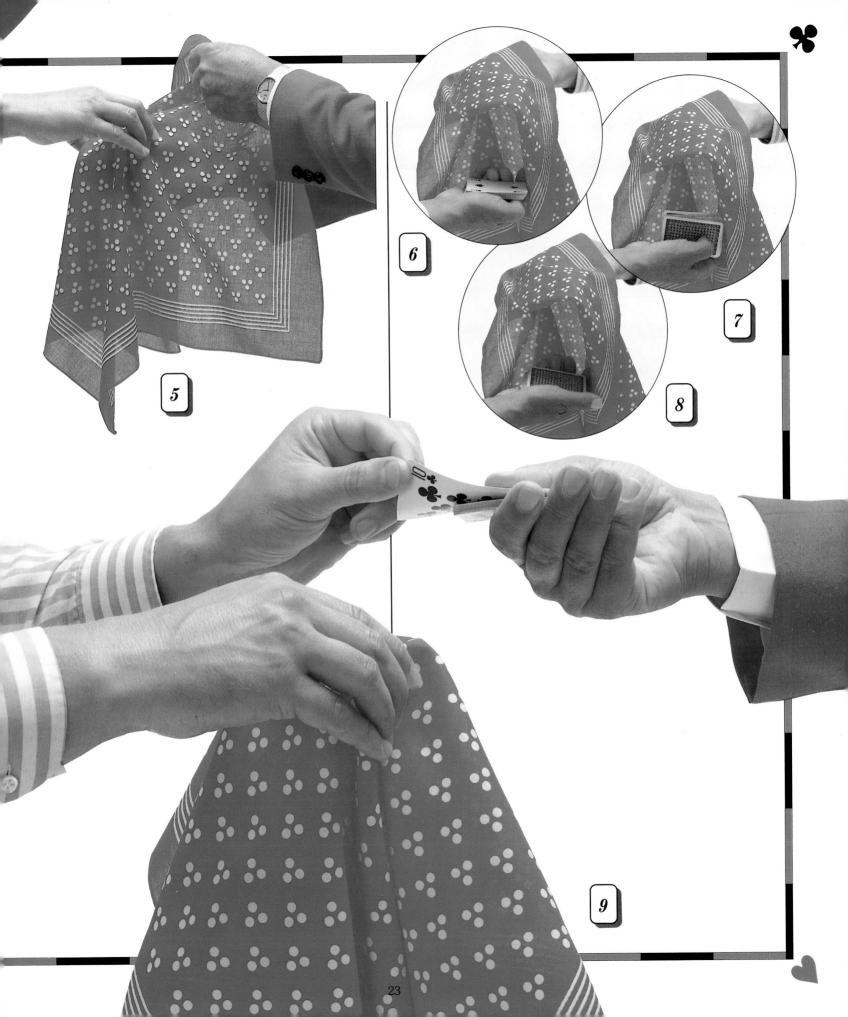

➤ FORCE 4: CROSS HAND FORCE ◀

False shuffle the cards. Hold the deck in your left hand.

"I am going to do this trick without looking at the cards."

Put the cards behind your back (**1**). As soon as they are out of sight, slip the card to be forced off the top and slide it over into the palm of your right hand (**2, 3**) and cover it over with your left hand (**4**). Turn around so that your back is now facing the spectator.

"Now, I want you to take the deck (5). Give the cards a very good shuffle (6), then put them back on my hand again (7)."

As soon as you get the deck back, turn around to face the audience and secretly slide the concealed card back on top of the deck again (**8, 9**). With a little practice you should be able to do this without anyone noticing your arms move.

"Did you really give them a good shuffle?"

"Yes" says the spectator. Turn your back on her again (**10**).

"Right, take off the card that you have shuffled to the top . . ."

She does so (**11**) and you have successfully forced the top card (**12**)!

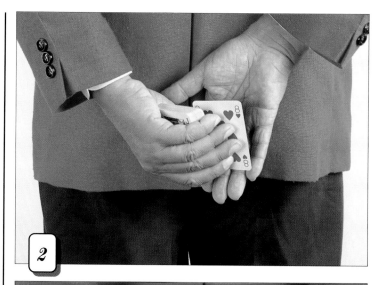

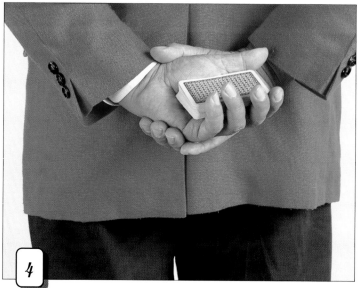

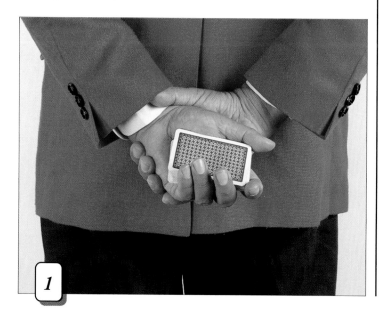

24

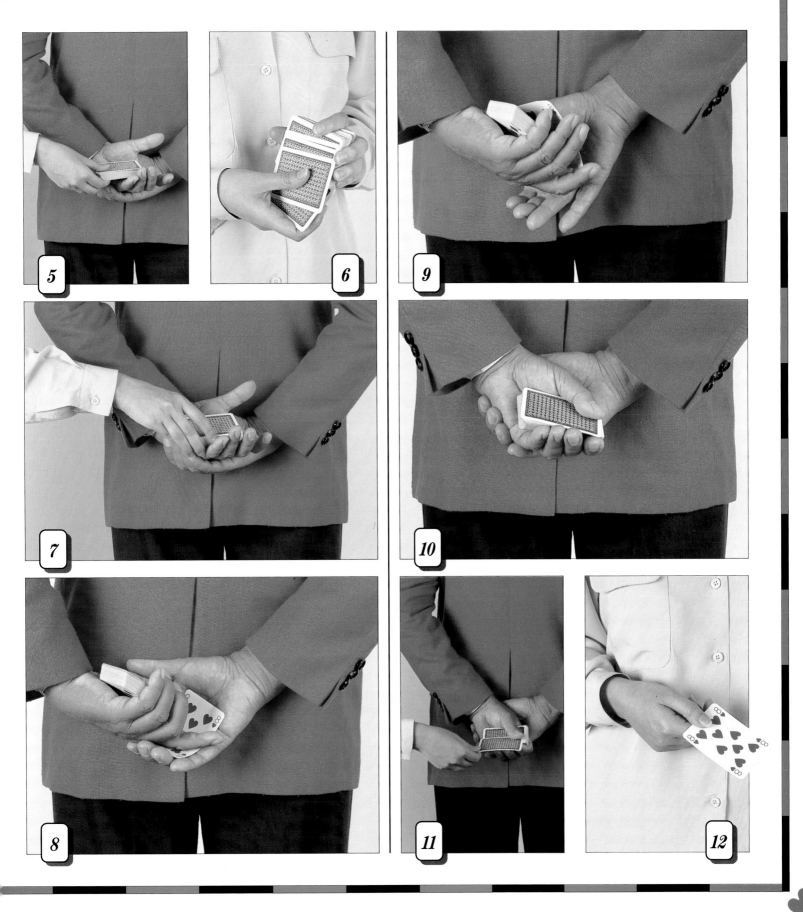

5

6

9

7

10

8

11

12

25

PART TWO

SELECTED CARD TRICKS

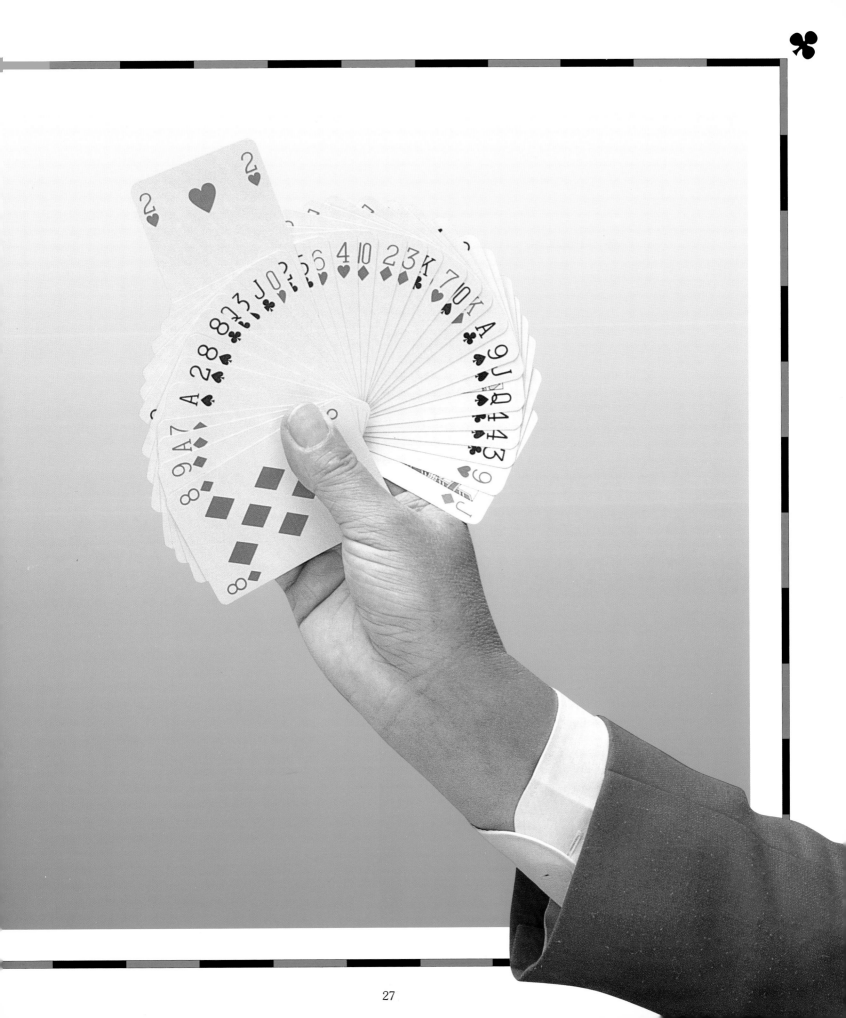

ACROBATIC ACES

I will start you off with a favorite theme among card magicians. Four Ace tricks always create interest – especially among card players!

♣ EFFECT ♣

The four Aces demonstrate their acrobatic ability by disappearing from the deck and appearing in a spectator's pocket!

WHAT YOU DO

Remove the four Aces and lay them face up on the table (**1**). Hold the rest of the deck face down in your left hand. Ask a member of the audience to tell you which Ace is the best. As I am sure he has never been asked that question before it should take him a couple of seconds for the question to sink in and for him to make his choice.

While he is making up his mind, secretly lift up the edge of the top *three* cards and insert the tip of your little finger in the gap, holding a break (**2**). When he has chosen his Ace (say the Ace of Hearts), pick it up and place it *face up* on top of the deck (**3**). Place the other three Aces on top of it (also face up) (**4, 5**). Then, with your right hand, pick up the Aces, together with the three cards above your finger break *as one block* (**6**).

You now have to show these *seven* cards as if they are only *four*! This is how you do it.

At the moment you are holding a block of seven cards in your right hand, (three face-down indifferent cards covered by the four face-up Aces). Hold these over the deck, covering about half of it. Do not let go of your grip. Drop your left thumb on the top Ace and press lightly.

REQUIREMENTS
Just a deck of cards and a spectator

1

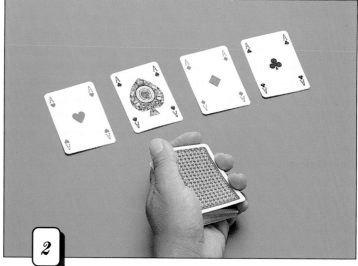

2

3

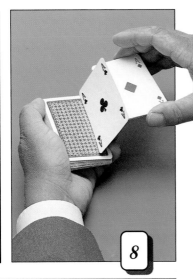

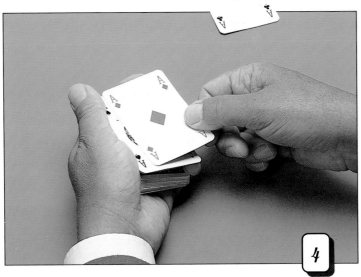

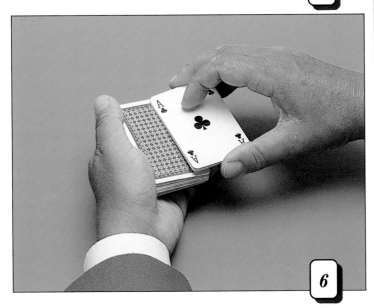

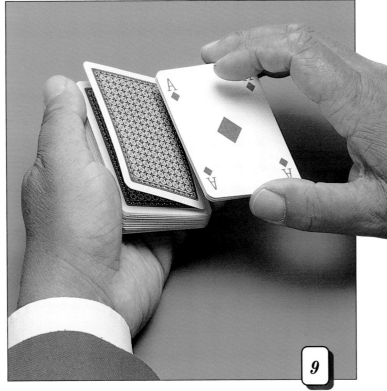

Move your right hand and the remaining (six) cards away to the right again (**7**). The left thumb's pressure prevents the top Ace from moving with them. It stays put. Just before the six cards clear the right hand edge, you use them to flip this Ace over so that it ends up face down on top of the deck (**8, 9**). These three actions should be practiced until they blend into one smooth movement – the act of just flipping a card over.

Repeat the action with the next Ace making sure that you keep the cards aligned so that the extra three are not revealed in any way. Now flip the third Ace over. This leaves you with the chosen Ace face up (**10**). Hidden beneath it, unknown to the spectator, are the three odd cards. Drop the whole pile on top of the deck (**11**) and then instantly flip the last Ace face down (**12, 13**). This *looks* exactly like the movement you have performed three times already – only this time you have secretly placed three odd cards under the top Ace.

The order from the top should now be the chosen Ace, then the three odd cards, and then the other three Aces (**14**). From your point of view you have just completed the technical 10 per cent of the trick. The dirty work has been done! Now comes the *presentation* – the other 90 per cent – which will turn this into a great trick. Deal the top four cards face down in a row from left to right (**15, 16**).

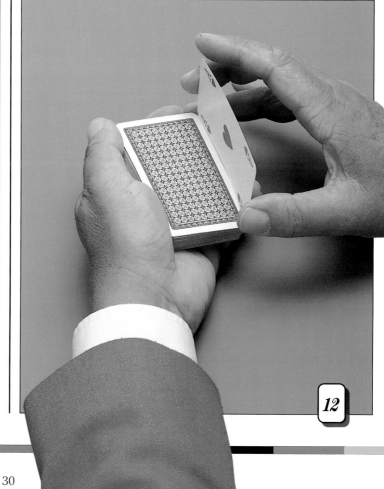

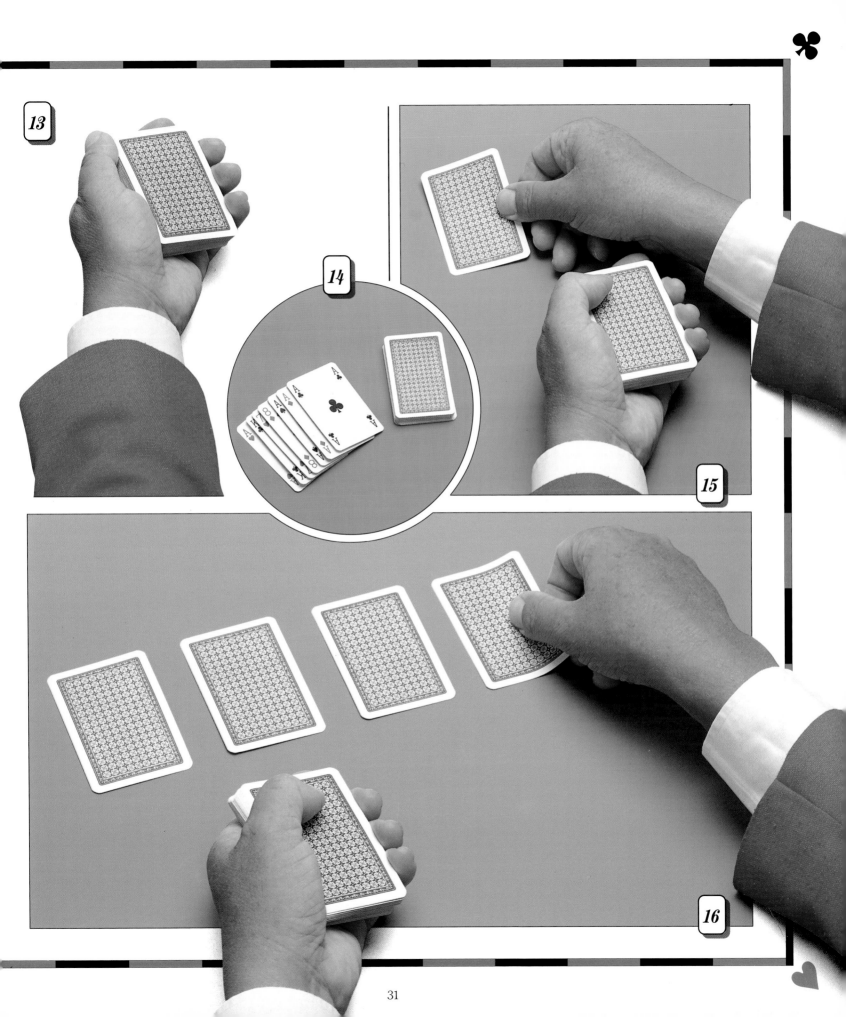

"I'll just deal the Aces onto the table."

In reality there is only one Ace (the chosen one) in the row – at the extreme left. *False shuffle the deck keeping the three Aces on top.*

"I will now deal three odd cards onto each Ace."

Suit your actions to your words by dealing three cards face down onto each card. The first three go on the left hand pile (**17, 18**), the second three on the next pile, and so on. The table now looks like this (**19**). Pick up pile number 1. Square the cards up and turn the pile face up – showing the chosen Ace – the Ace of Hearts (**20**).

"Let me put your Ace and the three odd cards into your pocket."

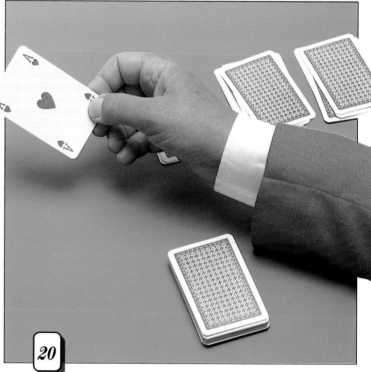

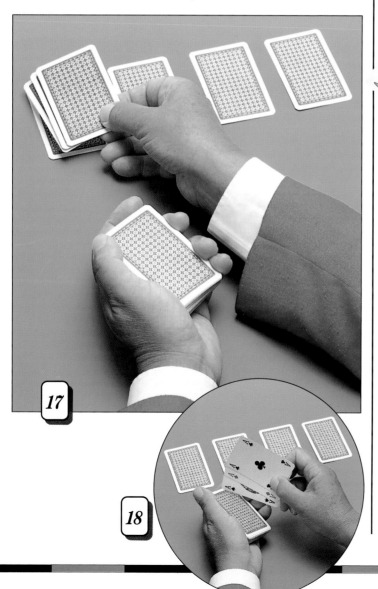

Be careful not to expose the other three Aces at this point. If he has not got a pocket, get him to stand up. Put the cards face down on a chair, then ask him to *sit* on the cards!

"Now watch very closely!"

Pick up one of the remaining piles and start to turn the cards face up, counting as you do so (**21**).

"One. Two. Three – odd cards. And an Ace."

21

22

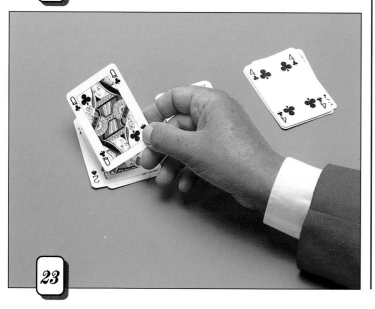

23

Turn the last card face up with a flourish (**22**).

"The Ace has gone!"

Repeat with the other two piles (**23**). Now all three Aces have mysteriously disappeared! Bring the trick to a stunning climax by having the spectator remove the four cards from his own pocket (**24**)! What has he got?

"The acrobatic four Aces!"

24

➤ AFTERTHOUGHTS ◀

Notice how the *false shuffle* enhances this trick. It subtly emphasizes the apparent randomness of the odd cards that are used to cover the four Aces. Part Three of this book contains a collection of self-working tricks – in other words, tricks that require no sleight-of-hand for their performance. Once again our fabulous false shuffle can be used to enhance many of these; in the process, turning them from perplexing puzzles into outstanding magical effects.

AMBITIOUS CARD TRICK

This is a "classic" card trick. Audiences love to see it because so many "magical" effects are created within it. It is fast and furious card magic at its best! From our point of view, it gives you a marvelous opportunity to practice your skills of false shuffling, double lifting, gliding and general card control. I guarantee that somebody will say,

"Wow! I wouldn't like to play cards with you!"

◆ EFFECT ◆

A freely chosen card keeps repeatedly returning to the top of the deck – no matter how often the deck is shuffled.

REQUIREMENTS
A deck of cards
A spectator

◀ WHAT YOU DO ▶

Spread the deck out and have the spectator choose a card (**1**). Make sure he remembers what it is otherwise you will feel very foolish. Have the card returned to the deck (**2**) and, in the process of an overhand shuffle, control it to the top. False shuffle keeping his chosen card on top (**3**). Flip the top card face up with a flourish to show his card (**4**)! (*First effect*).

Turn it face down, false shuffle again (**5**), flip the top card over to show that it has again returned to the top (**6**)! (*Second effect*).

Turn it face down. Undercut the deck. Run one single card on top of the chosen card, then injog the next card (**7**), shuffle off the rest, undercut at the injog and throw the block on top.

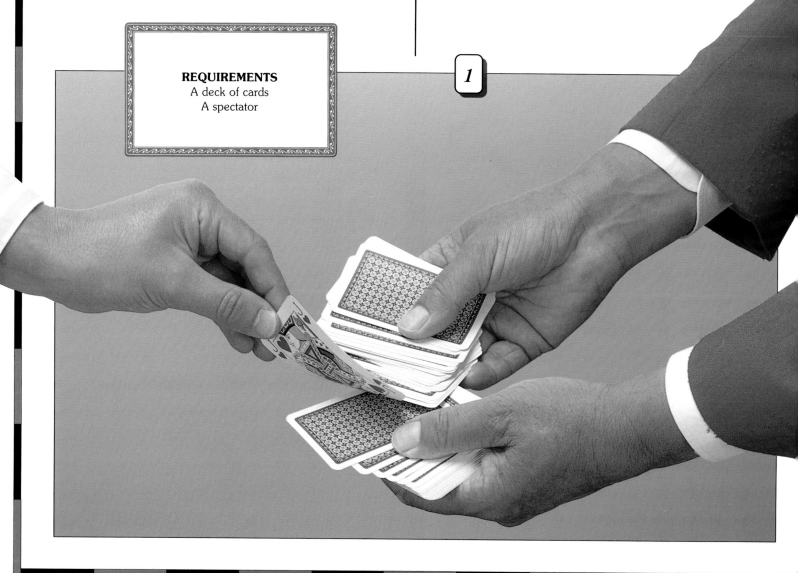

1

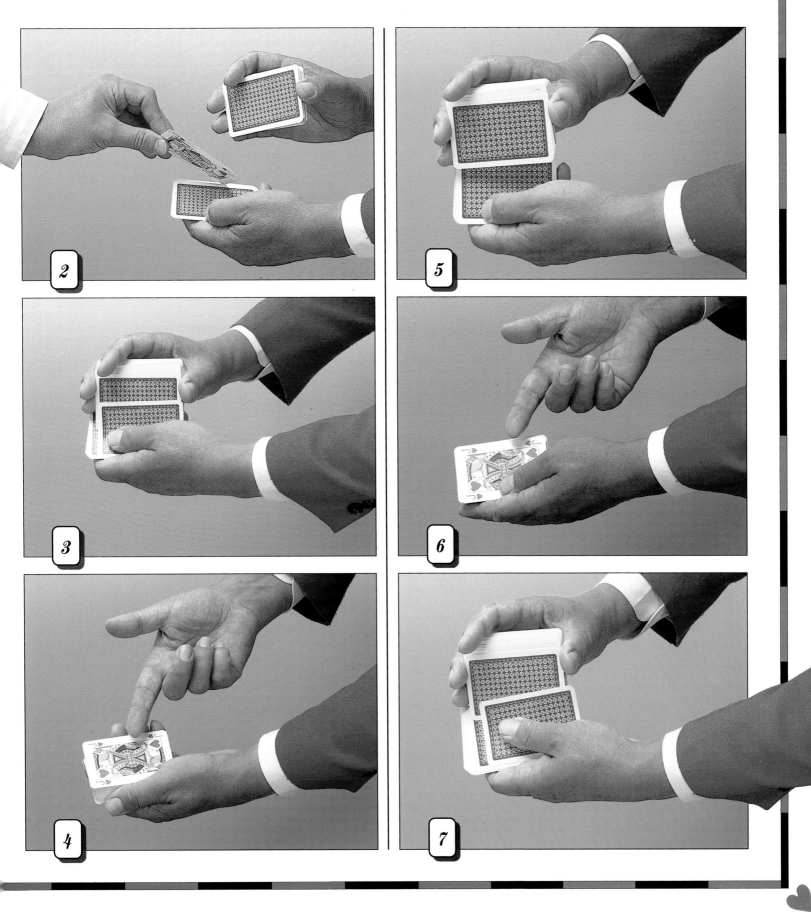

The spectator's card should now be second from the top! *Double lift* (**8, 9**) to show his card is back on top again (**10, 11**)! (*Third effect*).

Replace the two cards (**12, 13**). Take off the top card only (**14**) and, without showing its face, bury it somewhere in the center of the deck (**15**). Make a flourish with your right hand, then turn the top card over (**16**). His card is back! (*Fourth effect*).

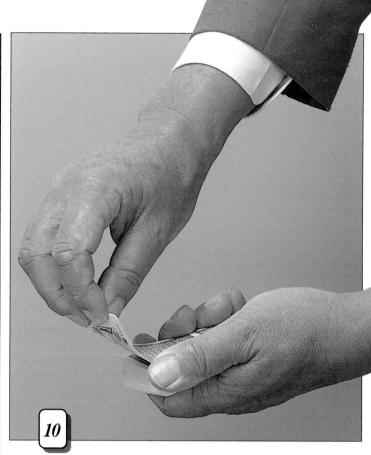

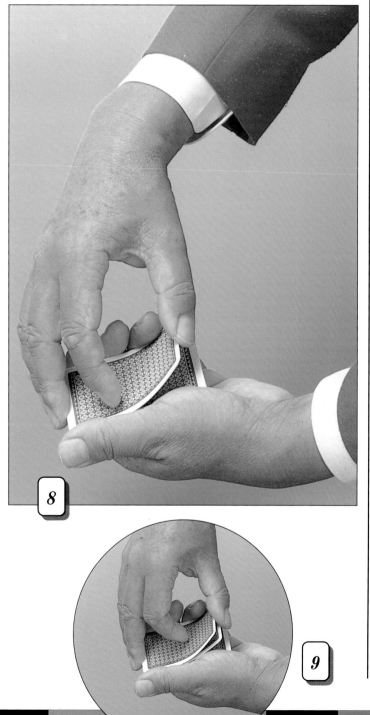

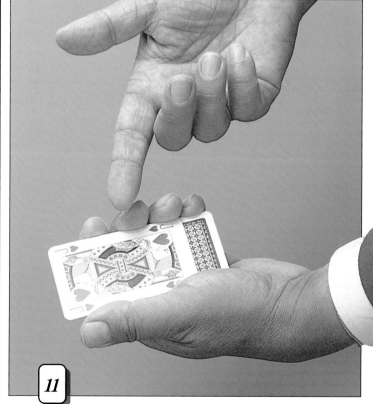

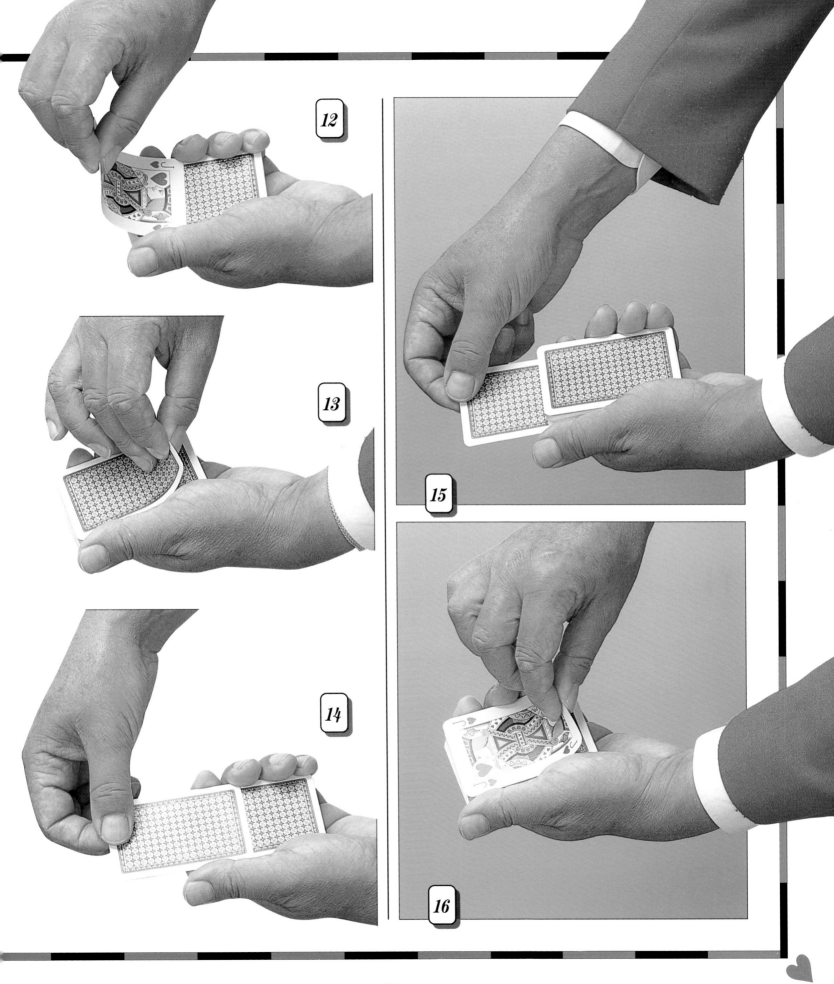

Put it face down on top again. This time false shuffle his card to the *bottom* (**17, 18**). Turn over the top card. Act surprised that it is not his card (**19**). Then slowly turn the whole deck over to show his card resting on the bottom (**20, 21**)! (*Fifth effect*).

Twist your wrist so that the deck is turned face down. In the process, execute *the glide* and apparently deal his chosen card face down off the bottom of the deck onto the table (**22**). Now false shuffle the deck to bring his chosen card to the top (**23**). Place the deck face down on the table (**24**). Bring the routine to a startling climax by showing that his chosen card is *not* the single card that you dealt down (**25**). Once again his "Ambitious Card" has risen to the top of the deck (**26, 27**)! (*Sixth effect*).

So there you have it. A dynamic card trick with no less than *six* strong surprises built into it. No wonder it has been a favorite of professional and amateur magicians for over a hundred years!

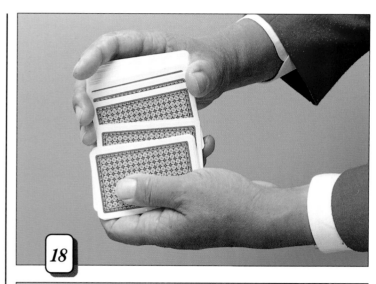

18

19

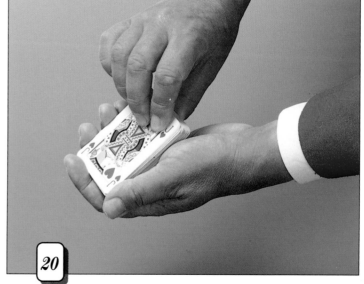

20

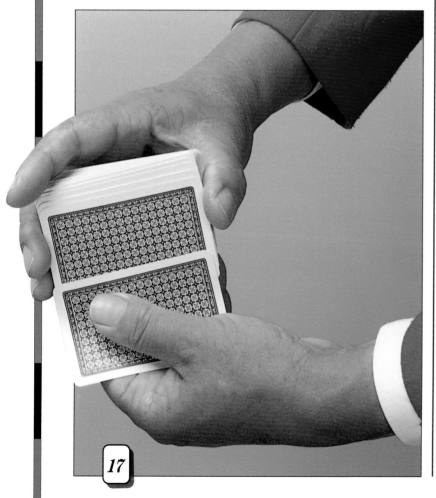

17

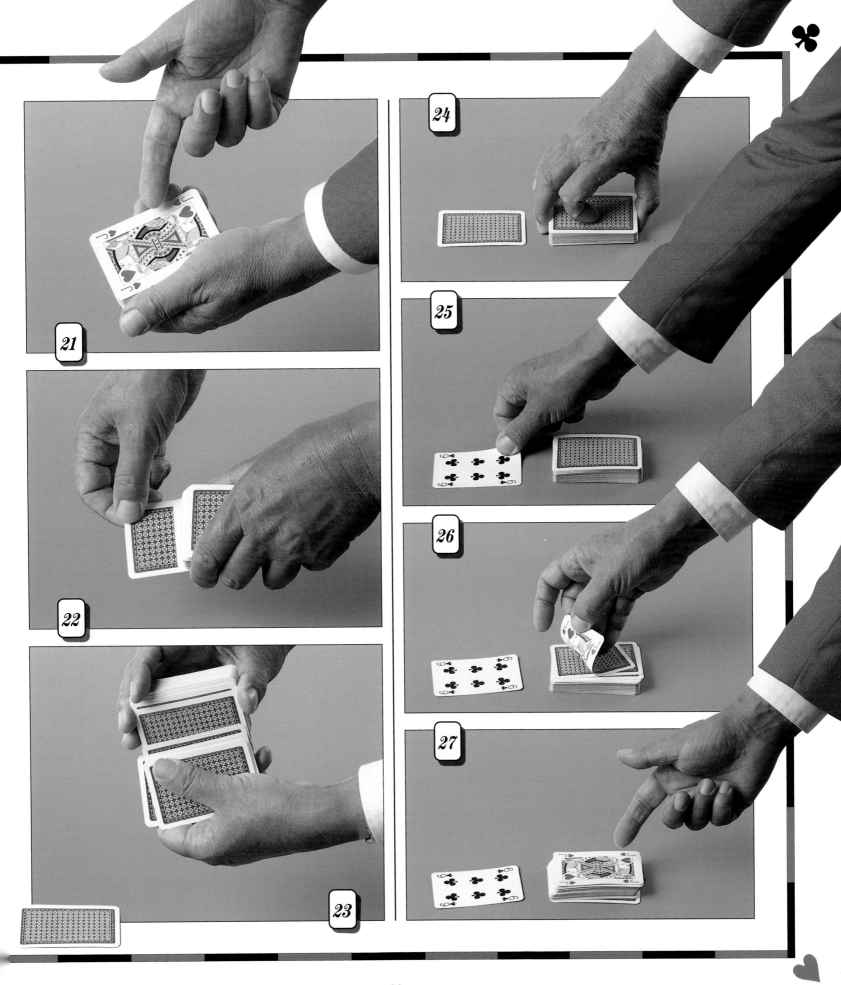

HERE TODAY – GONE TOMORROW!

Any trick where the "magic" happens in the hands of the spectator has got to be good. The effect this trick has upon the spectator is *dynamic*! The plot is good, the method *very* simple and the handling *extremely* deceptive.

◆ EFFECT ◆

A card is selected and returned to the deck, which is then shuffled. An indifferent card is then placed on a spectator's palm. The magician then says that by tapping the deck three times on the back and then three times on the front, the spectator's chosen card will magically reverse itself in the deck. After tapping, he fans out the deck face up and one card is seen to be reversed. The spectator is asked to reveal the identity of his chosen card for the first time, and then the magician turns over the reversed card. It turns out to be *not the selected card, but the indifferent card that the spectator is supposed to be holding*! The spectator turns over the card in his hand and is dumbfounded to find that he is holding *his own selected card*!

```
REQUIREMENTS
A deck of cards and the assistance
of a spectator
```

❮ WHAT YOU DO ❯

Have a card chosen and returned to the deck (**1, 2, 3**). In this case it is the three of Clubs. Control it to the top during the course of an *overhand shuffle* (**4**).

Explain that during the shuffle his chosen card may have arrived at the top of the deck. Execute a *double lift* (**5, 6**) and lay the card(s) face up on top of the deck with its right long edge overlapping the deck by about an inch (**7**). In our demonstration the visible card is the Queen of Diamonds (**8**).

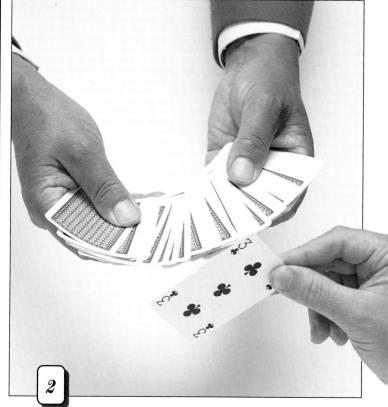

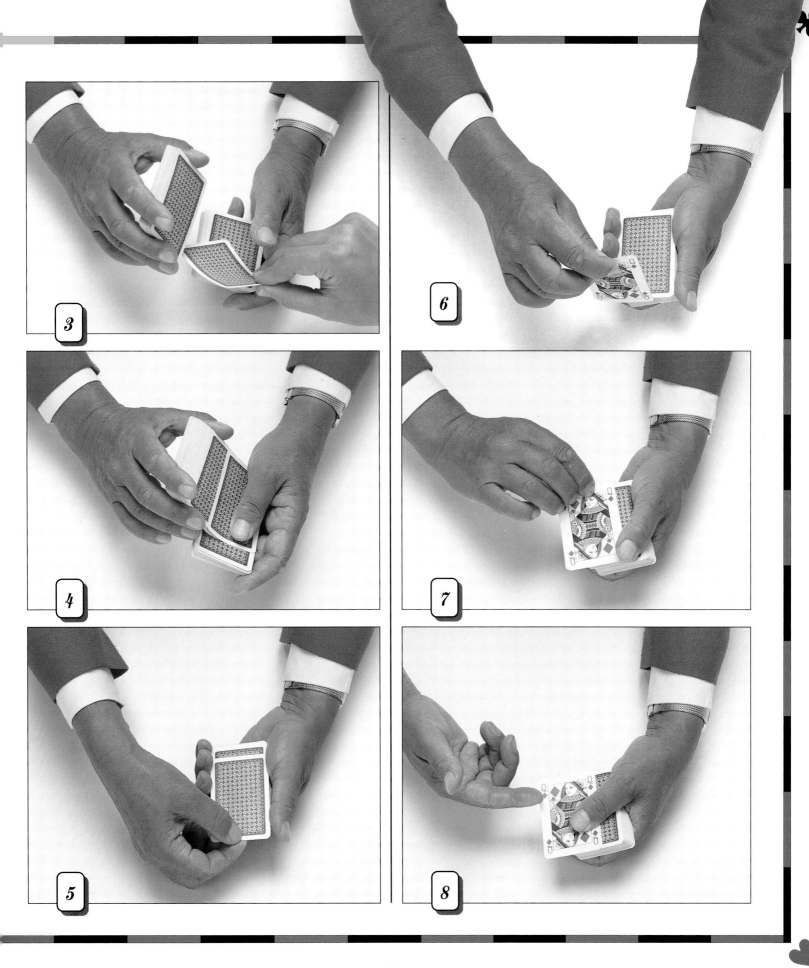

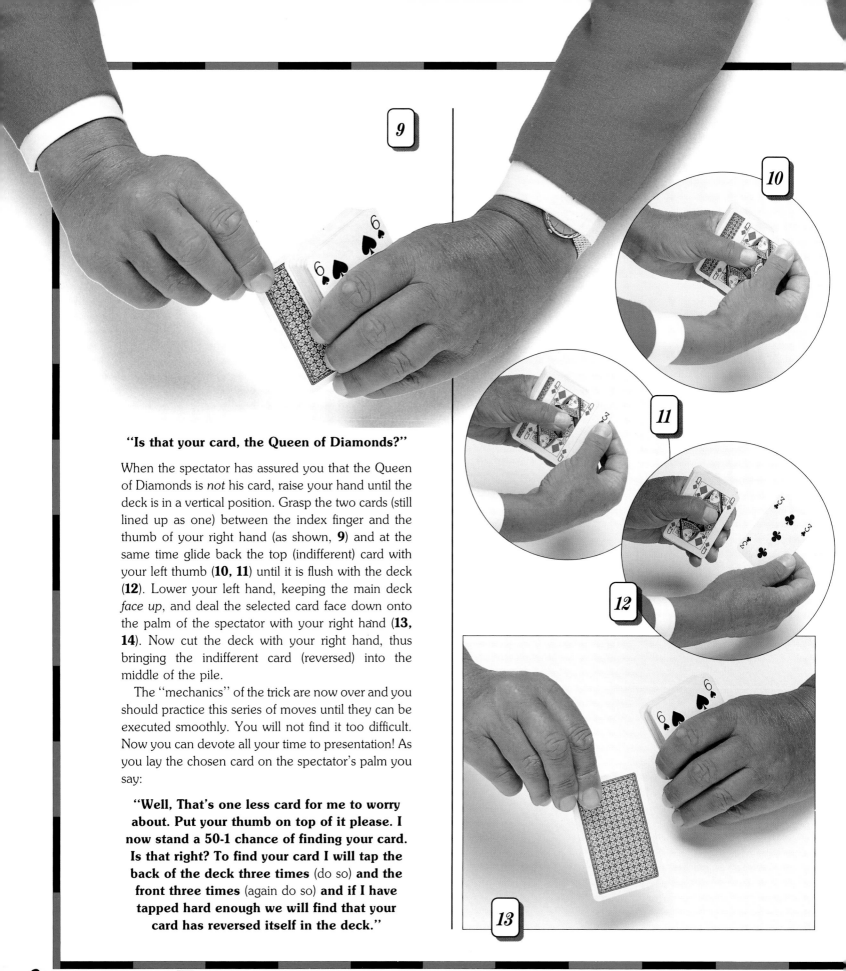

"Is that your card, the Queen of Diamonds?"

When the spectator has assured you that the Queen of Diamonds is *not* his card, raise your hand until the deck is in a vertical position. Grasp the two cards (still lined up as one) between the index finger and the thumb of your right hand (as shown, **9**) and at the same time glide back the top (indifferent) card with your left thumb (**10, 11**) until it is flush with the deck (**12**). Lower your left hand, keeping the main deck *face up*, and deal the selected card face down onto the palm of the spectator with your right hand (**13, 14**). Now cut the deck with your right hand, thus bringing the indifferent card (reversed) into the middle of the pile.

The "mechanics" of the trick are now over and you should practice this series of moves until they can be executed smoothly. You will not find it too difficult. Now you can devote all your time to presentation! As you lay the chosen card on the spectator's palm you say:

"Well, That's one less card for me to worry about. Put your thumb on top of it please. I now stand a 50-1 chance of finding your card. Is that right? To find your card I will tap the back of the deck three times (do so) **and the front three times** (again do so) **and if I have tapped hard enough we will find that your card has reversed itself in the deck."**

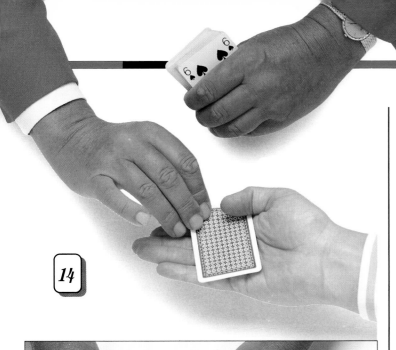

14

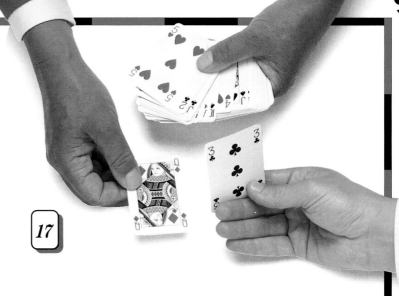

17

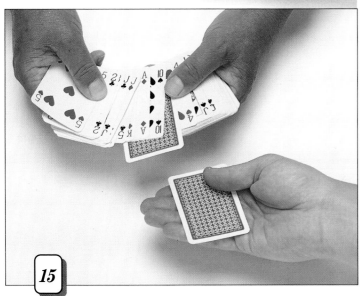

15

18

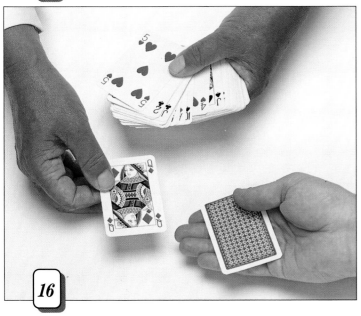

16

Fan the cards *face up* (**15**). Draw attention to the one reversed card. Take it out and hold it up without showing its face for the moment.

"It seems that I have been successful. You are holding the Queen of Diamonds; what was the card that you chose?"

He says it was the three of Clubs. Turn the card that you are holding over to show that *you* are now holding the Queen of Diamonds (**16**)!

"Well, I've now got the Queen of Diamonds which you are supposed to be holding! What have you got?"

He turns over the card that has been on his palm all this time (**17**) and finds to his amazement that he is now holding his chosen card, *the three of Clubs* (**18**)!

CARDS ACROSS

Because playing cards are fairly small they are not normally used by stage and cabaret magicians. This trick is a notable exception. It is an impromptu trick that you can present absolutely anywhere. It will have the same remarkable effect whether your audience consists of one or a hundred and one people.

❖ EFFECT ❖

You use two assistants. Each deals out ten cards and then stands on them. You make three cards magically jump from beneath one spectator's foot to reappear under the other spectator's foot! One now has seven cards – the other has thirteen!

```
REQUIREMENTS
A deck of cards
A small table or stool
Two spectators (we will call them
Suzy and Kate).
```

♣ WHAT YOU DO ♣

Stand Suzy to your right and Kate to your left. The small table is in front of you. Turn to Suzy.

"Can you count to ten?"

"Of course I can."

"Education is a wonderful thing, isn't it?! You must have gone to a private school. I want you to count ten cards out loud onto the table like this . . ."

Demonstrate by dealing and counting about three cards onto the table by way of illustration (**1**). Then gather up all the cards again and give them to Suzy (**2**).

"Off you go – ten cards please – out loud – onto the table."

4

5

Suzy deals out ten cards (**3**) and is left holding the rest. Pick up the ten cards as you say

"I'll just check that you have counted correctly."

Count them yourself from hand to hand (**4**) and, as you square them up, get a little finger break under the top three cards. Push them slightly forward in preparation to palm them but *don't do anything else at the moment*. The timing of the palm is critical and, providing that you synchronize the following actions, it will be beautifully deceptive.

"Suzy, you were only *just* absolutely correct! You were nearly wrong! Give the rest of the cards to Kate . . ."

Just as she reaches across to do this, *palm the three cards in your right hand* (**5, 6, 7**).

6

7

8

Your left hand goes forward and across your body with the remaining seven cards (in a block) as you say (**8**)

". . . and put your ten cards on the floor over there and stand on them – preferably using your foot!"

She takes the cards from you and follows your instructions (**9, 10**). Your right hand, with the three cards secretly palmed, comes to rest casually by your hip. This natural action gives perfect cover for the palmed cards! Turn to Kate.

"Kate, I want you to do the same. Count ten cards onto the table (11) – out loud so that we can all hear you."

Our next "task" is secretly to add the three palmed cards to her pile of ten cards without anybody realizing. Once again the timing is all important! I will divide this sequence into three phases, A, B and C. (**A**) With your left hand, gesture to any free surface on your left, (such as another table, a chair or a sideboard) and say (**12**)

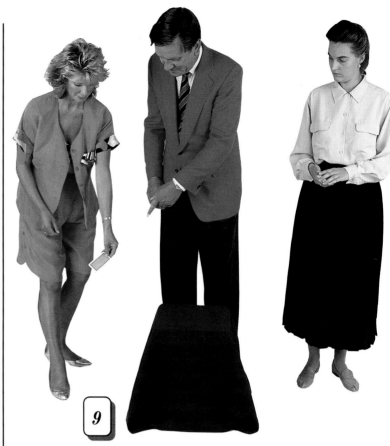

9

10

"Would you please put the rest of the deck over there, out of the way . . ."

(**B**) At the same time as she turns to do this (**13**), you push the ten cards (the ones she has just dealt) forward a little with your right hand, secretly adding the three palmed cards to the top of this uneven pile in the process (**14, 15**).

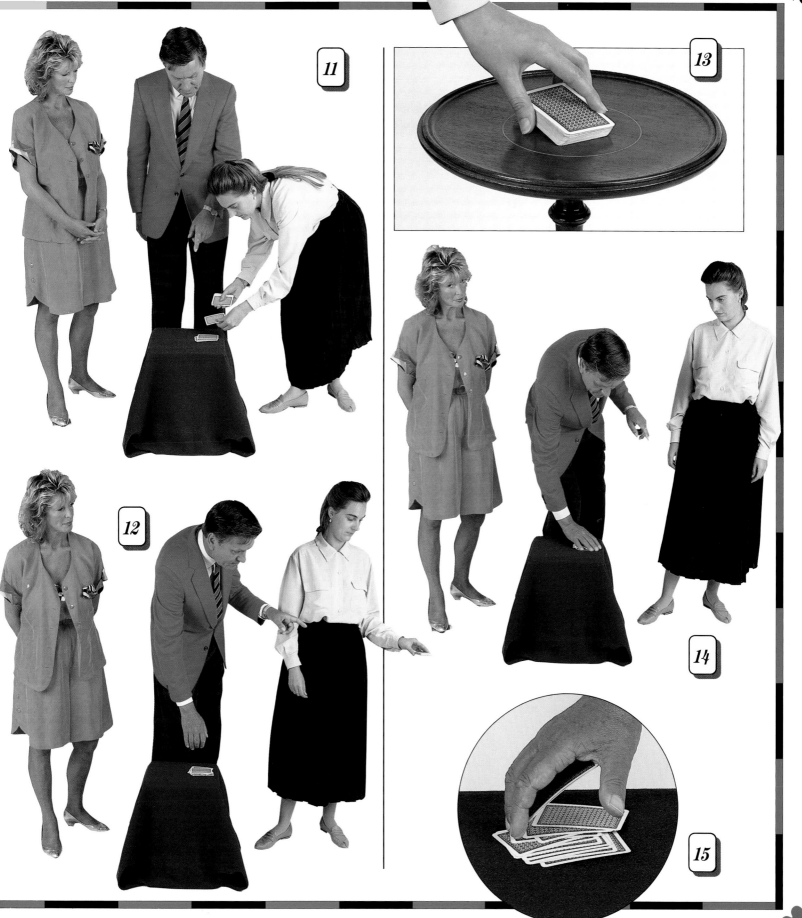

47

The extra cards will never be noticed. As you do this, you say (**16**).

> **". . . and then take your ten cards, put them on the floor over there . . ."**

Gesture to a spot to your left (**17**) with your now empty *right* hand (**C**)

> **". . . and stand on them (18)."**

I have separated these three stages intentionally. Practice the moves and try to get a *rhythm* going. A *slow* "A – B – C." The naturalness of these actions creates the deception. It is bare-faced impudence, really! Now, with the "distraction" achieved, we must build the effect with *presentation*. Talk to Suzy again.

> **"I need a very long hair from your head!"**

Reach up and *mime* plucking a hair from her head (**19**). Whatever you do, *do not* actually pluck a hair – just pretend! Pretend also that the hair just continues to come (**20**). The more you pull, the longer it gets! In fact it is so long that it reaches right across from Suzy's to *Kate's* head! Mime the act of fixing the end of the

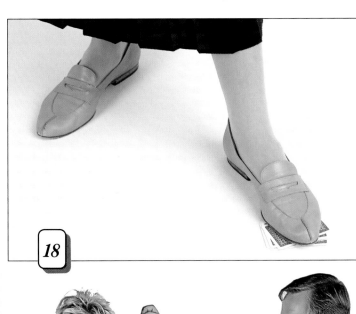

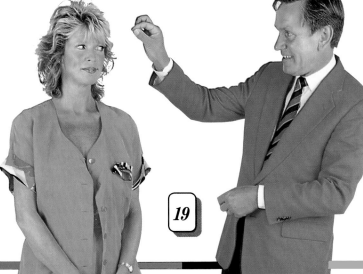

hair to Kate's head (**21**)! When I present the trick, I use an imitation mallet made from sponge rubber to hammer the end of the hair home! I give the lady a couple of gentle taps on the head with it! All good fun!

You have created a bizarre, farcical situation. Two grown-up people each standing on ten cards and joined together by an invisible hair (**22**)! Only a magician could get away with it! Hold your hands in a praying position:

> **"You are now joined together by holy hairlock! Now, this is the trick. Under your foot, Suzy, are ten cards. Under your foot, Kate, also ten cards and in between you is this incredible invisible hair!**
> **I will now make three cards fly from your pile, Suzy. They will travel up your leg, up your back and onto your head. Then, without the aid of a safety net, they will crawl slowly across the invisible hair until they reach your head, Kate! They will travel down your back and down your leg until they arrive on the pile of cards under your foot! They will travel over one at a time, and the first one will go *now*!''**

Pretend that you can actually *see* the first card leaving Suzy's pile (**23**), and traveling upward onto her head. "Trace" its course across the invisible hair onto Kate's head (**24**), then down her body and eventually to her foot (**25**).

"Did you feel it arrive, Kate?"

She will think you have gone out of your mind!

"That was the first one! Let's try the second!"

Trace its invisible path as before.

"That's two. Now the third card is *really* difficult!"

Act as if you really have a struggle to make the last card maneuver its invisible course. Once it has apparently arrived under Kate's foot, breathe a large sigh of relief

"Wow! That was very tricky! Now Suzy, if this trick has really worked, you would not have ten cards under your foot would you? You would only have seven. Pick them up from under your foot, bring them over to the table and count them out loud onto the table."

Suzy counts out her cards and is amazed to find that she now has only *seven* (**26**). Have her check beneath her foot once again to make sure that there are not any cards stuck to her foot! Turn to Kate.

"If this crazy trick has worked, Kate, you would not have ten – you would have the extra three to make thirteen! Bring them over here and slowly count them out loud so that we can all hear."

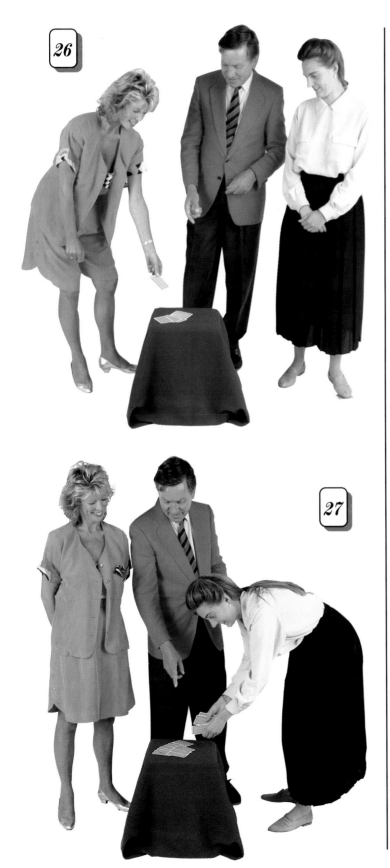

You join in as she counts. Count even louder when she reaches **"Eleven. Twelve. Thirteen."** This strongly emphasizes the appearance of Suzy's three cards (**27**)!

➤ AFTERTHOUGHTS ◄

Well, there you have it. A zany, very entertaining card routine that really packs a punch at the end (**28**). Nor is it difficult to do, once you have got the hang of the timing. Notice how the simple act of palming three cards results in a chance for you to indulge in some delightful humor. It is a great exercise in *presentation*. The patter that I have given you *is* funny. However, I would suggest that you adapt it to suit your own personality. If you use words and phrases that you would not normally use in everyday speech, your performance will become stilted and less convincing. Never be afraid to introduce ideas of your own. That is how new tricks are born.

THE PIMPERNEL QUEEN

This famous trick, usually called "Find the Lady", has a checkered history. It is a swindle common on city sidewalks. Basically the idea is that you have to find the Queen which is one of only three cards used. The three cards are shown face up, you are asked to note the position of the Queen. The cards are then turned face down and very slowly mixed around. *You* (the "mark") are invited to say which one of the three face-down cards is the Queen. The only problem is that you are asked to put your money where your mouth is and back up your choice with hard cash!

Needless to say, you always lose. You may see someone else win and thus be encouraged to try your luck too! Beware! The winner that you saw was "in" on the scam – a member of the gang – he is known as a "shill." Two or three more members of the team will be positioned around to keep an eye out for the police so that a quick getaway can be made if it becomes necessary! So the racket is "feeding" at least four people and is, of course, strictly illegal.

Even to this day you will come across gangs fleecing unwary people at racetracks and on the city sidewalks with "Find the Lady." It is also sometimes known as "The Three Card Trick," "Three Card Mark," or "Chase the Ace." If you ever come across such a team *please keep your money in your pocket* – cross the street – walk away – do not get involved. This simple gambling game is not a "game" at all, but an outright con. There is no way for you to win. The operator ("thrower") of the cards will be an extremely expert sleight-of-hand merchant! *You have been warned*!

Magicians always cheat fairly! I will now teach you an entertaining routine that has been inspired by the traditional swindle although the methods that we will use will be very different! Your audience will credit you with having incredible skill! I call it The Pimpernel Queen.

REQUIREMENTS
Two identical Queens
Three identical Jokers
One trombone-type wire paper clip
Double-sided adhesive tape

♣ EFFECT ♣

While performing a "Find the Lady" routine, the Queen repeatedly disappears only to be found in the performer's pocket! Even with the restraints of a paper clip placed upon her, the Lady vanishes yet again!

◆ WHAT YOU DO ◆

Stick a Joker and a Queen together, *back to back*, using the double-sided tape. Glue would do, but the sticky tape gives a better finish (**1**). Put the ungimmicked Queen in your right hand pocket. Place the double-faced Joker/Queen between the two ordinary Jokers with the Queen side showing.

Lay the three cards on the table (**2**).

"This is a trick called 'The Pimpernel Queen.' I use two Jokers . . ."

Pick up the two Jokers and hold them face up in your left hand.

" . . . and a Queen."

Pick up the Queen (being careful not to "flash" its Joker side) and place it next to the two Jokers (**3**).

"You must keep your eye on the Queen at all times. Are you watching?"

Close up the small fan and in so doing get a little finger break under the top two cards (the double-sided Queen and the first unprepared Joker) (**4**). Push them forward (**5**) and then turn both cards face down as one (**6, 7**).

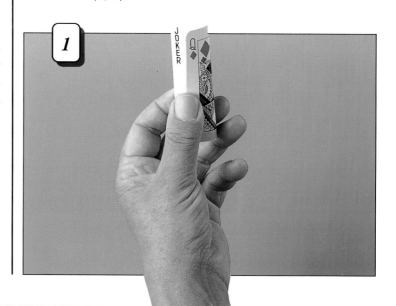

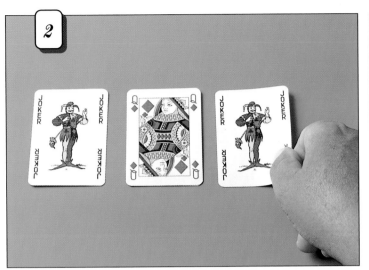

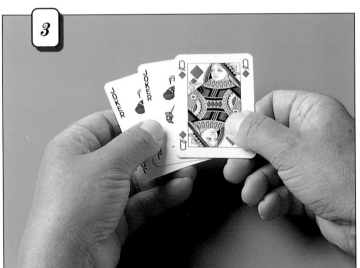

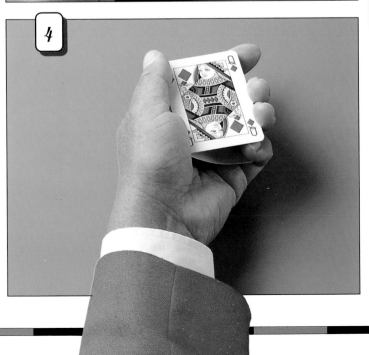

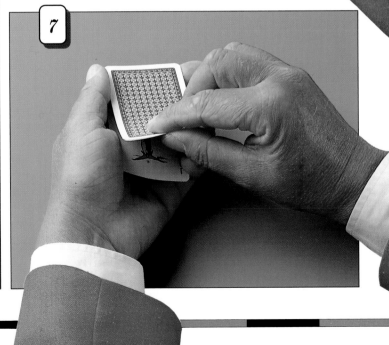

Now spread the cards out again (**8**). Apparently the Queen is now face down on top. Actually, the back that can be seen is the back of the Joker. Our double-faced card is now in the middle with its Joker face showing and its Queen face hidden! Transfer the face-down card to the center of the spread (**9**). Now address one of the spectators and say,

"No matter how I mix the cards up now, you will have no problem keeping track of the Queen because it is the only face-down card! Take out the Queen for me please. Turn it over."

He does so (**10**) and is flabbergasted to find that it is not the Queen but another Joker (**11**)!

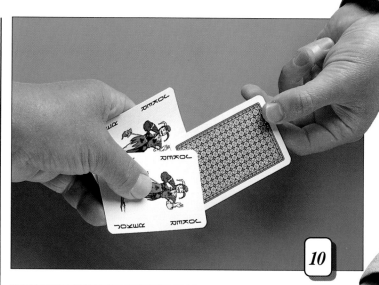

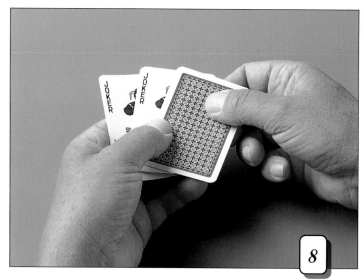

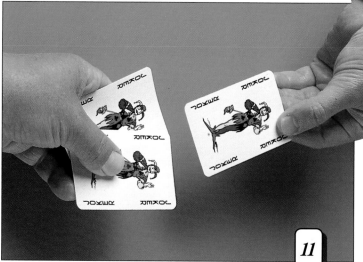

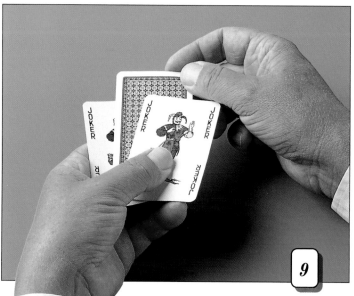

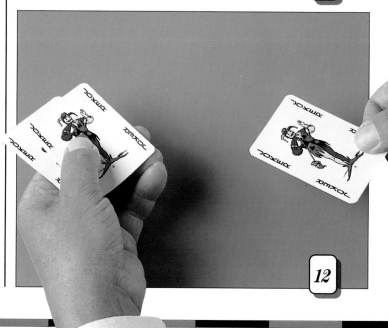

54

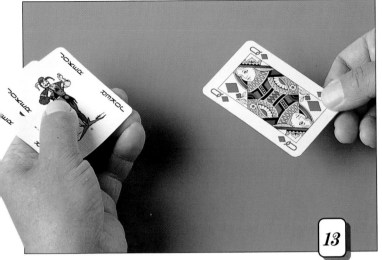

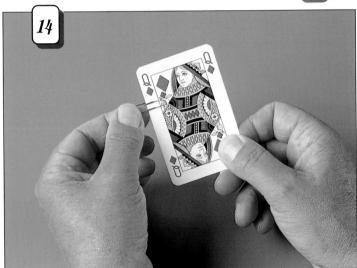

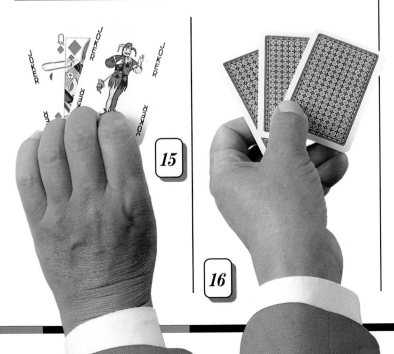

"I had another Joker in my pocket and, when you were not looking, my hand shot into my pocket like a flash with the Queen and changed it for the Joker!"

As you say this, pick off the top Joker (**12**) (really the double card), put it, and your hand, into your pocket and turn the double card over bringing the same card out again only with its *Queen* face showing again (**13**)!

"I'll do it again!"

Repeat all the previous moves, but this time when your hand goes to your pocket with the double card, *leave it there and bring out the ungimmicked Queen which you previously placed there*! You are now, as we say, "clean!" You now add an extra refinement by introducing the paper clip.

"Just to help you keep track of the 'Pimpernel Queen' I will put a paper clip on her."

Slip the paper clip on the long side of the Queen (**14**) and then hold the three cards in your left hand as shown, with the paper-clipped Queen in the middle (**15**). It is important that the cards are held *exactly* as shown. The first two fingers are placed near the lower left corner of the top card and the thumb immediately behind. The three cards are first shown face up, and then face down by turning the hand over (**16**).

Show them face up and then face down again. Now remove the card immediately under your thumb (Joker) and place it face down on the table to your right (**17**). This leaves two cards in your hand.

"If I place a card over there . . ." (gesture towards the tabled card) **". . . what cards have I got left? Yes, that's right, the Queen with the clip and the Joker."** (Show their faces, **18**) **". . . and the card over there is a . . . ?"**

You distract the spectator's attention by asking this question and pointing to the card on the table again. As soon as he looks toward the card, turn your left hand over (**19**), bringing the two cards into a face-down position, *and at the same time* twist your two fingers and thumb that are holding the cards so that the two cards slide past one another (**20**) and change positions (**21**). As this happens, the Joker will automatically engage the clip and "steal" it from the Queen (**22**)!

This is a very sweet move and with a little practice you will soon get the hang of it. The transfer of the clip from one card to the other is disguised by the greater movement of the hand as it turns the two cards face down. The eye is incapable of taking it all in at once. Place the newly clipped card onto the table (**23**) and tell your chosen spectator to keep his eyes firmly on it.

Now lay the card without the clip (Queen) on top of the free card on the table and in the same action pick them both up and put them away in your pocket (**24**).

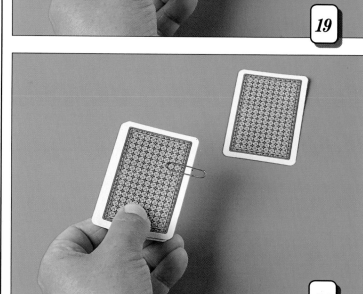

56

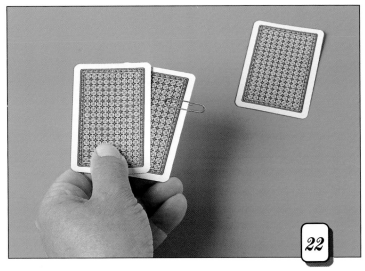

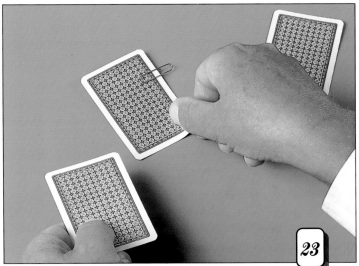

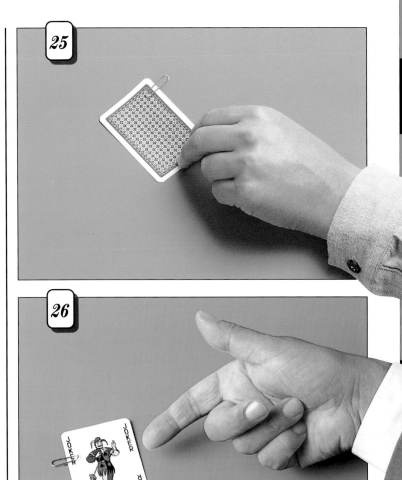

"I'll just put the Jokers in my pocket out of the way. Do you know why I call her 'The Pimpernel Queen?'

They seek her here,
They seek her there,
They seek her almost everywhere!
Is she in heaven?
Is she in hell?
That darned elusive Pimpernel!

Turn her over please!"

He turns over the card with the paper clip (**25**) and finds, to his utter astonishment, that the Pimpernel Queen has flown! The Joker (that's you) has the last laugh (**26**)!

CHANGE OF IDENTITY

This is a cute, snappy trick with some remarkable magical changes actually happening in the hands of two spectators!

◄ EFFECT ►

Two spectators each hold a card. On your command the cards change places!

REQUIREMENTS
A deck of cards
One extra card (say an Ace of Spades)
Two spectators (we will call them Kate and Suzy)

➤ WHAT YOU DO ◄

Arrange the deck so that the top three cards are: Ace of Spades, Queen of Hearts, Ace of Spades (**1**). Put the cards in the case and the case back in your pocket.

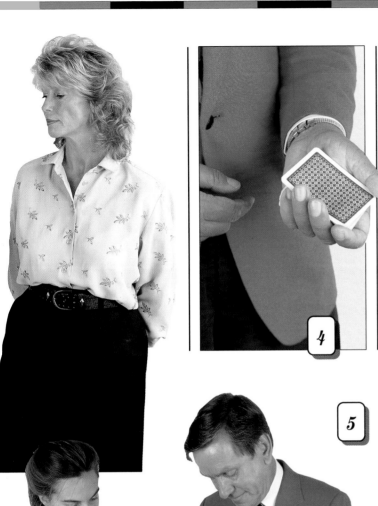

Stand Kate to your right, Suzy to your left. Take out the case, remove the cards (**2**) and *return the empty case to your pocket* (**3**). This is important – you will see why later. Give the deck a couple of *false shuffles* keeping the top three cards in place. Secure a little finger break under the top *two* cards (**4**) in preparation for a *double lift*. Turn to Kate (**5**).

"What is your name?" ''Kate.'' **"Well, Kate, I am going to change your identity!"**

Double lift, showing the Queen of Hearts (**6**) and lay the two cards, (still aligned) on top of the deck (**7**).

"From now on you are going to be Miss Queen of Hearts (8)!"

Turn the two cards face down again (**9, 10**) and deal the top card only (Ace of Spades) (**11**) onto Kate's outstretched palm. Have her cover the card with her other palm (**12**). She thinks that she is holding the Queen of Hearts!

"What is your name now?" "Miss Queen of Hearts" says Kate. **"That's right!"**

Give the cards another couple of false shuffles and then prepare for another doubt lift as you turn to Suzy.

"What is your name?" "Suzy." Double lift showing the Ace of Spades (**13**). **"From now on you will be known as Miss Ace of Spades! O.K.?"**

Turn the card(s) face down as before and deal off the single top card onto Suzy's palm (**14**). Have her cover it with her other hand too (**15**). It is really the Queen of Hearts but she *thinks* it is the Ace of Spades. The reason for asking them both to hold their respective cards sandwiched between their palms in this way is to stop them fiddling with them and exposing their faces prematurely. This would rob you of the climax that you are working up to.

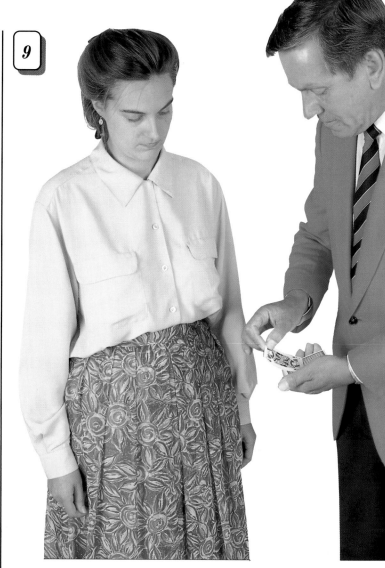

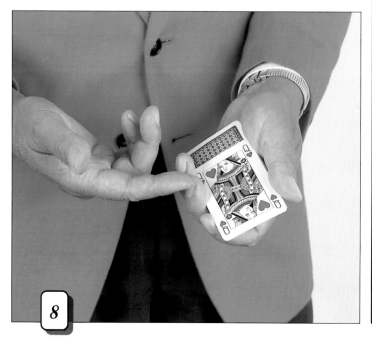

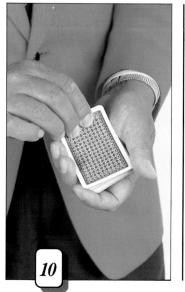

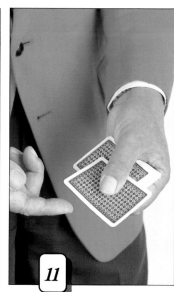

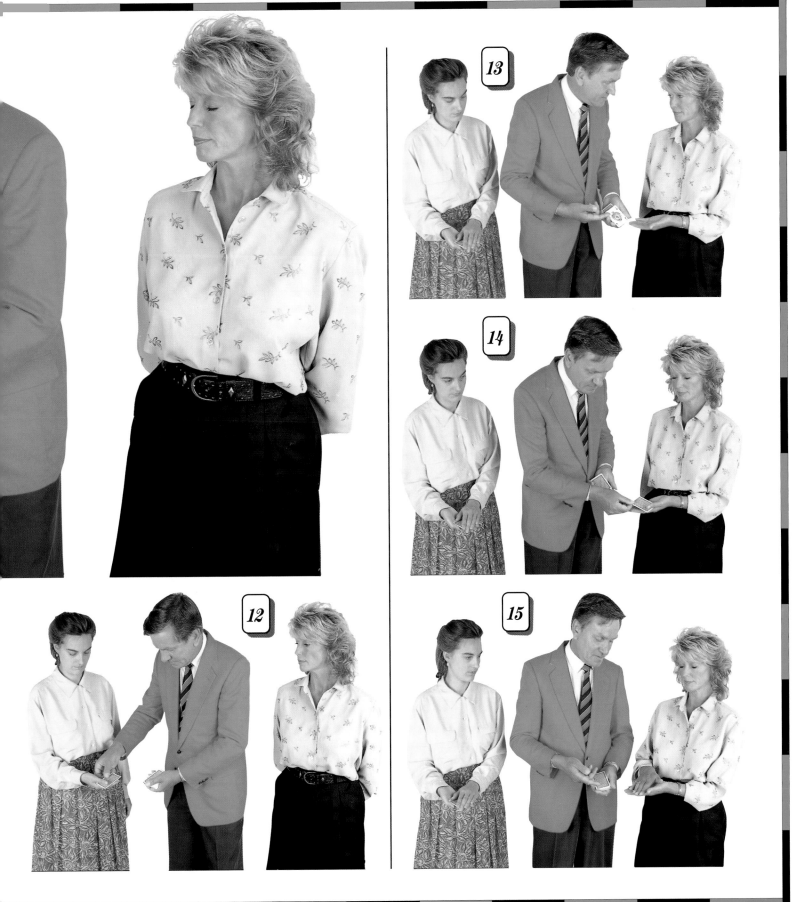

"What is your name now?"

"Miss Ace of Spades" laughs Suzy.

"If I can change your identity so easily, I can probably do it again. Shall I try? Miss Queen of Hearts – you will now become Miss Ace of Spades! You, Miss Ace of Spades, will now become Miss Queen of Hearts! You don't believe me, do you? When I snap my fingers, turn over your cards and show them to everyone!"

Watch their faces! The two cards have somehow changed places (**16**) even though they were holding the cards themselves! Unbelievable!

While *everyone* is concentrating on the revealed cards, *palm off* the top card (the spare Ace of Spades) with your right hand and immediately shove your hand into your right pocket (**17, 18**). *Leave the Ace of Spades there* and bring your hand out again holding the empty card case. Put the cards into the case (**19, 20, 21**) and then casually toss it onto the table. If anyone should want to examine the cards later, all is now "clean!"

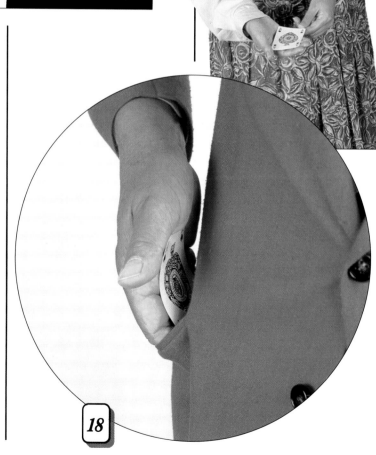

◆ AFTERTHOUGHTS ◆

Like all the best tricks, this one has a very simple plot and is quite easy to do. We magicians often put thoughts into the minds of our audiences. Notice how the two false shuffles very subtly emphasize the apparent fairness of it all, so that at the end there is no logical explanation. It must be magic!

Although, at the end , the deck may be examined by any curious spectator, *you should not openly invite such scrutiny*. It is bad psychology and puts the wrong type of thoughts in people's minds. The deck should be above suspicion. We remove the extra card so that, should you wish to perform another trick, you will not be embarrassed by the sudden appearance of five Aces! People have been shot for less!

THE PHOENIX CARD TRICK

This trick will ruin two cards. Having said that, I think you will find that it has such a fantastic effect upon the spectators that you will consider it worth the expense. I keep two decks of cards aside just to enable me to perform this trick. That's how good *I* think it is.

♣ EFFECT ♣

A card is selected and torn up. One corner piece is given back to the spectator, who then sets fire to the rest of the pieces! In a flash, the destroyed pieces reappear inside your wallet which has been on the table throughout. To cap it all, the corner that she has been looking after fits perfectly!

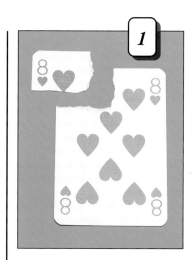

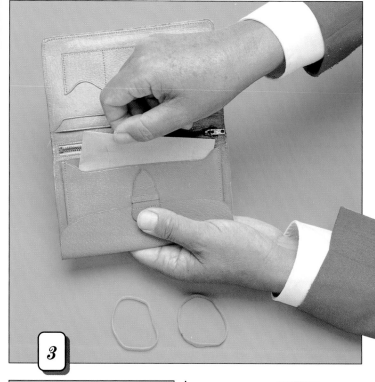

> **REQUIREMENTS**
> Two cards the same (say both eight of Hearts)
> Your "working" deck of cards
> A wallet
> Two rubber bands
> Two good quality thick envelopes
>
> Matches and a large ashtray
> A spectator (we will call her Jill)

♣ PREPARATION ♣

Tear a corner off one of the cards so that it looks like this (**1**). Seal the rest of the card inside one of the envelopes (**2**) and place it inside your wallet (**3**). Place a rubber band around the wallet (one each way) effectively "locking" it (**4**).

Hide the piece that you tore off the eight of Hearts in the corner of the other envelope (**5**). *Do not seal it down.* Place the other eight of Hearts on top of your deck. Put the deck back in its case. Before you start, the loaded wallet, the envelope containing the hidden corner, the deck of cards in its case, the matches and the ashtray should all be ready on the table.

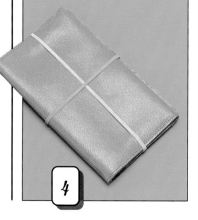

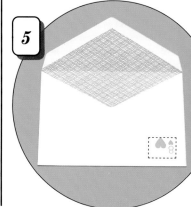

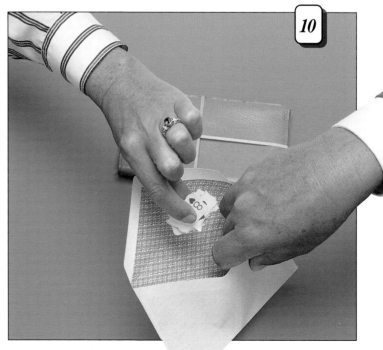

➤ WHAT YOU DO ◀

Take the cards out of the case and give them a quick *false shuffle*. Now force the eight of Hearts (**6, 7**). I would suggest that the *slip cut force* is probably the best one to use for this trick. Try to give the impression that the choice of the card is of no real significance to you.

"I want you to tear your card into eight pieces. I know it will ruin the card but don't worry, there's no expense spared when I'm around!"

While she does this (**8, 9**) , pick up the envelope and hold it in readiness as shown with your fingers inside concealing the spare corner that you previously placed there (**10**).

"Drop the pieces into this envelope please, Jill."

As soon as she has dropped the pieces into the envelope begin to lick the flap to seal the envelope down. Then before you press the flap down, and *almost as an afterthought*, take out the extra piece and give it to Jill to look after (**11**).

"Please look after this piece until the end."

Now seal the envelope, pick up the matches and set fire to it. It is best to start at one corner and let the flames lick up the sides of the envelope (**12**). It goes without saying that you do this over the large ashtray that you have readily at hand. Try to reduce the whole thing to ashes (**13**). You must ensure, at the very least, that all the pieces of torn card are completely destroyed. Once the flames are out and things have cooled down, pick up a handful of ash and crumble it between your fingers (**14**).

"You know, Jill, nothing in this world is ever completely destroyed. Even this card. It is now floating through the air invisible to the human eye. In this state, however, it is possible to resurrect the card. Watch!"

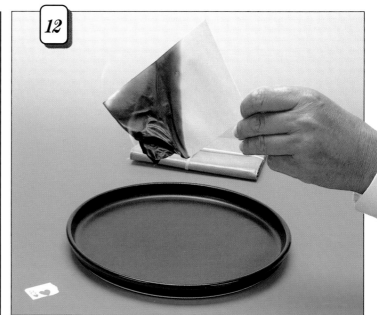

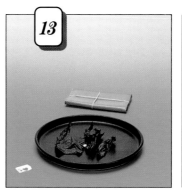

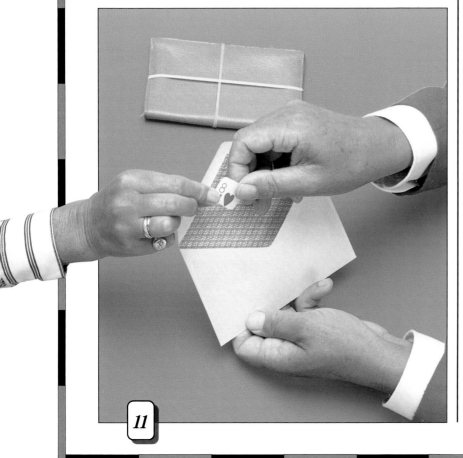

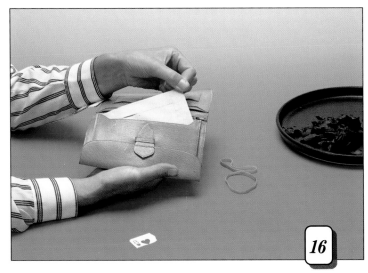

16

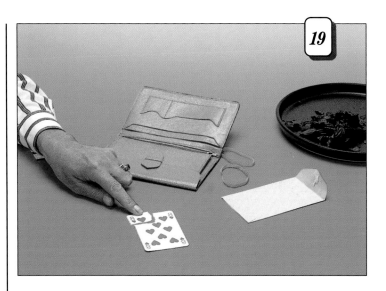

19

17

20

18

Grab handfuls of fresh air and make magic passes with them toward the wallet, which you will remember has been in full view throughout.

"This is called the Phoenix Card Trick. Your card, like the mythical bird, has now risen from the flames and is completely restored! Open up my wallet. Remove the sealed envelope from inside and see what it contains!"

Jill does all this (**15, 16, 17**) and finds the "restored" eight of Hearts (**18**). Minus one corner!

"See if the corner that you kept fits the gap, Jill."

She does (**19**). It does (**20**)!

67

THE GHOSTLY CARD!

The time that you have spent learning to false shuffle and palm cards will be rewarded once you have mastered this beautiful trick. It is very popular among card magicians.

◆ EFFECT ◆

A spectator freely chooses a card, returns it to the deck and then shuffles the cards himself. You wrap the cards in a handkerchief and hold the parcel high in the air. The spectator names his card and you gently shake the parcel. His selected card is seen slowly to penetrate through the handkerchief, finally being shaken clear and falling to the floor. The rest of the deck is still securely wrapped up in the handkerchief!

This short description cannot hope to do justice to this fine trick.

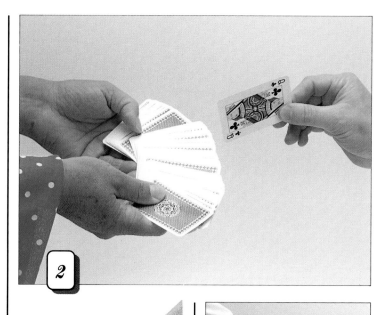

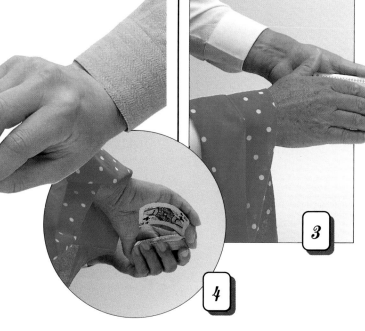

REQUIREMENTS
A deck of cards
A clean, good quality handkerchief
A spectator (we will call him Paul)

♣ WHAT YOU DO ♣

Drape the handkerchief over your right arm, waiter fashion! Have Paul choose a card (**1**) and remember it. Have it returned to the deck (**2**) and then control his card to the top of the deck during the course of an overhand *false shuffle*. Prepare to palm his card off the top. *Do not do it yet!*

Please don't forget the name of your card, Paul. To be absolutely fair, I'd like you to give them all a good shuffle too!''

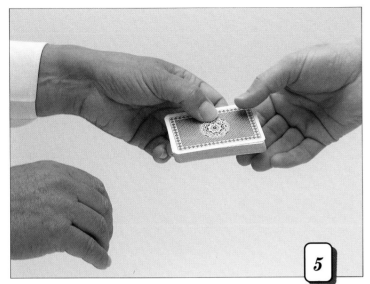

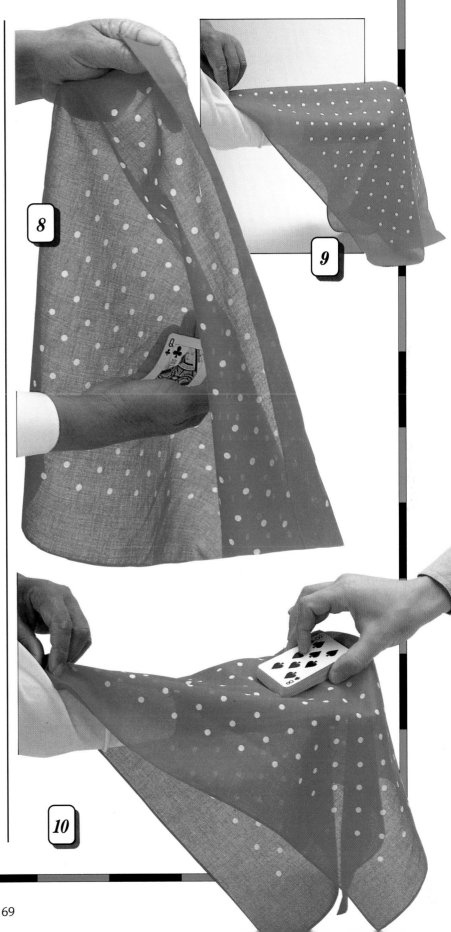

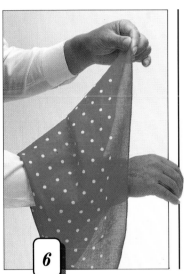

Paul will look at your face as soon as you start to talk. *Palm the card now (3, 4)*, taking the rest of the cards away with your left hand and giving them to him to shuffle (5). As soon as he has taken the cards, remove the handkerchief that is hanging over your arm (6) and drape it over your right hand (7). In the same action, turn the hand palm upward (8) and cover your hand with the handkerchief (9). *These four actions that must be practiced until they flow and blend into one.*

"Paul, now that you have shuffled the cards, I want you to place them face up on top of the handkerchief (10)."

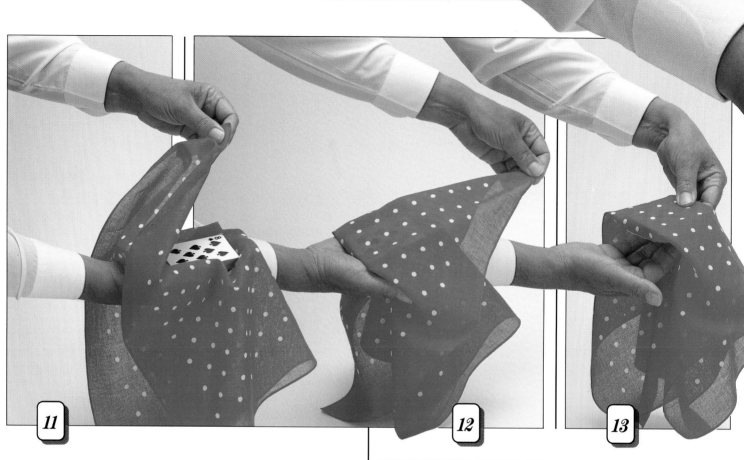

He does this. You now have to wrap the cards up in the handkerchief. It is very important how you do it. The end result will be that the deck will be on the *inside* and the palmed card will be on the *outside*!

With your left fingers pull the fold of the handkerchief that is draped over your right wrist *forward* (**11**) to cover the cards (**12**). Take a grip on the deck, the handkerchief *and* the hidden card beneath it, with your left fingers as illustrated (**13**). You can now take your right hand away.

The left and right sides of the handkerchief are hanging down on their respective sides. Fold these sides down and underneath the deck and take any surplus material forward, twisting it rope fashion (**14**). The deck should now look like this (**15**). This is an exposed view and not one that is seen by the spectators. The parcel is now casually shown on both sides. Your right fingers cover the otherwise visible end of the selected card! Hold the twisted part of the package in your left hand at about head height (**16**).

"What was the name of the card you chose, Paul?"

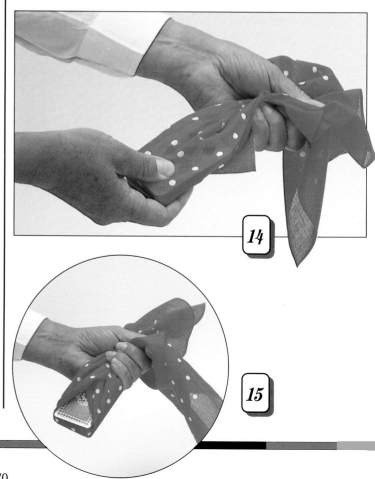

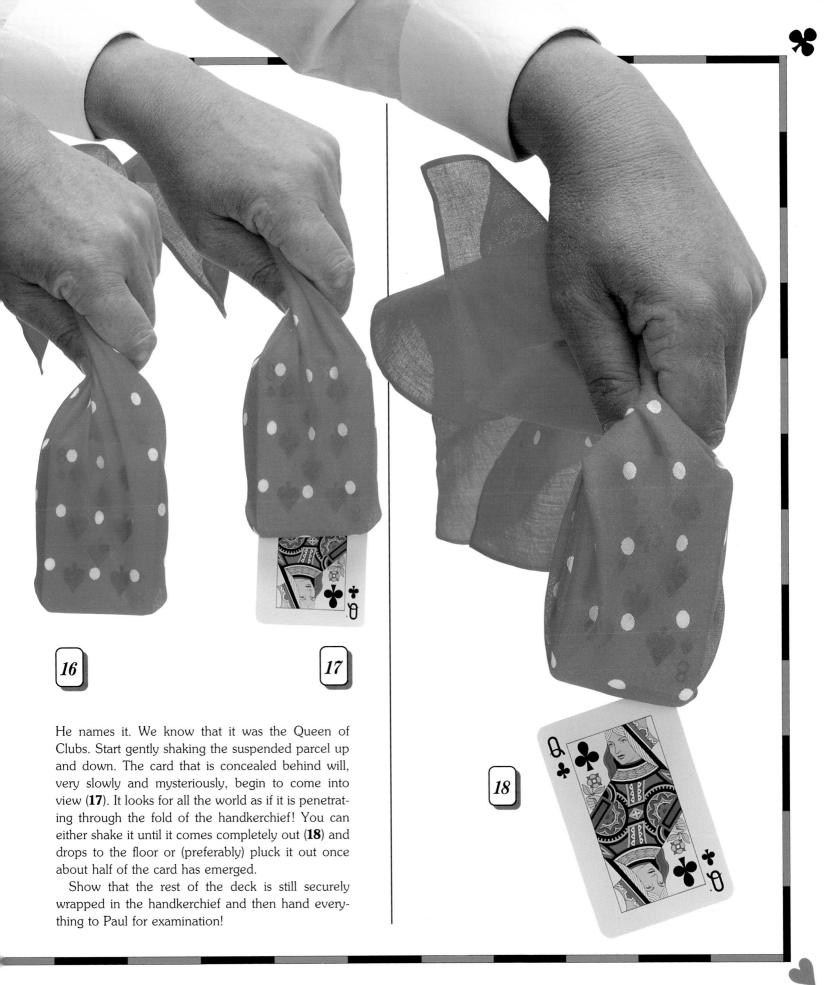

16

17

18

He names it. We know that it was the Queen of Clubs. Start gently shaking the suspended parcel up and down. The card that is concealed behind will, very slowly and mysteriously, begin to come into view (**17**). It looks for all the world as if it is penetrating through the fold of the handkerchief! You can either shake it until it comes completely out (**18**) and drops to the floor or (preferably) pluck it out once about half of the card has emerged.

Show that the rest of the deck is still securely wrapped in the handkerchief and then hand everything to Paul for examination!

CLEOPATRA'S NEEDLE

This spectacular trick ruins a card each time you perform it – so use your own deck, not a borrowed one. You do not want to lose your friends, even in the cause of magic!

◀ EFFECT ▶

A freely chosen card is shuffled back into the deck which is then wrapped up in a paper package. The spectator is invited to stick a darning needle (that has been threaded with ribbon) into the edge of the deck at any point that he wishes. It is pushed right through and out the other side, thus threading the ribbon through at the same point.

The spectator holds each end of the ribbon with the paper package suspended from its center. He is asked to name his card (say the two of Clubs). The paper is now ripped away. All the cards drop to the floor – all that is except his chosen card, the two of Clubs! It remains suspended with the ribbon penetrating right through its center!

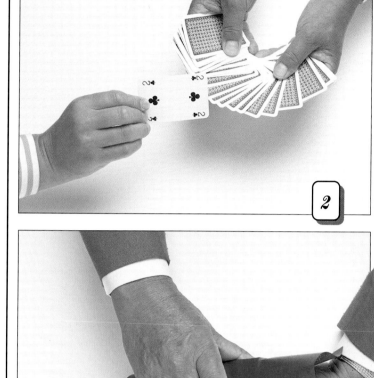

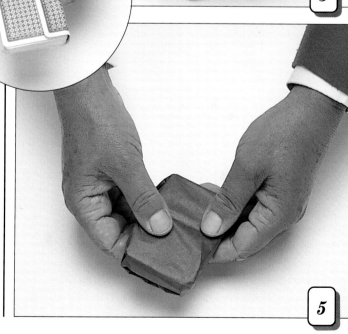

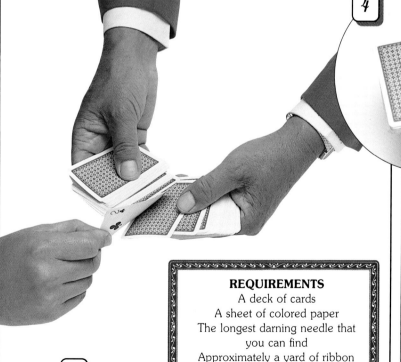

```
REQUIREMENTS
A deck of cards
A sheet of colored paper
The longest darning needle that
you can find
Approximately a yard of ribbon
(red looks best)
```

1

2

3

4

5

You hold the package while he does this (**7**). Offer him the clear long edge first and help him guide the needle into the package and then out the other side. Make sure that he realizes that you are in no way trying to influence where he puts it. He will not notice the slight extra pressure needed to push the needle through the other side. Pull the needle completely through (**8**) and keep pulling until the paper package reaches the center of the ribbon. Then remove the *needle* completely.

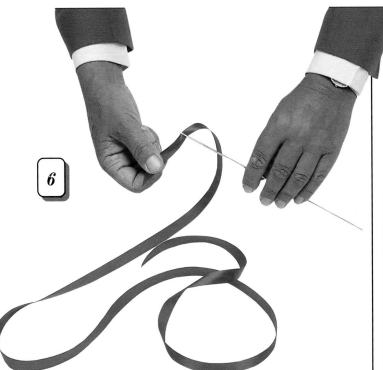

◆ WHAT YOU DO ◆

Pick your spectator. Let us call him Oliver. Have him choose a card (**1**), look at it and remember it (**2**).

Always emphasize that a card should be remembered. You would feel very foolish if you got to the end of the trick and the spectator could not remember the name of his card! I know! It has happened to me!

Get the card returned to the deck and control it to the top in the course of an overhand *false shuffle*. Now wrap the deck up in the paper (**3**). As you do so, slide the top card over and around the long side of the deck (**4**). You will find this quite easy to do – although a few practice rounds would be advisable to perfect your technique. The card should be slipped over *secretly* under cover of the wrapping process (**5**) and will not be suspected.

"Now Oliver, take this darning needle (6) and stick it into the package. I want it to go through the paper, pass between any two cards, and then come out the other side. So, I want you to thread the package onto the ribbon. Please be careful of my fingers!"

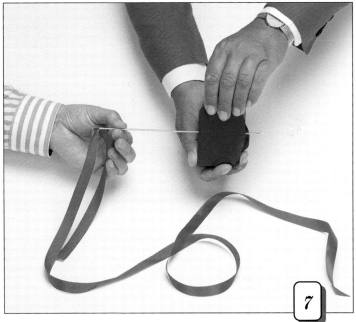

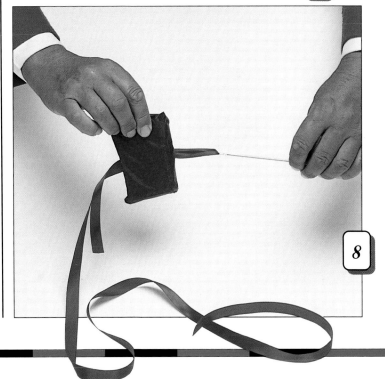

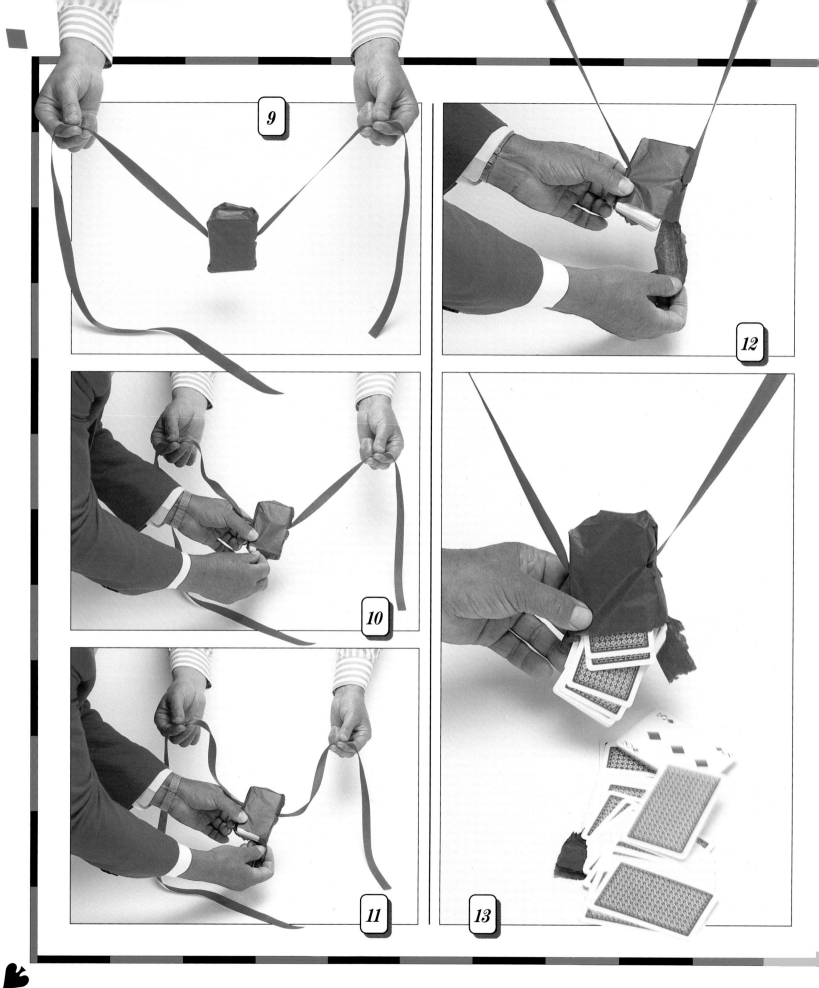

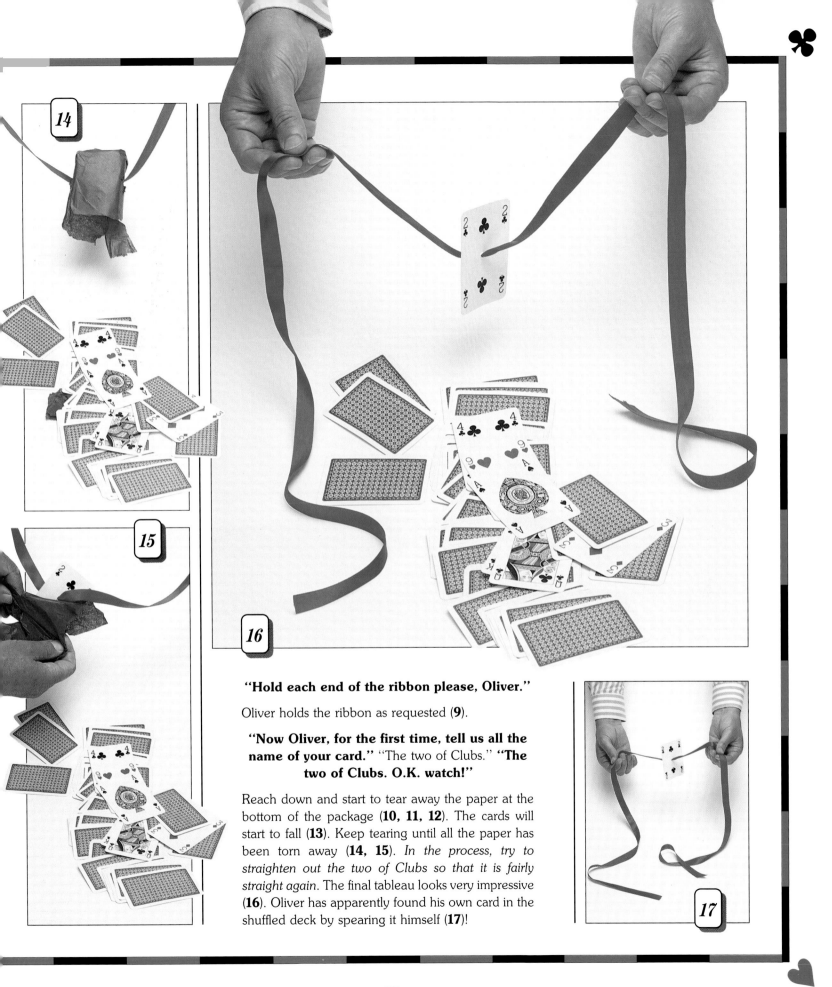

"Hold each end of the ribbon please, Oliver."

Oliver holds the ribbon as requested (**9**).

"Now Oliver, for the first time, tell us all the name of your card." "The two of Clubs." **"The two of Clubs. O.K. watch!"**

Reach down and start to tear away the paper at the bottom of the package (**10, 11, 12**). The cards will start to fall (**13**). Keep tearing until all the paper has been torn away (**14, 15**). *In the process, try to straighten out the two of Clubs so that it is fairly straight again.* The final tableau looks very impressive (**16**). Oliver has apparently found his own card in the shuffled deck by spearing it himself (**17**)!

THE GOBSMACKER CARD TRICK

After performing this trick, your friends will think that you are totally brilliant, super skilful, and a Master Magician!

♣ EFFECT ♣

The name of a spectator's chosen card is found written on a piece of paper that is concealed in your shoe!

REQUIREMENTS
A deck of cards
A piece of paper bearing the appropriate message

◀ PREPARATION ▶

Write these words on a piece of paper and sign it at the bottom:

**You are thinking of the Queen of Hearts!
signed Mystery Man**

Fold the paper up and slip it in your right shoe! Place the Queen of Hearts on top of your deck of cards and you are all set.

➤ WHAT YOU DO ◀

Get a volunteer. Let us call him Simon. Give the cards an overhand *false shuffle* retaining the Queen of Hearts on top. Now perform the *cross hand force* which, very effectively, forces the Queen of Hearts (**1**). Do not forget to emphasize the fairness of everything to Simon. (You cannot see the cards, he shuffles repeatedly, etc., etc.)

Ask him to remember the card (**2**) before he returns it and loses it in the deck when he shuffles them (**3**). Turn around to face him while he is still doing the final shuffle. Now we lead him up the garden path a little!

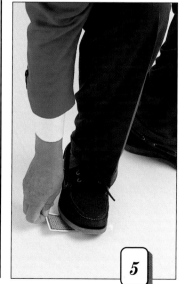
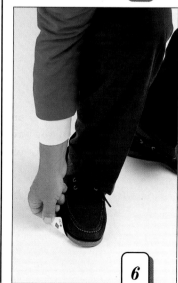

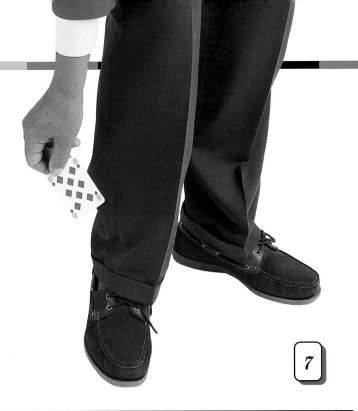

7

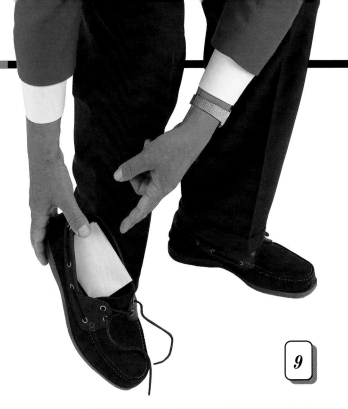

9

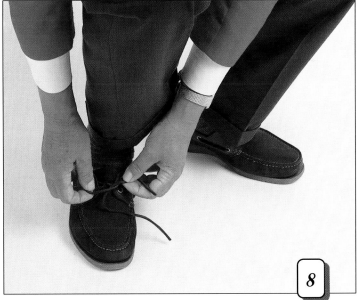

8

10

"You shuffled the cards, chose one, returned it to the deck and shuffled yet again. Obviously, Simon, nobody knows now where your card is, do they?"

He agrees that it would be impossible. Take the deck back and start to look through them as if you are trying to find his chosen one. Then, with a look of triumph on your face, take out any card (**4**) (*not* the Queen of Hearts) and, without showing it, place it face down *under* your right shoe (**5**).

"Your card is now under my right foot!"

(*Don't say "shoe"*). Pick it up (**6**). Turn it over (**7**) and say

"Tell me – yes or no – is that your card?"

"No."

"Oh dear! Can I try again?"

Take off your shoe (**8**), pick up the piece of paper (**9**), and give it to Simon to read aloud (**10**). *He will be absolutely gobsmacked!*

THE SEE-THROUGH CARD TRICK

If you are in the right place at the right time this classic of card magic is an absolute stunner! You will, however, have to choose your location and moment very carefully. Never attempt to do it unless the conditions are 100 per cent favorable. It is too good to be ruined by bad presentation.

◆ EFFECT ◆

A spectator chooses a card, returns it to the deck and shuffles the cards himself. You go to a window in the room and hold the deck against the window pane. The spectator is then invited to take your place, holding the deck in position. You walk a few paces away, turn and then ask the spectator to name his card. You ask the spectator to return the cards to you. He does, but he appears to leave one card stuck to the glass. It is his chosen card! You ask him to pull it off so that you may show it to the rest of the audience. To his utter amazement he finds that he cannot.

His chosen card is actually on the other side of the glass, outside the window!

REQUIREMENTS
The window must be suitable, with curtains that can easily be pushed aside. This is an "after dark trick."
A duplicate of any card in your deck. We will assume that it is the five of Spades.

♣ PREPARATION ♣

Long before you do this trick you must stick the duplicate card to the outside of the window so that it faces inward (**1**). A small piece of double sided sticky tape does the job nicely. If you are in an upstairs room and you have the opportunity secretly to open the window, you just reach around as far as you can, stick the card in position and then close the window and re-draw the curtain.

❯ WHAT YOU DO ❮

You start with the five of Spades on top of the deck. *False shuffle* a few times and then *force* the spectator to choose the five of Spades by your favorite method. The slip force or the cross hand force are both very suitable.

Once the spectator (let us call him Jim) has remembered his card, returned it to the deck and given it a shuffle, give the deck to him to shuffle again. This is

3

4

5

always a good policy when you do not have to keep track of a selected card. Just make sure he loses it in the deck. If you notice that he has shuffled the force card to the bottom ask him to give the cards another little shuffle!

"Let me have the deck now, Jim."

You take it from him and walk over to the window. Your left hand pulls the curtain to one side while your right hand (which contains the cards) quickly puts the deck directly over the card that is outside the window (**2**). Your back helps conceal what is actually happening and as Jim has no idea what you are trying to do, you will find it an easy matter to set yourself up in the correct position. The cards, of course, must have their faces toward the room.

"Now Jim, I want you to take over from me. Come and hold the cards against the window for me please"

You swap places (**3**) and walk a few paces away, then turn to face him.

"What was the name of the card that you chose?" "The five of Spades."
"Please bring the cards to me now, Jim."

He does so (**4**).

"Look Jim! You seem to have left one card behind stuck to the window. Good gracious! It is your card! The five of Spades . . . would you fetch it for me please!"

In a daze, Jim goes back to the window and tries to peel off his card (**5**). To his utter amazement he finds that, somehow, his chosen card has passed through the glass and is now on the *outside* of the window!

➤ AFTERTHOUGHTS ◄

Although I do not think it vital, if you have the opportunity during the mayhem to palm the other five of Spades and secretly pocket it, do so! An alternative "insurance" would be to keep the other deck of cards from which the duplicate card was originally moved in one of your pockets and just casually swap the decks as the spectator goes to retrieve his card from the window.

TIMES FOUR

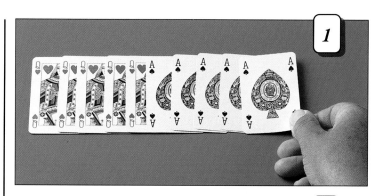

This lovely routine is very close to my heart. It is well worth the practice and effort needed to perfect it. If you have digested the technical section at the beginning of this book you will be in possession of all the skills required to make this trick very special.

◆ EFFECT ◆

A pile of Aces instantly changes places with a pile of Queens, only a split second after all the cards have been shown!

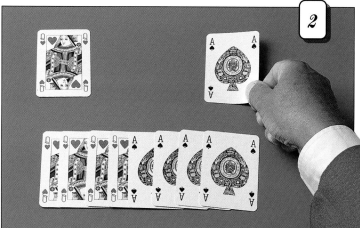

```
REQUIREMENTS
Five identical black Aces
(say Spades)
Five identical red Queens
(say Hearts)
```

◆ WHAT YOU DO ◆

Arrange the Aces and Queens as shown in the photograph (**1**), and spread them out across the table. Gesture toward the table.

"I have five Queens and five Aces – all left over from last night's poker game!"

Pick up a Queen from one end and an Ace from the other and lay them on the table just above the spread (**2**).

"These two cards will act as our 'markers'."

Scoop the rest of the cards up with your right hand *but* (apparently accidentally) miss the first two Queens – leaving them on the table (**3**).

"Oops! Sorry!"

Pick the last two Queens up and place them on top of the Aces (**4**) – *not in their original position!* This is a very casual, laid-back sequence of actions and should not attract suspicion. Turn the block of cards face down. Very slowly and deliberately deal the first four

cards face down in a pile just beneath the Ace marker, counting them as you go (**5**). The first two will be Queens, so make sure that you do not inadvertently flash the faces of these to the audience. The third and fourth cards dealt are actually Aces, so you can flash the faces of these if you wish. Don't make a big thing of it – just be casual.

"We have one, two, three, four Aces."

Deal the remaining four cards face down beneath the Queen marker in the same way (**6**). As before, be careful not to flash the first two.

"And over here we have one, two, three, four Queens." Pause. **"Let's see what happens if we change the positions of our two markers!"**

Switch the two markers over so that the Ace is now above the left hand pile and the Queen above the right hand pile (**7**). Pick up the four cards from the left hand pile. Turn them face up and hold them in your left hand as shown (**8**). The spectator will probably be surprised to see the face of the Ace instead of the Queen that he was expecting!

3

6

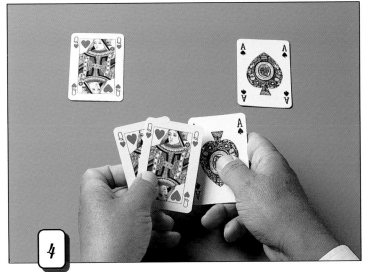

4

7

5

8

This next move has four separate parts which must blend into one. (**A**) With your right fingers and thumb pull the top Ace to the right until it is clear of the other three cards (**9**). (**B**) Turn your left wrist so that its cards are now face down (**10**). (**C**) Place the Ace in your right hand face down on top of these three face-down cards (**11**). (**D**) Twist your wrist back the other way so that the cards are face up again. You count . . .

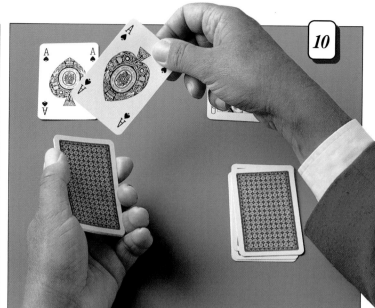

"One."

All you have done is to transfer an Ace from the face of the packet of cards to the back of the packet. You must do it exactly as I have described because next time we do it, although everything will *look* the same, we are actually going to cheat a little!

Secretly *glide* back the bottom card (**12**). Grip the remaining three cards as one and pull them to the right just as you did with the single card a moment ago (**13**). Turn your left wrist to bring its card face down (**14**). Deal the three cards (as one) face down upon it (**15**). Twist your wrist to bring the cards face up again (**16**). *This should look exactly the same as before.* You count . . .

"Two."

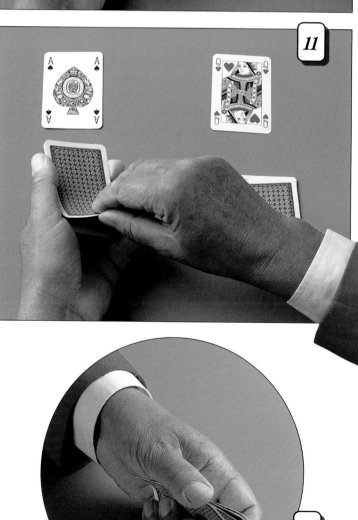

13

16

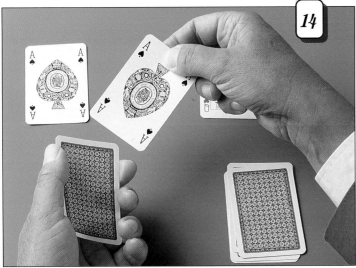

14

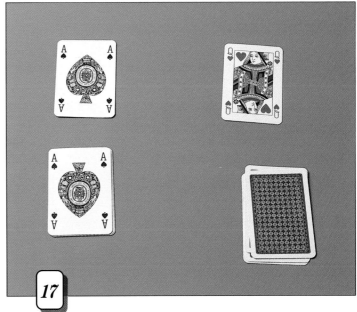

15

17

Now transfer a single card again as you count . . .

"Three"

. . . and finally do the *treble lift* version again as you count . . .

"Four Aces!"

Square the four cards up and place them *face up* beneath the Ace marker (**17**).

"Where we had the Queens, we now have the Aces . . ."

18

20

19

21

Pick up the left hand pile and repeat all the above sequences with these cards (**18-23**), showing that you have (apparently) *four Queens*!

". . . and where we had the Aces, we now have the four Queens."

Once you have shown them, place this pile face up *on top of the other pile* (**24, 25**). Pick up all eight cards, turn them face down and then start to deal them one at a time casually onto the table, counting them as you go . . .

". . . and all we use are the one, two . . ."

You break off after you have dealt the first two (**26**) and throw the remaining six cards on top of them (**27**).

22

23

26

27

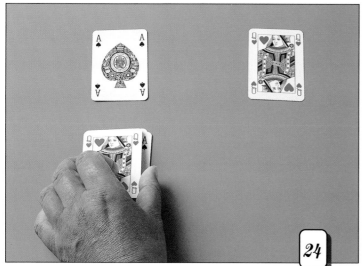

24

28

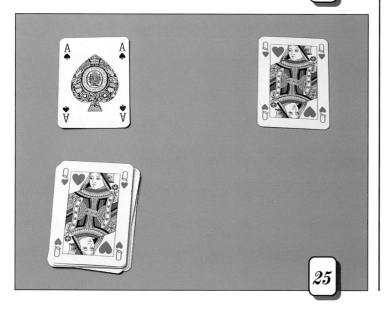

25

". . . Oh! Here, examine and count the eight cards yourself!"

With this natural and casual action you destroy all the evidence because the eight cards are now back in their original order (**28**) and can be examined until kingdom come!

◆ AFTERTHOUGHTS ◆

For my money, this trick has everything. It has a simple plot, it is short, quite easy to do, and is extremely deceptive when correctly performed. It means having to buy a few decks of cards in order to get the cards necessary for the trick, but you cannot have everything, can you? You will find that, as a magician, you cannot have too many decks of cards either!

PART THREE

SELF-WORKING CARD TRICKS

THE DREAM CARD

I learned to do this trick forty years ago and still perform it today. Unlike me, it has aged very well!

◀ EFFECT ➤

The spectator finds *your* chosen card and yet has no idea how she does it! She handles the cards herself throughout.

REQUIREMENTS
A deck of cards

♣ WHAT YOU DO ♣

Give the deck of cards to the chosen spectator (we will call her Suzy) and ask her to give them a thorough shuffle.

> **"Last night I had a dream. In this dream I could see a playing card. Hold the deck up in front of me and pass them from one hand to the other, one at a time, so that I can see their faces. I want to find the card that I dreamed about. Just stop when I tell you."**

At this point you do not really have a card on your mind. Instead you pay particular attention to the *first two cards* that she shows you (**1**). They dictate which card you will pretend to be dreaming about. You use the *value* of the first card and the *suit* of the second card to determine your choice. For example: if the first card that she shows you in the *nine* of clubs, and the second the Queen of *Hearts* – you must look out for the *nine of Hearts*, which will become your "Dream Card." When it appears (**2**) you call out . . .

"Stop!"

Reach out and take the nine of Hearts (**3**). Place it face down on the table without showing its face (**4**). Because she has been passing the cards individually

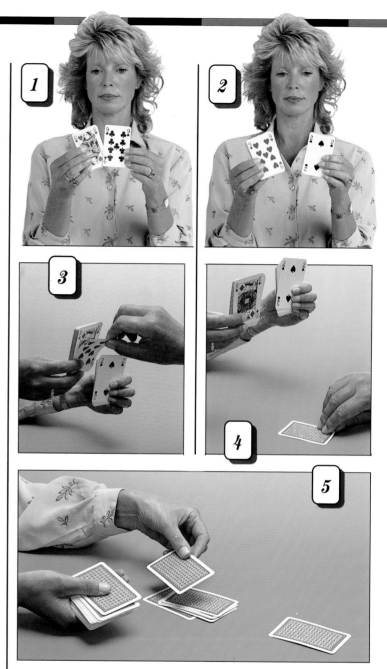

from hand to hand, the order of the deck has actually been reversed and the nine of Clubs and Queen of Hearts are now the top and second card from the top respectively.

> **"Let's see if you can find out what my dream card is without looking at it! Start dealing the cards *one at a time* onto the table in a pile . . . stop whenever you get the urge to."**

Suzy will deal the cards as instructed and will stop after a while (**5**). Our two "key" cards are now on the bottom of this pile.

6

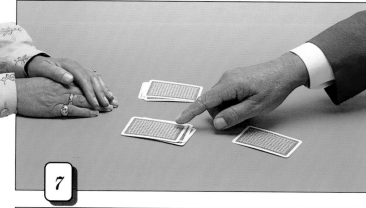

7

8

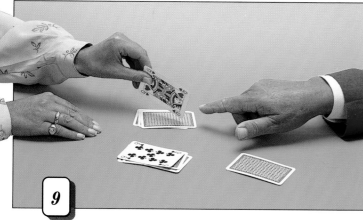

9

"Pick up the cards that you have dealt, Suzy. Deal them evenly, one at a time, into two piles. One of the piles will represent the value of my Dream Card and the other will represent its suit!"

Notice where the very last card goes (6)! Point to that pile (**7**).

"This pile will represent the value of my Dream Card – and the other pile the suit. Please turn the top card of each pile face up."

The first card that she turns over is the nine of Clubs (**8**).

"This is the value pile – so you say that my Dream Card is a *nine*. Right . . . Now turn over the top card on the suit pile."

She turns over the Queen of Hearts (**9**).

". . . and the 'suit' is Hearts. So you reckon that my Dream Card is the nine of Hearts! Turn it over and see if you are right.

She turns over your Dream Card (**10**). It *is* the nine of Hearts! Because it is self-working, the Dream Card Trick works like a dream every time!

10

➤ AFTERTHOUGHTS ◄

If the first two cards that she shows you are of the same suit, just ask her to give the cards another shuffle. If, after that, you still get two like-suited cards, get her to cut the cards. The odds of the first two cards still being of the same suit after all this are *extremely remote*.

OUT OF THIS WORLD

Don't miss this one! It is far too good to pass up! "Out of this World" is recognized by magicians the world over as the finest self-working card trick ever invented. It is Earth-shattering in effect! Quite frankly no card trick can follow it. Your audience will be too dumbfounded to concentrate on anything else anyway!

◆ EFFECT ◆

All credit must go to its creator Paul Curry. His original concept of having a *spectator* deal a deck of cards *face down* into two piles – one containing all the black cards (Clubs and Spades) and the other all the red cards (Hearts and Diamonds) *without once looking at the faces of the cards* is a masterpiece. I have been performing the effect successfully for nearly forty years and, during all that time, the trick has never failed completely to dumbfound those who have witnessed it.

REQUIREMENTS
A deck of cards, prepared as described

♣ PREPARATION ♣

Arrange your deck of cards from the top (**1**) as follows:

24 red cards
24 black cards
1 red card
2 black cards
1 red card

You need two assistants: (Betty and Edward)

◄ WHAT YOU DO ►

Hold the deck *face up* in your left hand. The face card will be a red card. This will be followed by the two odd black cards, another red card, then the rest of the secretly prearranged deck.

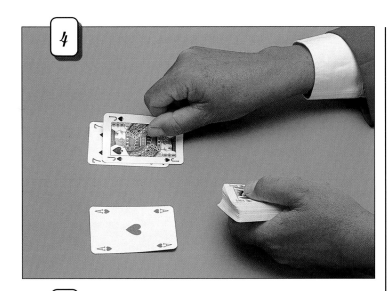

"If I were to ask you to take the deck and deal the cards into two separate piles – one pile containing all the red cards and the other containing all the black cards – you would have no difficulty at all . . . because you have learned to tell red from black!"

As you are saying this, and by way of demonstration, you deal the top red card onto the table to the left (**2**), the next two black cards onto the table to your right (**3, 4**), slightly overlapping each other – then the next red card to the left on top of and slightly overlapping the red card (**5**).

"Well, that is exactly what I want you to do. The only difference is that I do not want you to look at the *faces* of the cards – *only the backs!*"

Pick up one of the two black cards that you have dealt and casually stick it back somewhere in the *top half* of the face-up deck (**6**) – then pick up one of the two red cards and slide it back somewhere in the *bottom half* of the deck (**7**). The deck is now arranged with 25 red cards followed by 25 black cards.

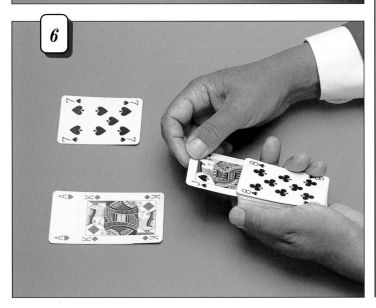

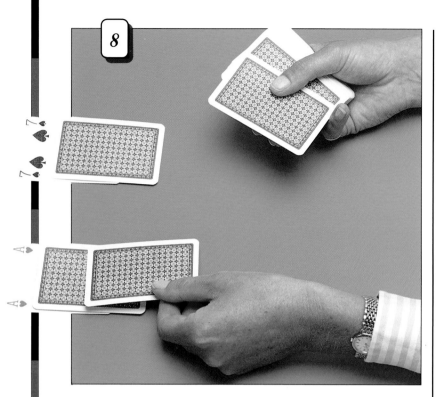

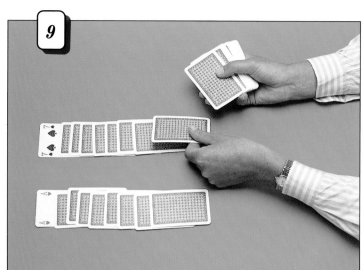

"I have left a red and a black card out to act as 'markers.' Take the deck from me. Keep it face down. I want you to start to deal the cards, one at a time, face downward onto the two markers. If you think that the card that you are about to deal is a red one, deal it onto the left hand pile beneath the red marker. If, however, you think that it is a black card, deal it to the right beneath the black marker. Deal them one at a time and please don't go too fast because I have to keep up with you in my mind!"

Betty takes the cards and starts to deal them out haphazardly beneath the two markers (**8, 9**). As she does this, you must secretly count the cards. *Stop her as she deals the 24th card.*

Take back the rest of the deck from Betty. The top card will be a red one, followed by 25 black cards. Give the cards a little shuffle.

"Let's give Edward a try!"

Look through the cards without letting anyone else see their faces. Locate and remove the single red card (**10**) and lay it *face up* overlapping the last card that Betty dealt in the right hand (black) pile (**11**).

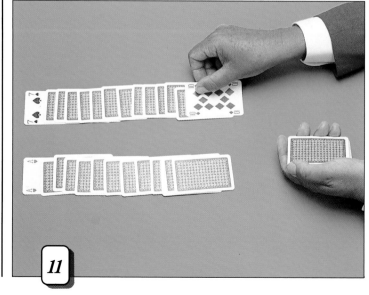

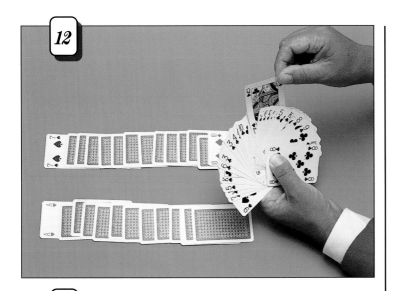

"We will change the markers over so that we can see where Betty left off and Edward begins. Let's find a black card as well"

Sort through the cards again as if searching for a black one! Finally remove one (**12**) and place *face up* on top of the last card in the left (red) pile (**13**). Give the balance of the cards to Edward and have him distribute them between the two piles, dealing them one at a time in any order he wishes (**14, 15**). This time you do not have to count. After he has dealt about a dozen cards, wait until he deals one beneath *his* red marker, the right hand pile. Shout out . . .

"Stop!"

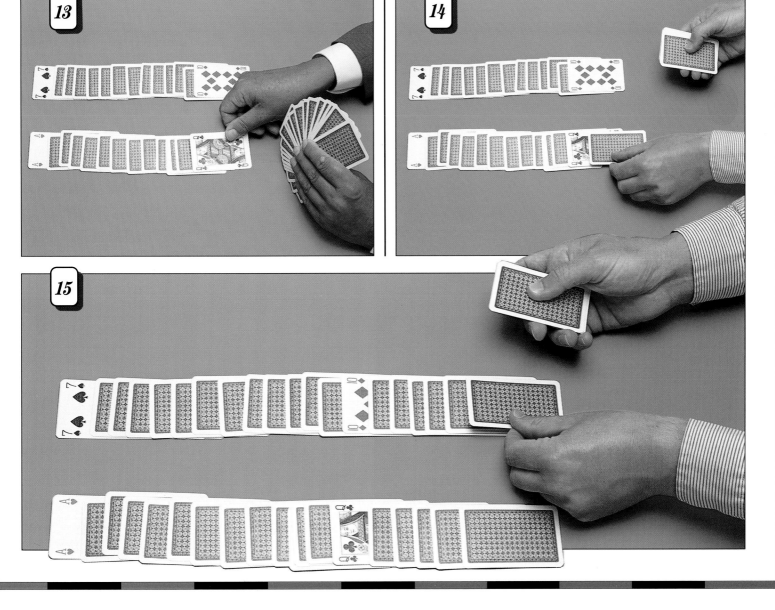

Pick up the card that he has just dealt (**16**) – turn it face up showing that it is black card (**17**) – then transfer it face down onto the other pile beneath the black marker (**18, 19**)!

"That one was wrong. But don't worry – you are doing very well!"

This little "subtlety" is most effective. Now have Edward finish the distribution of the remaining cards (**20**). The situation now is that the *left* pile is in the correct order with all face-down red cards beneath the red marker and all face-down black cards beneath the black marker. The *right* hand pile, however, is wrong. Black cards are at present beneath the red marker and red cards beneath the black marker. A minor problem for you, the Wonder Worker!

Scoop up all the cards in the right hand pile *except for the top black marker* (**21, 22**). Square the cards up and hold them in full view in your left hand (**23**).

"Let's just recap what has happened so far. First, the deck was shuffled. Second, it would not really matter if the deck was in a prearranged order because you both decided where each card should go. Is that right! Third, even if the cards were secretly marked on their backs, it would not make the slightest difference to the trick because, once more, *you* dealt the cards yourself. That's right, isn't it? How then do you explain this?"

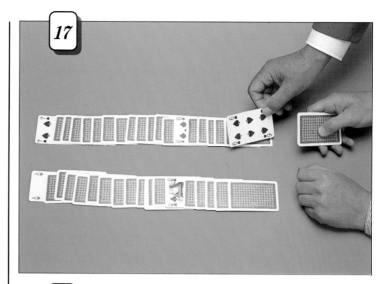

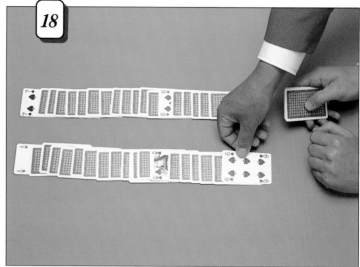

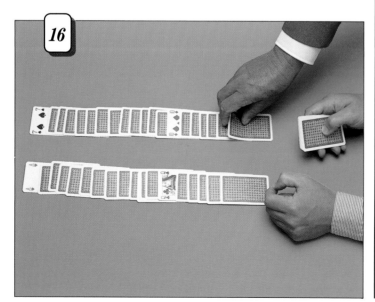

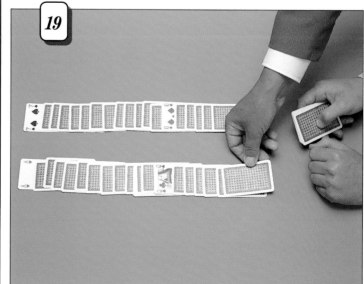

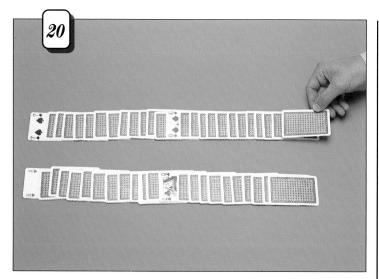

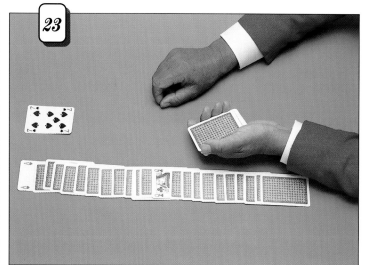

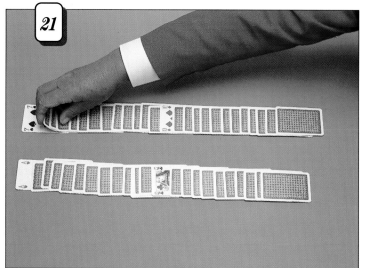

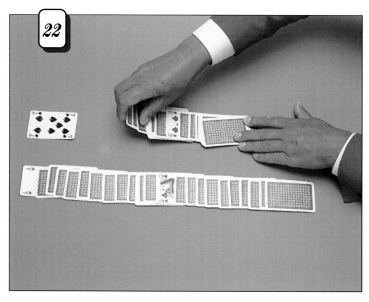

By setting the scene in this way you divert the spectators' concentration so that you can now get away with the following extremely bold move.

Thumb off the top face-down cards into your right hand (**24**) (just stop when you reach the face-up red marker)!

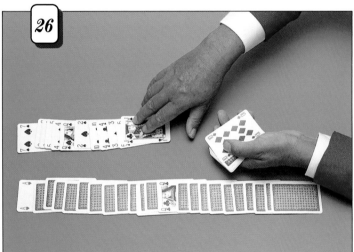

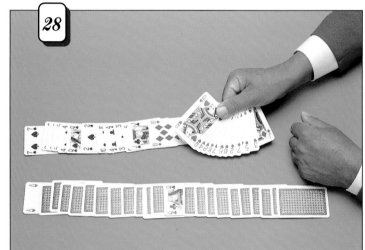

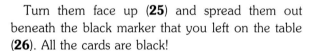

Turn them face up (**25**) and spread them out beneath the black marker that you left on the table (**26**). All the cards are black!

"... all these cards are black ..."

The *red* marker is now on top. Take it off and place it face up on the table (**27**). This leaves you with a pile of *red* cards in your left hand. Turn them face up and spread them out casually beneath the red marker (**28**).

"... and all these are red! Now for the cards in the other pile? Let's see how successful you have been!"

Turn over the cards in the left hand line and show that they have in fact done the impossible! All the black cards are beneath the black marker (**29-31**) and all the red ones beneath the red marker (**32, 33**)!

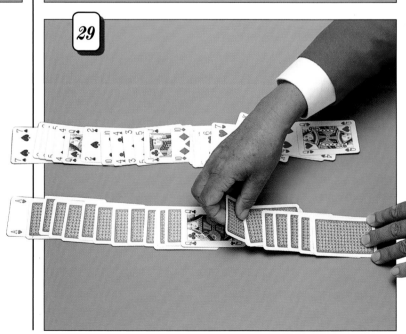

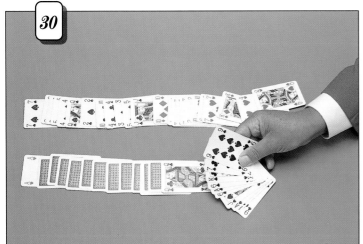

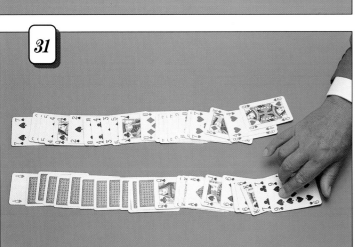

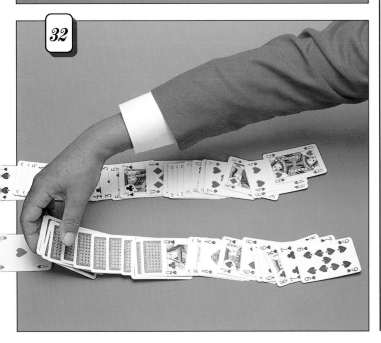

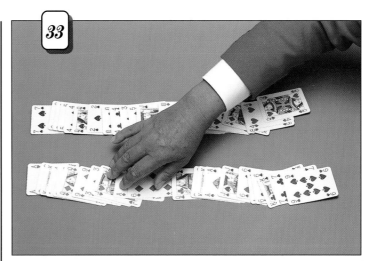

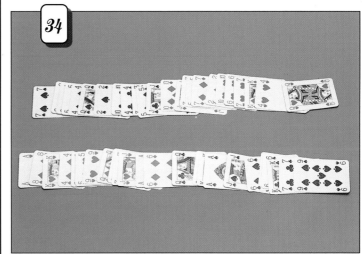

They have successfully color-separated the entire deck without looking at the face of a single card (**34**)!

✦ AFTERTHOUGHTS ✦

1. Make sure that the dealers keep the cards low while dealing so they do not inadvertently "flash" the faces of the cards to the other spectators.

2. In my opinion, it is a mistake to be too perfect in an "mental" effect of this type. The trick can be greatly enhanced by making a couple of small errors. I usually prepare the original set-up by burying one black card among the red half and a couple of red cards among the black so that they will eventually be dealt out incorrectly. The psychology here is that if *all* the cards are separated perfectly it *must* be a trick. If, however, just a few of the cards are wrongly placed, there must be something in this mind-reading business after all!

TIME GENTLEMEN PLEASE

This unusual trick is very "visual" and will create quite an impression. You will be accredited with superior mental powers by anyone who witnesses it.

◆ EFFECT ◆

A spectator (Vicky) thinks of a number. You successfully tell her what number she is thinking of and also predict which card she will choose long before she makes her choice!

REQUIREMENTS
A deck of cards
A sheet of paper
A pen

❥ PREPARATION ❤

Decide upon a card to use. Any one will do but, for the sake of our explanation, we will assume it to be the three of Clubs. Mark the back of the card with a light pencil dot in the white margin at the top left and bottom right corners (**1**). Put this marked three of Clubs *thirteenth* from the top and put the deck back in its case. On one side of the paper boldly write:

You will choose the three of Clubs

♣ WHAT YOU DO ♣

The spectators should *not* be aware of your prediction at this point, so place the paper (message side down) on the table. Put the card case near it and also have the pen nearby.

Take the paper and draw a large circle on it (**2**) and then fill in the numbers from one to twelve around the edge like a clock face. Put a bold dot in the center (**3**). Turn to Vicky as you remove the cards from the case.

"This is a clock face, Vicky. Around it are twelve numbers. In a moment I will turn my

back on you – if you will forgive my bad manners. While my back is turned, I want you to think of any one of the twelve numbers."

Hand her the deck of cards (**4**).

"When you have thought of the number, I want you to remove the same number of cards from the top of the deck and, without looking at them, I want you to sit on them!

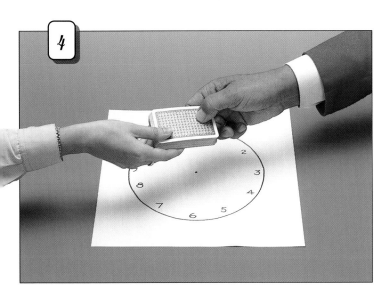

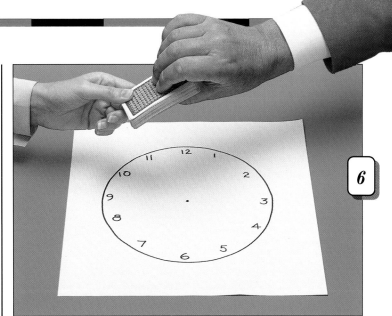

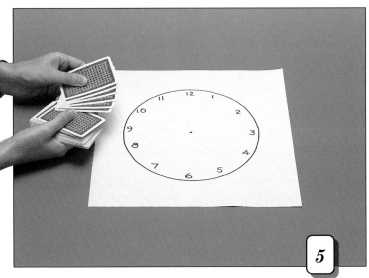

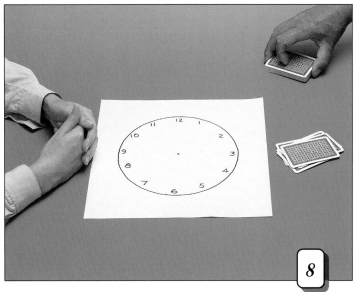

For example, if you thought of "three" – you would just remove three cards from the top of the deck and sit on them! Right?"

Turn your back so that you are obviously unable to see what she is doing. She does your bidding (**5**) and you turn to face her again when you are sure that she has completed the task. Take back the deck (**6**).

"We have twelve numbers."

Deal twelve cards from the top of the deck one at a time onto a little pile on the table (**7**), counting them out aloud as you do so. This action reverses the order of the twelve cards and, as you will realize later, is the reason the trick works. Put the rest of the deck to one side (**8**) and pick up the block of twelve cards.

Deal them out alongside the twelve written numbers on the clock starting at 1 o'clock with the first card (**9**), 2 o'clock with the second and so on until all twelve cards are in place (**10, 11**).

Watch for your secret pencil dot. Your marked card will now be indicating the number she was thinking of! It could actually be dealt in any one of the twelve positions but to assist a clear explanation of the trick we will assume that it has dropped on position number *seven*. Pick up the pen and place the point on the center dot of the clock face circle.

"Vicky, I want you to think of your number. Don't call it out. Just think of it."

Slowly start to draw in a clock hand pointing directly at the number 7 (**12**). At the same time, say

"I think that you are thinking of the number 7! Am I right?"

In utter amazement she confirms this to be true! Have her remove the cards that she is sitting on. There are, indeed, seven cards (**13**)! Reach over and turn over the card in position 7. It is the three of Clubs (**14**). Clear away all the other cards (**15**).

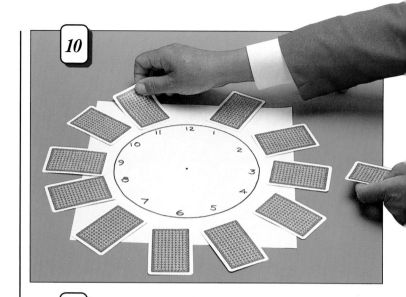

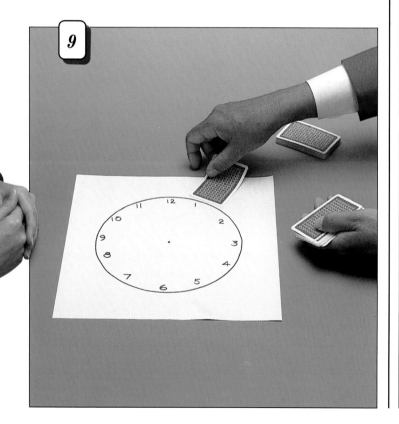

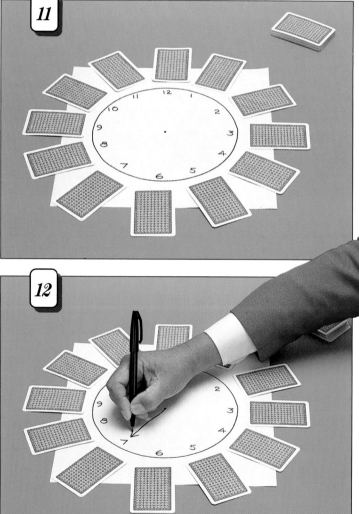

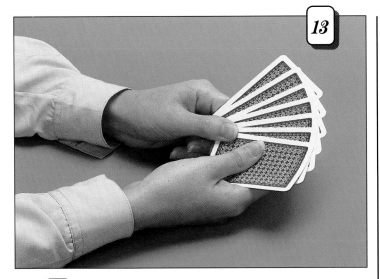

13

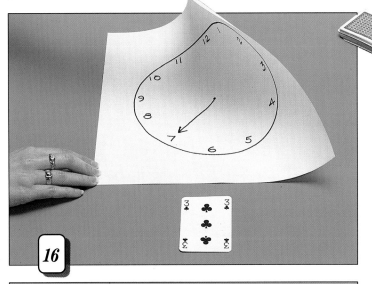

16

14

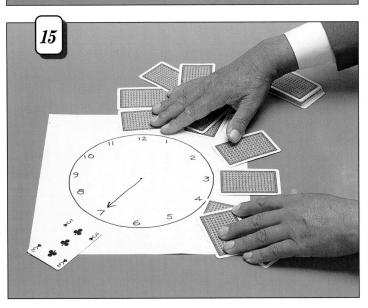

15

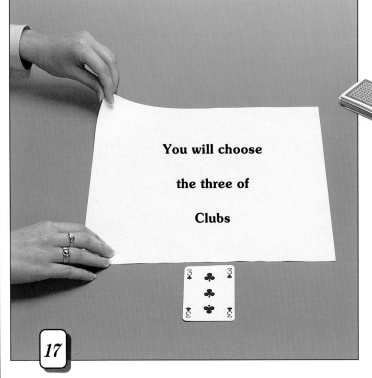

You will choose

the three of

Clubs

17

"The card that you have chosen is the three of Clubs. Now let me show you something really strange! Before we started I wrote you a message. That message is under the clock. Please pick up the clock. Turn it over and read what I wrote!"

She does as you say (**16, 17**). I think that you will agree that this is a mindboggling finish to a really amazing trick!

THE IMPOSSIBLE CARD TRICK

This is my favorite self-working card trick. It really looks "impossible."

◄ EFFECT ►

A spectator chooses a card in a scrupulously fair manner. You can have no idea what it is. The card is returned by the spectator and the deck cut by her as many times as she wishes. Even under these test conditions you are able to find the chosen card!

REQUIREMENTS
A deck of cards, one of which is secretly marked

♣ PREPARATION ♣

In the last trick we made use of a card that had been secretly marked on its back in the top left and bottom right hand corners. We are going to use the card again but this time as a "locator" card or, as we magicians call it, a "key card." It will not tell us *what* the chosen card is. However, it will tell us *where* the chosen card is, which in this trick serves just as well! Position the key card so that it is the 26th card from the top (**1**). Place all the cards back in the case.

➤ WHAT YOU DO ◄

Remove the cards from the case and place them face down in front of the spectator (Lucy).

"Lucy, I want you to lift off about two thirds of the deck (over half) and place them here . . ."

Point to a position to the left of the deck. When she has done that (**2, 3**), point to second pile.

". . . and cut this pile roughly in half and place the cards here . . ."

Point to a position slightly further to the left. She does as you say (**4**). Your key card (the 26th card) is now somewhere in the center of the middle pile. Point to the left hand pile again (**5**).

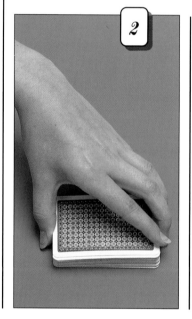

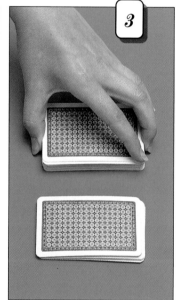

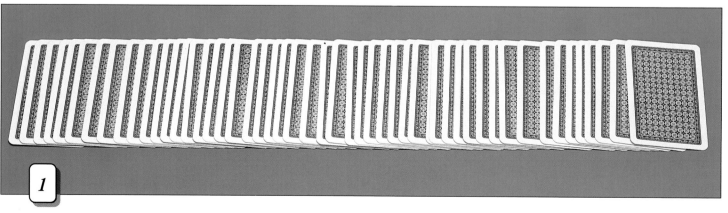

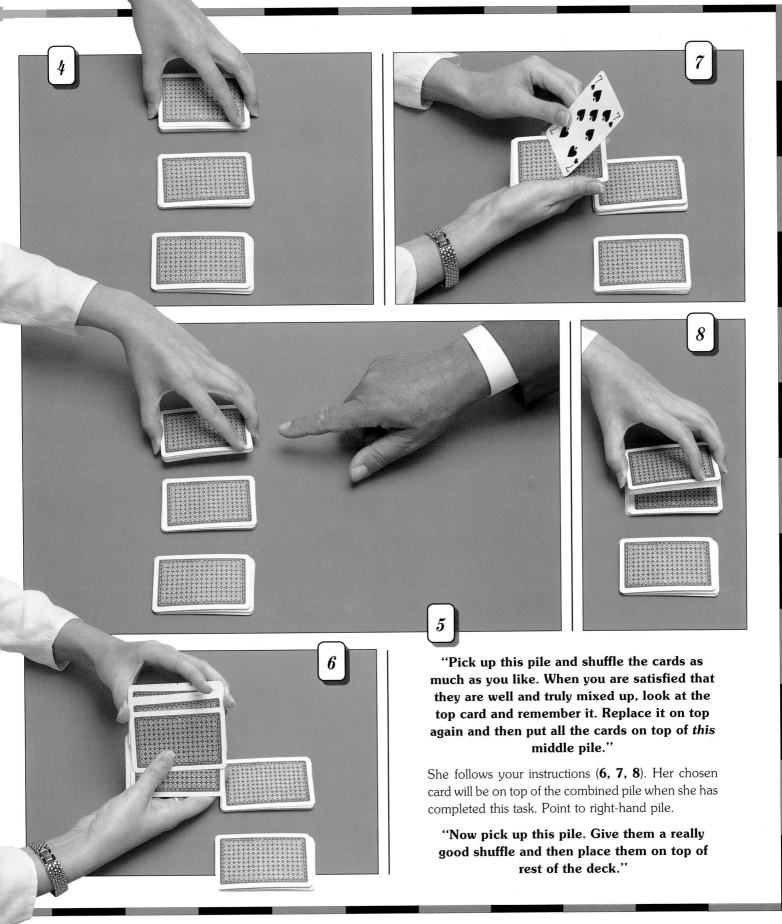

"Pick up this pile and shuffle the cards as much as you like. When you are satisfied that they are well and truly mixed up, look at the top card and remember it. Replace it on top again and then put all the cards on top of *this* middle pile."

She follows your instructions (**6, 7, 8**). Her chosen card will be on top of the combined pile when she has completed this task. Point to right-hand pile.

"Now pick up this pile. Give them a really good shuffle and then place them on top of rest of the deck."

Again, Lucy does as she is told (**9, 10, 11**). *She can now give the deck as many complete cuts as she wishes.*

"So far I haven't touched the cards at all. You have shuffled them – chosen one – shuffled again and then repeatedly cut the cards. It is quite impossible for me to know the name of your card."

Lucy has to agree because everything that you have just said is absolutely true! Now take the cards and spread them out face down on the table in a line from left to right (**12**). Make sure that no two neighboring cards stick together and that the edge of every card can be clearly seen.

"Hold my right wrist, Lucy. I am going to attempt to receive impulses from you and find your chosen card."

Extend your index finger and, starting from the *left* hand side (**13**), begin to move it slowly along the line of cards and about two inches above them (**14**). When you sight the pencil dotted corner (your key card) count this as number 1, and continue to count the cards *silently* to yourself until you have reached 26. This will be the chosen card! Do not pick it out right away though. Go a little past it. Hover over the cards in the vicinity as though you are beginning to receive an "impulse" from the cards. Then go back to the 26th card (**15**) and pull it clear of the spread, still face down (**16**).

"What card did you choose, Lucy?"

"The seven of Spades." Slowly turn the face-down card over to show that your "impulse" was correct (**17**)! The *impossible* has been achieved!

➤ AFTERTHOUGHTS ◄

If you reach the end of the line (the right-hand end) before you have reached the count of 26, merely continue the count back at the left-hand end. The chosen card will always be 26 away from your key card.

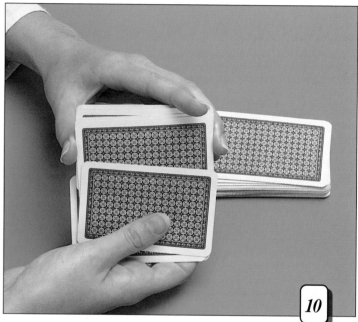

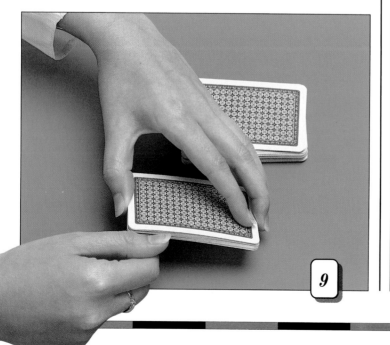

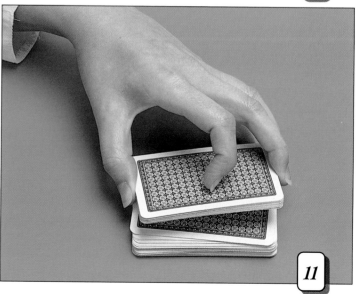

104

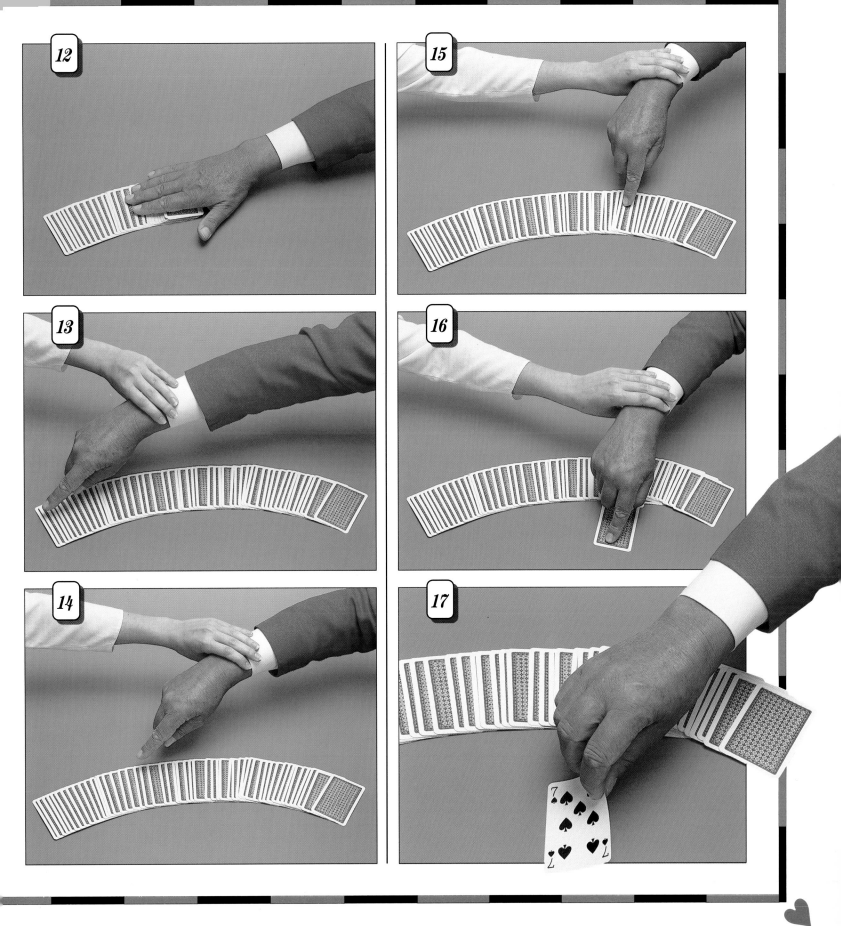

THE CIRCUS CARD TRICK

This is an old fairground "con" trick, often used to fleece the unwary!

◀ EFFECT ▶

When you attempt to find a spectator's chosen card, she is convinced that you have made a mistake. Convinced enough to bet all her money on it! You turn the tables on her in a very funny way.

> **REQUIREMENTS**
> A deck of cards

◆ WHAT YOU DO ◆

Let us call your friend Mary. Get her to shuffle the cards. As you take them back, secretly look at the bottom card and remember it (**1**). Do not make a big thing of this — just be casual. This card will be your key to finding the card that Mary is about to choose. We will assume that your *key card* is the three of Hearts, although it could be any card. Spread the cards out and get Mary to choose any card she likes (**2**). If there is anybody else watching she should also show it to them, because if she forgets the name of her card you will feel very foolish too!

Ask her to put her card back on *top* of the deck (**3**) and then cut the cards so that her chosen card is buried somewhere in the middle (**4, 5**). This puts your key card (the three of Hearts) right on top of it! Get her to cut the deck and complete the cut once or twice more, and, if anyone else is watching, let them have a cut too. *Just make sure each time that they merely cut off the top half and then put what was the bottom half on top of it.* Do not let the two important cards get separated. Your key card will still be right on top of her chosen card even after all these cuts.

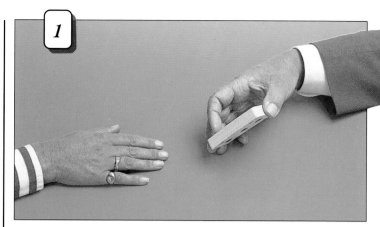

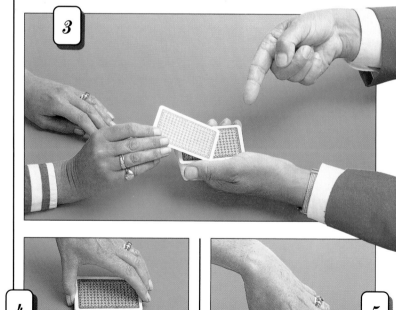

Tell Mary that you can read with your finger tips! You will be able to find her card without looking, by just feeling the raised patterns left by the printer's ink!

Hold the deck face down and start to deal the cards *face up*, one at a time, onto the table (**6**). In doing this, pretend that you are feeling the ink on each one before you turn it upward. Keep doing this until you spot your key card (3H) (**7**). *The next card that you turn over will be Mary's chosen one!* Take it off just like the others, feel its face and deal it face up too. We will assume that it is the four of Clubs (**8**).

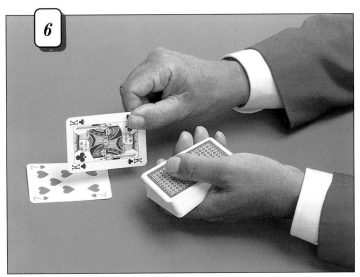

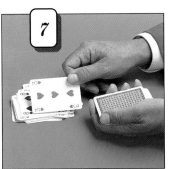

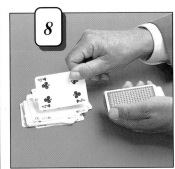

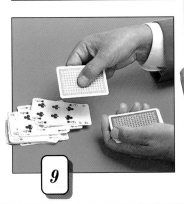

Do not let on that you know that it is her chosen one at this point. Keep a straight face and continue feeling and turning over another five or six cards. Now you must really act! Push off the next card (**9**). Feel it. Feel it again. Smell it. Hold it up to your ear as if you are listening to it, then feel it yet again! What you now say is very important – so practice until you get it right.

"I bet you $10 that the very next card I turn over will be the one that you chose!"

Give the card that you are holding another feel. Do you see what we are doing? Mary is being led to believe that you are going to turn over the card that you are holding. She has already seen the four of Clubs pass by, so she will be very eager to accept your bet! As soon as she agrees to the bet you reach down to the pile of cards already dealt and turn the four of Clubs face down (**10, 11**). You have done exactly what you said you would do!

This trick was originally used by swindlers in circus fairgrounds years ago. That is how it got its name. We, however, are entertainers, not cheats, so you must refuse to take Mary's money.

➤ AFTERTHOUGHTS ◄

If Mary should want to take the bottom card when she makes her original choice, let her! Your planned key card now becomes Mary's chosen card and as we already know what it is, we can continue as described above and just wait for the three of Hearts to show itself. You can even let her give the deck a thorough shuffle!

THE FABULOUS FOUR

Unlike "The Acrobatic Aces," this version is completely self-working. The spectator does all the work for you.

❖ EFFECT ❖

You do not touch the cards yourself. In this fabulous self-working trick, the spectator does all the mixing and cutting and yet still manages magically to find the four Aces – all by himself!

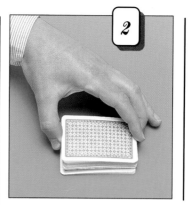

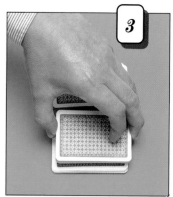

REQUIREMENTS
A deck of cards, prepared as described

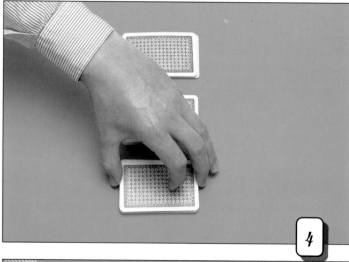

◆ PREPARATION ◆

Secretly place the four Aces face down on top of the deck (**1**). Place the deck on the table in front of the spectator and you are ready to begin.

♣ WHAT YOU DO ♣

Ask the spectator (James) to cut the deck into four more or less equally sized piles in a row by dropping off a section at a time (**2-5**). By doing this the original top section (with the Aces on top) end up in the fourth position (**6**).

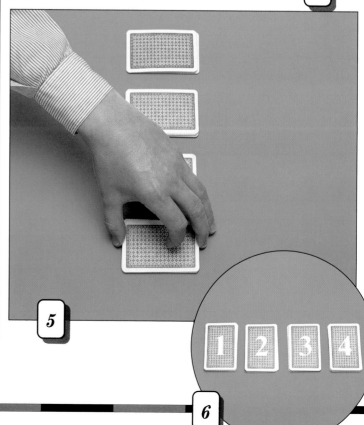

You have nothing to do now except tell James what to do – so please make your instructions to him very clear! You say,

"Pick up pile number one."

Point to it (**7**) so that there can be no mistake . . .

"Without looking at them, I want you to take three cards from the top of your little pile and put them at the bottom of your little pile. Now – also from the top of your pile – deal one card onto each of the other three piles."

When this has been done (**8-12**) . . .

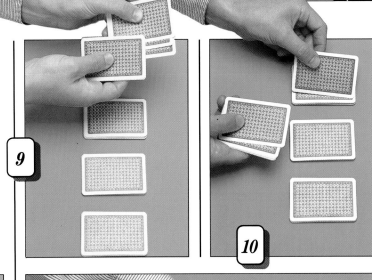

9

10

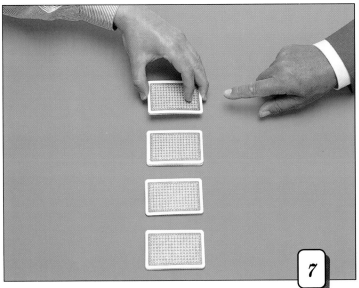

7

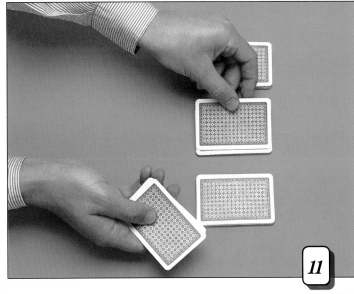

11

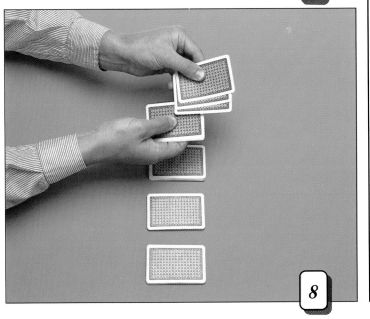

8

12

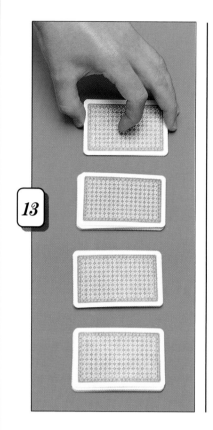

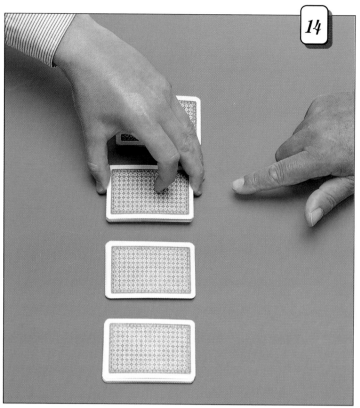

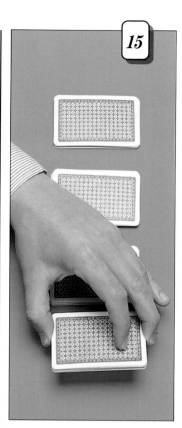

"Put your pile back on the table again." He does so (**13**) . . . **"Pick up pile number two (14) – again transfer three cards from the top to the bottom and then one card onto each of the other three piles."**

Have James do the same with the other two piles as well. You will notice that, when he gets to the last pile (**15**), the three cards that have been placed, one by one, on top of pile number *four* get transferred to the bottom by the spectator and then, unknown to him, he deals an Ace on the top of piles Nos. 1, 2 and 3 (**16**)! All four piles now have an Ace on top. Very sneaky!!

"You did all the cutting, shuffling and moving of the cards yourself. Is that true?"

James has to agree that this is so.

"I call this trick 'The Fabulous Four.' Do you know why? Please turn up the top card on each pile!"

Bingo! The four Aces now stare him in the face (**17-20**), and he did it all by himself. (Well – almost)!

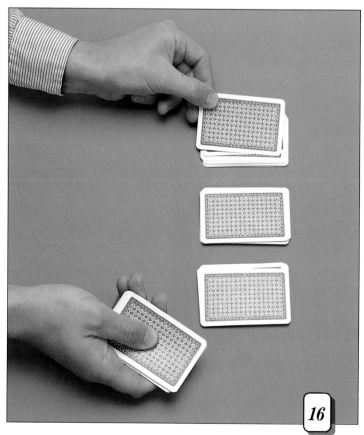

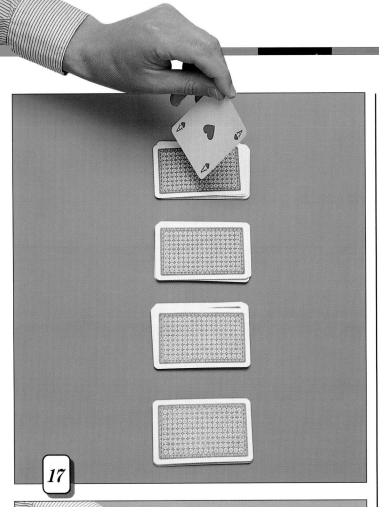

17

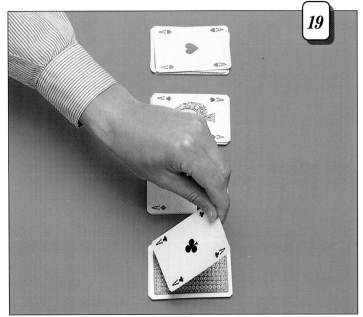

19

18

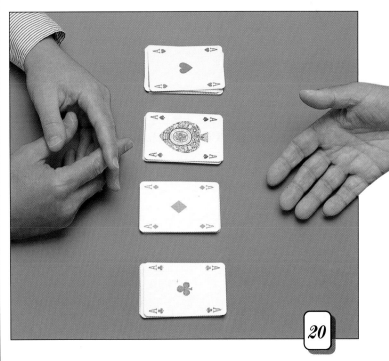

20

♣ AFTERTHOUGHTS ♣

The cutting – transferring – and dealing of the cards is cleverly designed to confuse the spectator so that he will be unable to remember the exact sequence of his duties. James will think that he just shuffled and then cut to the four Aces. A false shuffle (retaining the four Aces on top) at the beginning, *before* you place the deck of cards on the table, will enhance the overall effect.

A MATHEMATICAL CERTAINTY

For downright subtlety this classic takes some beating. The trick is a very good one and the misdirection – fabulous!

◆ EFFECT ◆

You correctly name the cards that a spectator hides in his pocket under what appear to be impossible conditions. This brief description does not do justice to this strong effect, so read on!

❥ PREPARATION ❦

You must know and remember the names of the third and fourth cards from the *bottom* of the deck. If you make the third one the three of Hearts and the fourth one the four of Spades while you practice, you will find them easier to remember (**1**). Once you get the hang of it, you should in fact use whatever cards you happen to find in those positions.

♣ WHAT YOU DO ♣

We will call our spectator Paul.

"Cut the deck into two piles and then touch one."

You do not ask him to *choose* one pile but merely *touch* one (**2**). This is most important because you must get the spectator to take the original bottom half of the deck, seemingly of his own free will. If he touches it, get him to pick it up while you pick up the other half (**3**). If, however, he touches the original top half of the deck, pick it up yourself and say,

"Thank you. You take the other half, Paul."

Diabolical, isn't it! This type of force is called *Equivoque*. Magicians regularly use such careful choice of words to achieve otherwise impossible results.

"I want you to duplicate everything that I do. Will you count your cards first?"

You count by dealing the cards one by one onto the table (**4**) thus reversing the order of the cards. The noted two cards will now be the third and fourth card from the top of his packet.

Announce the number of cards in your packet and then ask him how many he has. Behave as if the matter was important. This is just a valuable "misdirection." Whatever he announces, ask him to discard one card. *He will naturally discard the top one* (**5**).

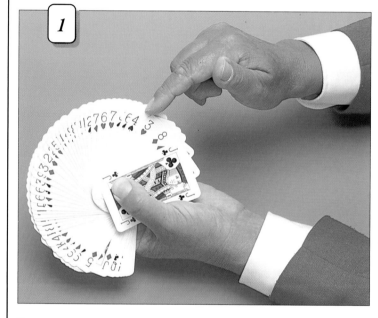

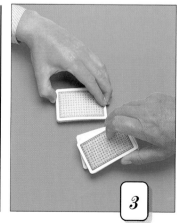

4

5

6

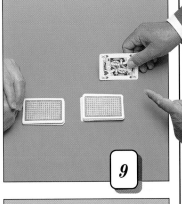

7

8

9

10

11

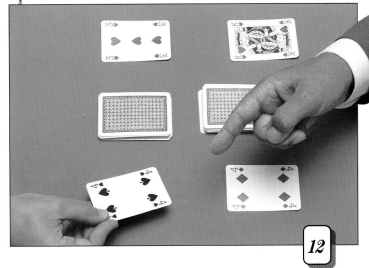

12

"Please continue doing what I do, Paul."

Take the top card of your pile and slip into the center (**6**). Wait while he does the same. Take a card from the bottom and push it into the center (**7**). Take another card from the top and put it into your *left* jacket pocket. Take another from the bottom and push it into the center of cards that you hold. Take one more card from the top and put it into your *right* coat pocket (**8**). Replace your half of the deck on the table.

These actions have been deliberately designed to drag as many "red-herrings" across the trail as possible! If Paul has been duplicating your actions with his own half of the deck, the card in his left hand coat pocket was originally the *third* from the bottom (three of Hearts), and the one in his right was originally *fourth* (four of Spades).

You bring the trick to a climax by saying . . .

"It is a mathematical certainty that this card in my right hand pocket being the . . ." You bring it out and name it as you show it (**9**) . . .
"The card in your *left* hand pocket is the three of Hearts!"

You name the first of the two cards that you remembered. And you are right (**10**)!

"And this one being the . . ." Remove the card from your other pocket and name it as you show it (**11**) . . . **"The one in your other pocket will be the four of Spades!"**

Name the second card that you remembered (**12**).

"Am I right?"

113

7-UP!

This trick really packs a punch, and builds up to an excellent climax. I am sure you will have fun with it.

◀ EFFECT ▶

The spectator finds the four sevens in a startling and amazing manner. They appear, one at a time, and each appearance is more startling than the last.

◆ PREPARATION ◆

Place two of the sevens on the top of the deck, one seven on the bottom and then turn the last seven face up and insert it, still reversed, about two thirds of the way down (**1**).

♣ WHAT YOU DO ♣

Hold the deck in your left hand in the dealing position. Take care not to "flash" the bottom seven. This time we will call your assistant Penny.

"Penny . . will you call out a number between 5 and 10 please."

It is a psychological fact that 80 per cent of the time people will say "seven" when asked to call out a number under ten. We will assume that Penny is no exception. The Afterthoughts section at the end of this trick's explanation will tell you how to continue should she be one of the other 20 per cent. So Penny, obligingly says . . . "Seven."

Deal out seven cards into two rows as illustrated (**2**). The second card dealt (a seven) goes beneath the first card dealt (also a seven). The third card goes to the left of the first card, the fourth goes to right of the

second, the fifth to the right of the first, the sixth to the left of the second and the last card to the left of the top row. Sounds complicated? It's not really – just take another look at the illustration (**3**) and all will be made clear. You have a row of four cards beneath which is a row of three cards and the sevens are both second from the right. Right? Right! Put the rest of the deck to one side, face down.

"Oh dear! I really wanted an even number! But don't worry, we will see if I can do the trick with seven cards. There are two rows of cards in front of you and, in a moment, I will ask you to choose one of the two rows. However, we need a row with four cards in it – so if you choose *this* row . . ."

Point to the row with just the three cards in it . . .

"We will just have to slide the last card that I dealt downward to make a row of four. O.K.?"

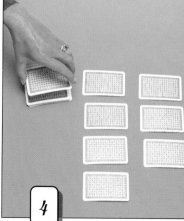

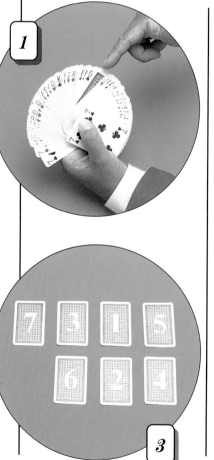

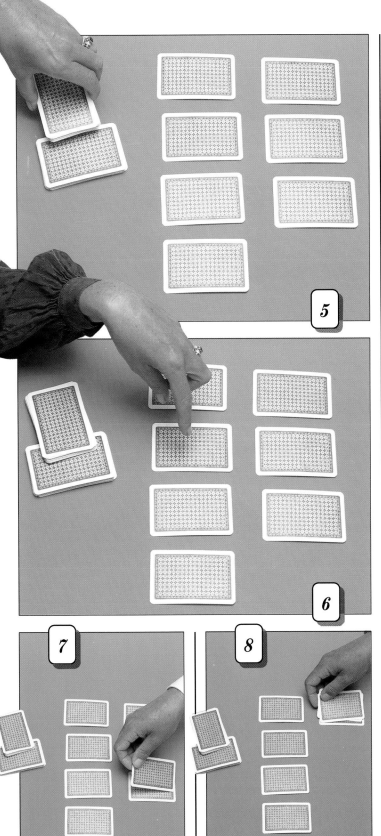

5

6

Slide the last card downward, and then back up again to its original place.

"Before you choose your row, I want you to cut the deck for me."

She cuts off about half of the deck. Ask her to pick up the bottom half and rest it across the cut-off section (**4, 5**). Of course, the original bottom seven is the bottom card of the upper half of the cut deck. Now bring her attention back to the two rows of cards.

"All right, now point to a row, Penny."

Once she has pointed to a row (**6**) and you have made sure that it has four cards in it, gather up the other three cards and place them, face down, on top of the upper section of the cross-cut deck (**7, 8, 9**). *In so doing, make sure that the center card (the seven) ends up as the top card. This is very important.*

Penny is now looking at the row of four cards spread out before her. Your task is to get her to choose the second card from her left which we know is a seven. Be careful not to use the word "choose." We are going to use the technique of *Equivoque* again, using a careful choice of vocabulary to create an inexplicable mystery. The seven is psychologically placed so that 70 per cent of the time it will be her first choice. Say

"I want you to point to one of these four cards."

If she points to the seven (**10**) – Bingo!

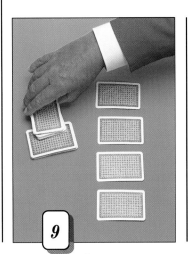

7

8

9

10

You need worry no more. Just ask her to turn it over (**11**) and then continue with the conclusion of the trick explained below. If, however, she points to one of the other three cards – say:

". . . and point to another one, too."

If she points to our Secret Seven this time, take the *other two cards away and discard them* leaving her two selections on the table.

"Place a finger on the back of each card, please . . . now lift up one of your fingers."

If she lifts her finger off the other indifferent card, take it away and discard it. You are home and dry again because her finger still rests upon the back of the seven. If she lifts her finger off the seven, say,

"Are you sure? O.K.!"

Push the seven closer to her – remove the other card from beneath her other finger and discard it! The other scenario is that her first two selections do *not* include the Secret Seven. In that case you just remove and discard the two cards and then proceed with the remaining two exactly as described above. You just cannot lose! Your "technical" work is almost complete. From now on it is *presentation* all the way. Well, almost!

"Penny, I want to show you a very remarkable thing. I asked you to call out a number. You said 'seven.' We dealt out seven cards and you chose one of them. Please turn it over!" She does (**12**). "Your chosen card is a *seven*!"

Lift up the top half of the cross-cut deck (**13**) and show the card at its face (the original bottom card)!

"You have cut the deck at a *seven*!"

Remove the seven and place it face up next to the one that is already there (**14**). Replace the rest of the cards squarely on top of the remainder of the deck (**15**) and then spread them evenly across the table to reveal the one *reversed* card (**16**)!

"The only reversed card in the deck is a *seven*!"

Gather up all the cards after removing the face-up seven, which goes down with the other two (**17**). The top card is now the remaining Secret Seven!

"That just leaves one seven to find! *Watch!*"

You are now going to drop the deck onto the table and the final seven is going to flip itself over and come to rest face up on the deck! You will have to practice this a few times before you get the hang of it. Believe me the practice will be well worth it because it is a very snappy way to reveal a chosen card!

Hold the deck in your right hand, fingers at the top short edge, thumb at the bottom short edge. Push the top card over with your left thumb, so that it projects over the long edge of the deck by about an inch (**18**). The back of your right hand prevents this from being obvious to the spectator. Hold the deck about 10 inches above the table top and drop the deck with a *very slight* downward thrust. This downward thrust will act against the air pressure and the projecting card will flip face upward (**19**)! Keep practicing until you get the "feel" for this. It is a very startling revelation and a great climax to this entertaining trick!

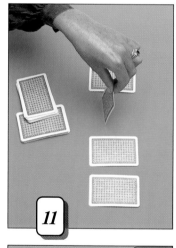

15

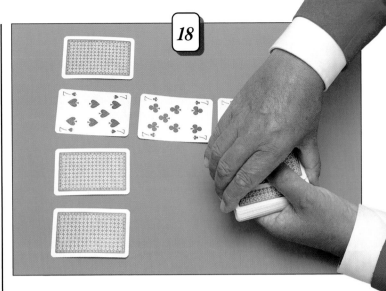

18

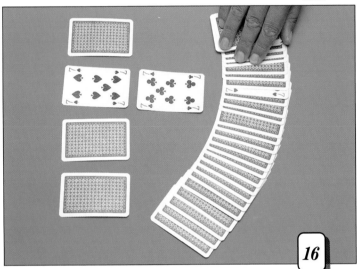

16

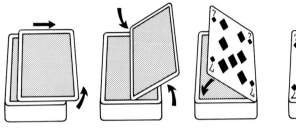

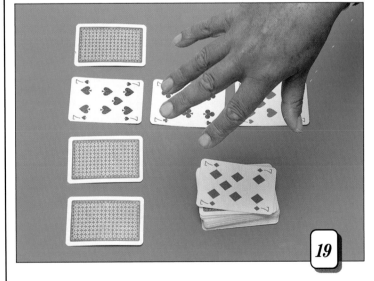

19

17

➤ AFTERTHOUGHTS ◄

If the number "seven" is not chosen, do not worry – just deal out the number of cards that the spectator nominates, keeping track of the two Secret Sevens, and then carry on as described. In your "winding up" speech you simply ignore the number as if it has no bearing on the trick. Just emphasize the appearance of the Mystic Sevens!

TOO HOT TO HANDLE

You will have great fun with this one! You achieve the impossible yet the method could not be simpler.

◆ EFFECT ◆

A spectator freely chooses a card from a shuffled deck and returns it to the center of the deck. In an instant her chosen card becomes the only reversed card in the deck!

REQUIREMENTS
A deck of cards with backs that have white borders
An assistant. We will call her Anne

➤ WHAT YOU DO ◆

Hand the deck of cards to Anne and have her shuffle them. Take back the deck and spread them between your hands so that Anne can remove one (**1**).

"Look at the card that you have chosen and remember it please (2). In a moment I will ask you to put your card back into the deck and then I will place the cards behind my back so that I can no longer see the cards."

While you are saying this, apparently by way of demonstrating, you put the deck behind your back. *As soon as it is out of sight* turn the whole deck *face up* (**3**) and then turn the first two cards *face down* (**4**, **5**). This should take little more than a second to do. Bring the deck into view again. Keep the cards well squared up. Now, what looks like a face-down deck is, in fact, a face-up deck with just two cards face down on the top!

"Push your card back into the deck, Anne — anywhere you wish."

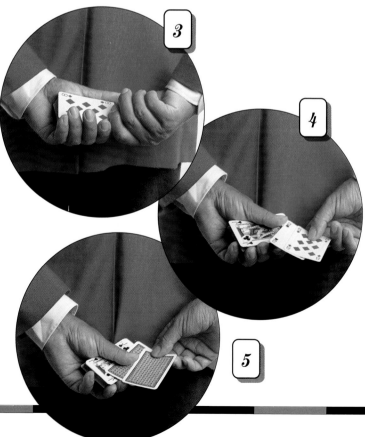

Anne does as you ask (**6**). Unknown to her she has returned her card to a face-up deck (apart from the couple of cards on the top)! Hold the deck firmly while she does this and the illusion will be perfect. Keep the deck fairly low so that she does not see the back of the bottom card.

"Because you have handled the card it should be slightly warmer than the rest! I will try to find your card with the aid of my very sensitive fingertips. It should feel 'red hot' to me!"

Put the deck behind your back. Once it is out of sight, turn the top two cards *face up again* (**7**, **8**)! Now her chosen card is the *only* reversed card in the deck! Flip the whole deck over (**9**) and bring it out again. Take your time over this. Pretend that you are having a bit of difficulty at first.

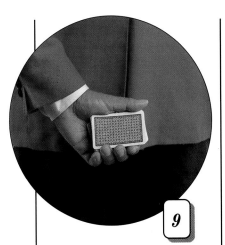

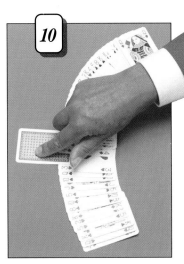

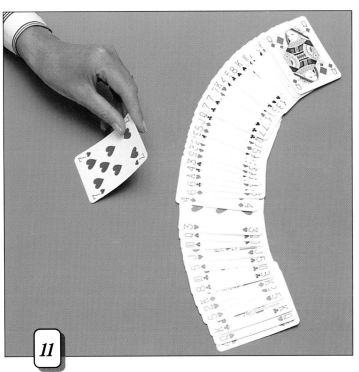

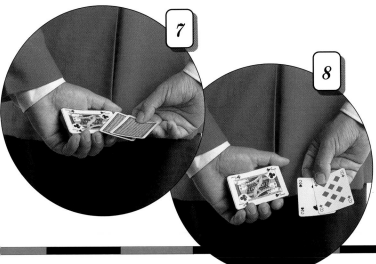

Spread the cards face up on the table in a curving sweep from left to right showing that there is one solitary face-down card in the deck. Push it slightly out of the spread (**10**).

"If I am right, this card will be the one that you chose. What was the name of your card. Anne?" Anne names her card.
"It's too hot for *me* to handle! Would *you* please turn the card over for me!"

She turns over the one reversed card (**11**). Q.E.D.!

DO AS I DO

Coincidence tricks are very popular with card magicians and this is one of the best.

♣ EFFECT ♣

Two decks of cards are used. The spectator selects a card from his deck – you remove one from yours. By an absolutely amazing coincidence, you both choose the same card!

REQUIREMENTS
Two unprepared decks of cards with different back designs

◆ WHAT YOU DO ◆

Put the two decks face down on the table side by side. Your assistant (Luke) stands on the other side of the table.

"Now Luke, this trick is called 'Do As I Do.' I want you to try to duplicate my actions as closely as you can. Do everything that I do."

Pick up a deck of cards. Luke will pick up the other one. Give your cards a thorough shuffle. Luke will do his best (**1**)! While Luke is absorbed with his shuffling, secretly look at and remember the card that you have shuffled to the bottom of your own deck (**2**). This will be your "key card." Let us assume that it is the two of Spades.

"You have just shuffled your deck and I have shuffled mine. So it must be true that I don't know the order of your cards and it is certainly true that you don't know the order of mine. So you take my deck and I will take yours." You take his deck and he takes yours (**3**). **"Now reach somewhere into the middle of the deck – remove any card – remember it – then place it on top of the deck. I will do the same."**

You show him how by removing any card and looking at it. Pretend to remember it and then place it on top of the deck. You can forget the card that you have just seen because it will play no further part in our trick. Luke does as you do (**4, 5**) only, you hope, he will remember the name of the card that he has chosen! You had better ask him again to remember it because if he does not, it will ruin the trick!

"Now cut and complete the cut."

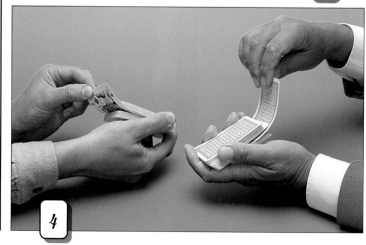

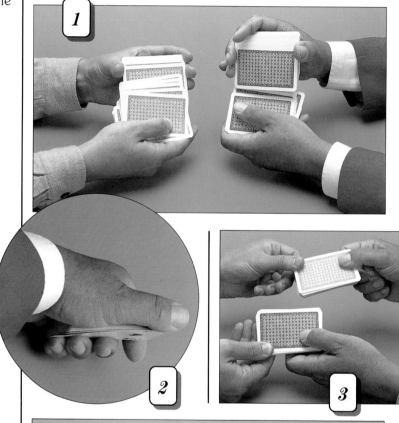

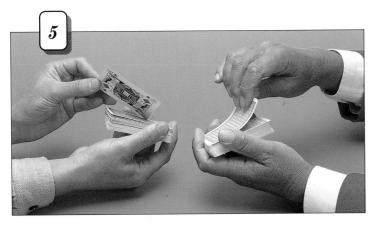

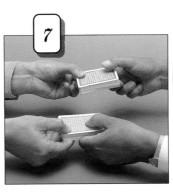

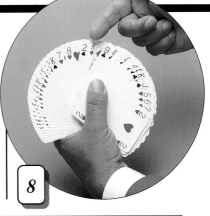

Show him how and in following your actions (**6**) he will unknowingly bring your "key card" to rest on top of his chosen card!

"Let's cut again . . ."

You both do another complete cut and then a third.

"Are you happy with that — or shall we cut again?"

Whatever he says, you oblige. Just make sure that each cut is a complete one that does not disturb the circular order of the cards. We do not want his chosen card and your remembered key card to be separated.

"Now that we have thoroughly mixed the cards, we will exchange decks again. You take mine – I'll take yours (7). Now this is want I want you to do. Look through the deck that you are holding and remove the card that you are thinking of and place it face down on the table – I'll look through this deck and remove the one that I am thinking of. Remember, this trick is called 'Do As I Do' so please let me remove my card first and place it on the table before you put down yours."

Thumb through the deck that you are now holding and search for "key card" (the two of Spades). The card next to and beneath it will be his chosen one (**8**)! Remove it and place it face down on the table without inadvertently showing its face. Luke does the same (**9**). All you have got to do now is wind up the trick (and Luke)!

"Do you believe in coincidence, Luke? We both chose a deck of cards. We both shuffled, and cut, and thought of cards at random. You tried to duplicate my actions to the best of your ability. Wouldn't it be amazing then if we both thought of the same card? Turn them face upward Luke (10)!"

PART FOUR

MONEY MAGIC

COIN MAGIC

Tricks with coins are great fun to do and, as most people carry loose change around with them in their pockets and purses, most of the time you will find that you will be able to borrow the coins that you need for your tricks. The ability to palm, vanish, and switch coins is a skill well worth acquiring and we are going to apply ourselves to learning these techniques now, before proceeding to the actual tricks.

♣ VOODOO COIN VANISH ♣

It is not necessary to be a great "sleight-of-hand" expert to perform interesting and mystifying tricks. However, if you take the trouble to master this simple coin vanish, it will mean that you will be able to add a special "sparkle" to many of your coin tricks. Hold the coin in your left hand as illustrated (**1**). Your other hand travels forward to meet it, the right thumb going *under* and the right fingers going *over* the coin (**2**). Make as if to grab the coin but as soon as it is hidden from the view of the spectator by your right fingers, let the coin drop secretly into your left palm (**3**). Complete the grabbing motion with your right hand, closing it into a fist (**4**) and move the hand away (**5**). *Do not move the left hand* – merely grip the hidden coin with the second and third fingers. The right hand is now slowly opened – the coin has vanished (**6**)!

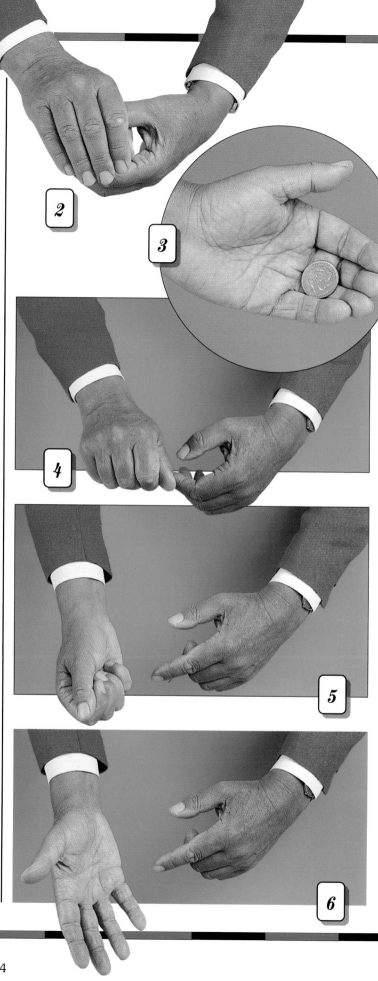

Well, that's it. Simplicity itself – but, I beg you please, please, practice this simple combination of moves until they become second nature to you. Try it in front of a mirror so that you can see how it looks from your spectators' viewpoint. You must *act* too, because if *you* do not appear to believe that the coin is in your right hand, you cannot very well expect your audience to believe it, can you?

◆ PALMING A COIN ◆

Concealing objects in your hand is called "*palming*." Two simple coin palms – the finger palm and the thumb palm – will suffice for your requirements at this stage. The Voodoo Coin Vanish (above) requires you to finger palm a coin. The coin is just lightly gripped by the bent second and third fingers. The first and fourth fingers are slightly extended in a natural manner and do not actually hold the coin. Look again at picture (**3**) to understand this.

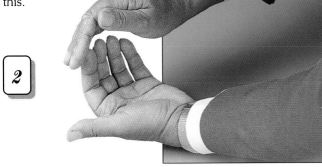

The thumb palm calls for a different type of manipulation. A coin is shown on your right palm in the position shown (**1**). You now, apparently, tip the coin into your left hand (**2**) which closes over it (**3**). On opening your left fingers, the coin is seen to have vanished (**4**). To achieve this vanish, you merely have to grip the coin in the skin fold at the base of your thumb as you turn your right hand over, as the reveal shot (**5**) shows.

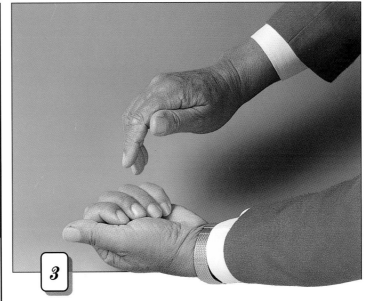

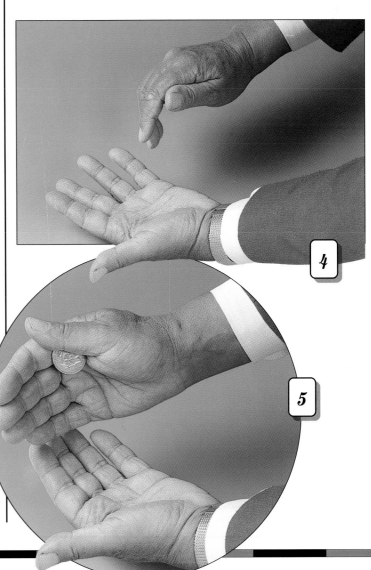

❥ THE COIN FOLD ❦

Place a coin on a square of paper as shown in picture (**1**). Now follow the sequence of actions illustrated until you have folded a packet to resemble picture (**7**). You first fold the paper upward crosswise from bottom to top (**2**), then fold the left and right edges behind the coin (**3, 4, 5, 6**). Finally you fold the top flap down behind (**7**). The coin now rests in the little packet which, unknown to the spectator, is open at the top.

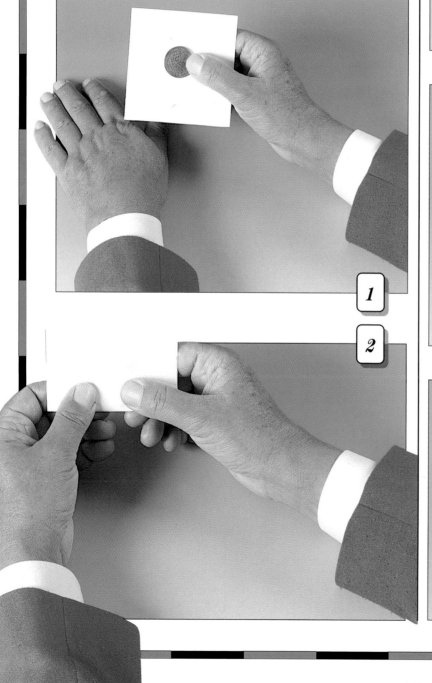

1

2

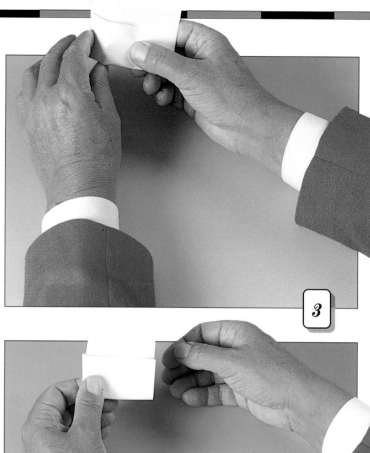

3

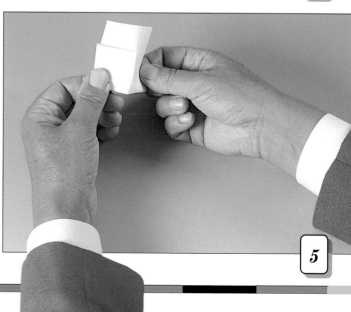

4

5

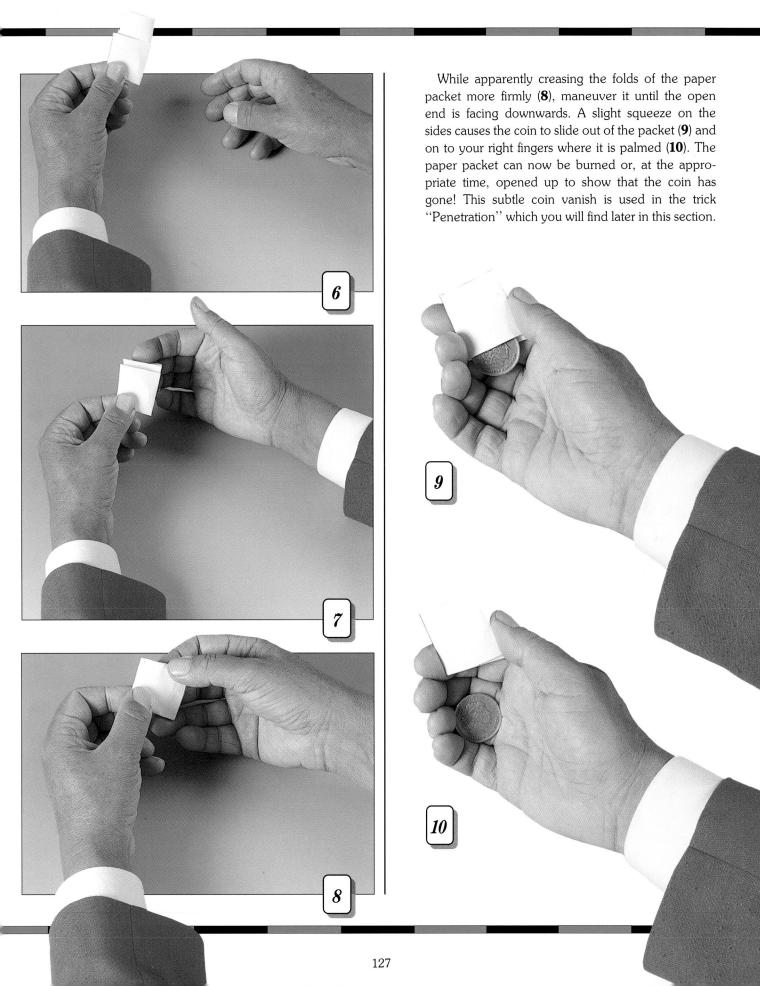

While apparently creasing the folds of the paper packet more firmly (**8**), maneuver it until the open end is facing downwards. A slight squeeze on the sides causes the coin to slide out of the packet (**9**) and on to your right fingers where it is palmed (**10**). The paper packet can now be burned or, at the appropriate time, opened up to show that the coin has gone! This subtle coin vanish is used in the trick "Penetration" which you will find later in this section.

← THE SITTING-DOWN COIN VANISH ➤

This subtle principle can be used to vanish any small object. It is particularly suitable for coins. All sleight-of-hand actions should *exactly* mimic *real* actions. The closer the imitation – the greater the deception. With this thought in mind we will learn the *real* action first – the action of picking up a coin from the table!

Sit yourself with your legs tucked well under the table and your thighs pressed together. Place the coin in front of you and about 4in from the edge of the table (**1**). Cover the coin with your right fingers and draw it toward you. As the coin reaches the edge of the table bring your thumb up so that you grasp the coin between your thumb and fingers (**2**). Close your hand into a fist and move it toward the center of the table (**3**). Open your hand and reveal the coin (**4**).

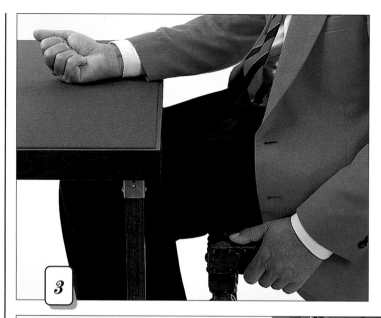

That is what you are supposed to do. Now let us look at what you actually do! When you make the coin vanish, your actions must look identical to those just described (**5**). The only difference is that as soon as the coin reaches the edge of the table (**6**), you just sweep it off and allow it to drop on to your lap (**7**). Your hand closes into a fist, as before, as if it really contained the coin and then moves forward to rest on the table (**8**). At the appropriate moment you open your hand to show that the coin has disappeared (**9**). This principle will be used with devastating effect later in a trick called "Gone."

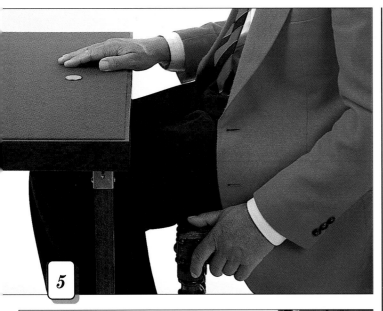

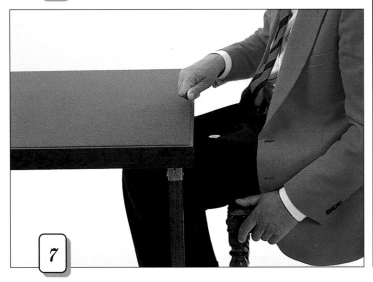

129

BRASS NECK AND ELBOW

This audacious coin trick is as bold as brass and involves you in a routine that uses your neck and elbow – hence its unusual name.

♣ EFFECT ♣

A borrowed coin is rubbed on your left elbow and then completely vanishes! Both hands are shown empty. The right elbow is now rubbed and the coin reappears! The "Voodoo Coin Vanish" plus a wonderful subtlety (about to be explained) enable you to show both your hands empty.

REQUIREMENTS
A single coin – the bigger the better

◆ WHAT YOU DO ◆

Borrow a coin and then seat yourself at a table (**1**). Hold the coin in your left hand in the position for the "the Voodoo Vanish" but when your right hand travels forward in the action of grabbing the coin, *you actually do take it in your right hand.* Rest your head on your left hand and rub the coin on your left elbow (**2**). After a couple of seconds let the coin drop onto the table with a clatter (**3**).

Pick up the coin with your *left* hand and now repeat the above actions, only this time actually execute "the Voodoo Coin Vanish" taking the coin away secretly in your left hand in a finger palm position. Rest your head on your left hand again (**4**) and get rid of the coin by tucking it down the back of your collar (**5**) while your right hand is apparently rubbing it into your left elbow! Then show both hands empty. The coin has vanished (**6**)!

To make it return you have to reverse the action. Rest your head on your left hand and start rubbing your left elbow with your right fingers, as before (**7**).

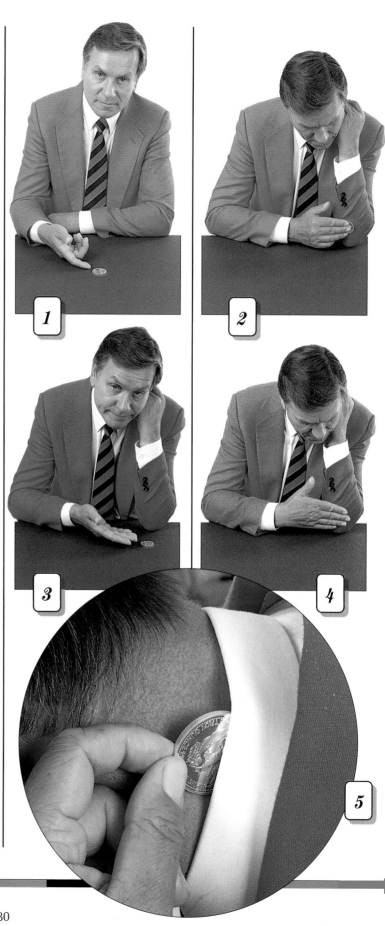

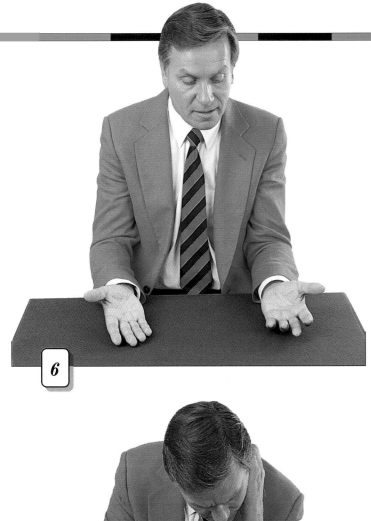

6

8

9

7

While all the attention is drawn to your left elbow, your left fingers secretly retrieve the coin from your collar and finger palm it again.

After rubbing your elbow for a while without success you give up (**8**) and change sides – this time resting your head on your right hand and rubbing the right elbow with your left fingers (**9**). After a few rubs, let the coin drop on to the table with a clatter (**10**)! Very bewildering!

10

HOW COULD YOU STOOP SO LOW?

Methods in magic are unimportant! How you achieve your "miracle" is really irrelevant. The only thing that matters is the ultimate effect on the spectator. Always remember this. The method used to bring about this wonderful trick is so blatant and impudent that you may be frightened to perform it at first. Trust me! Try it out. You will even amaze yourself!

➤ EFFECT ◀

A coin, apparently dropped accidentally, vanishes!

REQUIREMENTS
A borrowed coin

♣ WHAT YOU DO ♣

Borrow a coin and state that you will make it vanish (**1**). You make a "magic pass" over the coin and then "accidentally" (on purpose) let it drop on the floor at your feet (**2, 3**). While everyone is laughing at your clumsiness, you stoop down to retrieve the coin (**4**) but instead of picking it up, you flick it with your finger tips so that it shoots beneath your shoe (**5**)! Stand upright again with your right hand closed into a fist (**6**), as if the coin was really there. Make a "magic pass" (**7**), open your hand, the coin has vanished (**8**)! Now who's laughing?!

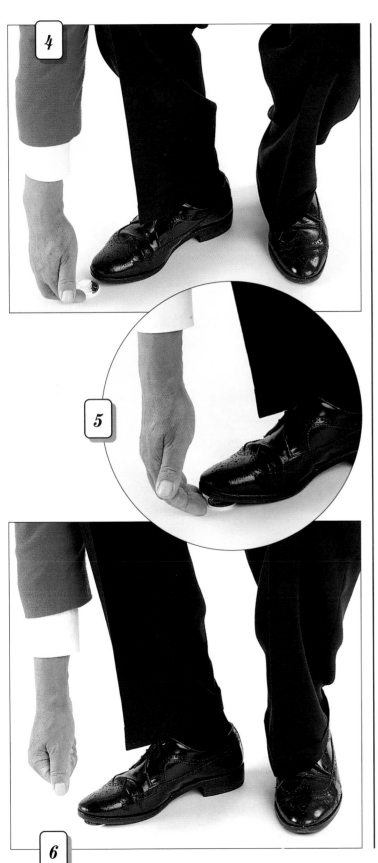

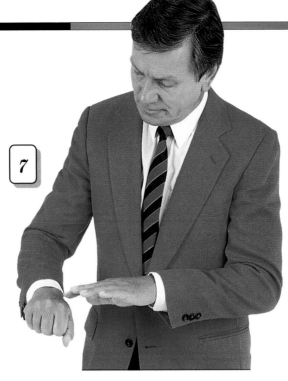

◆ AFTERTHOUGHTS ◆

If your pants have a cuff, you could actually pick up the coin from the floor and secretly drop it into the cuff as you straighten up. This little refinement means you can walk away casually after the trick and no one will know where the coin has gone.

THE BOLD COIN VANISH

This trick is so simple that a child of three could perform it (with twenty years' practice)! Seriously though, it is very bold indeed. Practice will make the actions smooth and the effect extremely deceptive.

❦ EFFECT ❧

A coin, apparently chosen from a handful of change, vanishes!

REQUIREMENTS
Just a handful of coins of various denominations

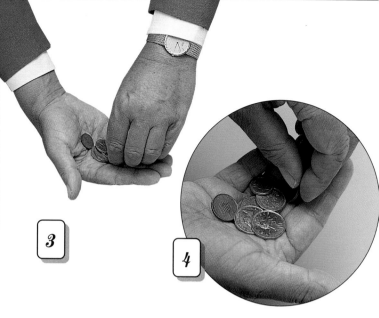

♣ WHAT YOU DO ♣

In order to perform this trick properly it is vital that the simple sequence of moves that are required of you exactly duplicate natural actions. So, first I will take you through the natural sequence.

Take all the coins out of your right pocket and display them on your right palm. Reach across with your left hand (with its back toward the spectator) and pick out one of the coins. Hold the coin between the fingers and thumb of your left hand and *at the same time* put all the other coins back in your pocket. Place the coin into your right hand, and close it into a fist. Open your hand and show the coin. This sequence of moves must be practiced until it becomes smooth – second nature to you. The success of our trick depends entirely on your ability to be natural!

To make a coin vanish, you must perform all these actions, only this time, when it comes to picking up the coin – *you don't*! Yes, it is as simple as that! Remove the coins as before and display them on your palm (**1**). Reach over to take the coin with your left hand (**2**) and, as soon as the back of your hand obscures the coins from sight (**3**), *pretend* to lift out a coin, but let it slip out of your fingers again (**4**). Close your fingers over the imaginary coin and at the same time put *all* the coins back in your pocket again (**5**)! Now *pretend* to pass the coin into your right hand (**6, 7**), and make a fist (**8**). Now, at your leisure, make the imaginary coin vanish (**9**)! Both your hands are empty (**10**)! If you cannot do that, you had better give up magic and take up knitting!

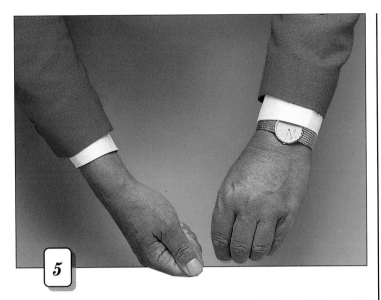

5

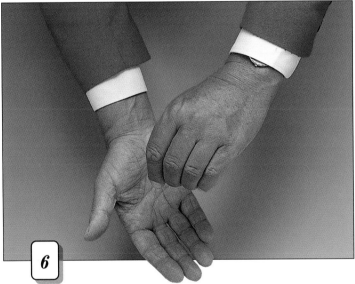

6

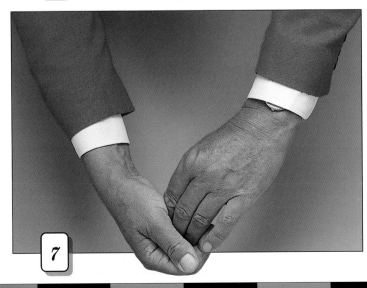

7

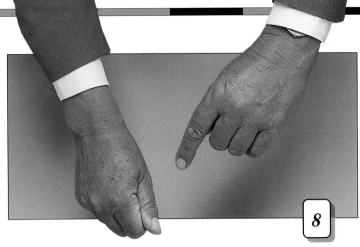

8

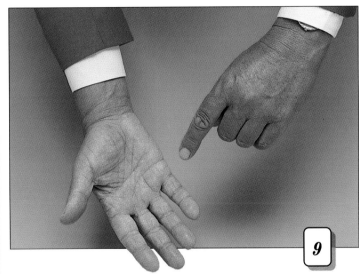

9

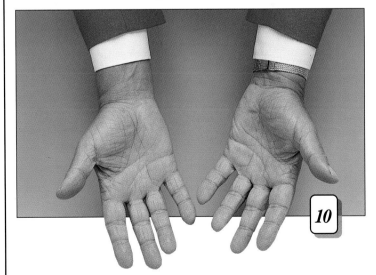

10

➤ AFTERTHOUGHTS ◄

Practice the sequence of moves in front of a mirror and you will see how deceptive they look. "Believe" the coin is there yourself and your audience will too!

PENETRATION

All the items required for this spectacular trick may be borrowed. No preparation is required, so it can be performed completely *impromptu*. You would be hard pressed to find a better bar trick.

➤ EFFECT ◄

A borrowed, marked coin is made to pass magically into a sealed glass tumbler, in full view.

REQUIREMENTS
A glass tumbler
A drink coaster
A coin (the larger the better)
A small piece of paper about 4in square – or even a dollar bill!
A pen

The pen will be used by the lender of the coin so that he can mark it for future identification. Coins, however, do not retain ink marks very well. Ink tends to smudge and rub off. For this reason I usually carry a strip of small, round adhesive labels in my wallet so that the spectator can stick one onto the coin and then write his initials easily upon it. Alternatively, the coin can be scratched with a knife, nail file, or similar sharp object to identify it.

◄ WHAT YOU DO ➤

Ask the spectator to loan you a coin for the trick. Try to get the largest one he has. Have him mark the coin for future identification, using whichever method best suits your situation.

"Let's wrap it up for safety"

You are now going to do the *coin fold*, as described earlier. After the folding, the packet is given a little squeeze and the coin drops on to your right fingers, which palm it (**1**). Take the packet away with your left hand and place it on the bar in full view. At the same time, with the coin still secretly concealed in your hand, pick up the coaster with your right thumb and index finger (**2**).

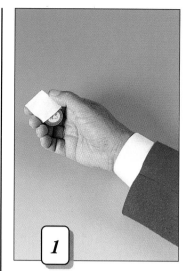

5

6

7

8

"Where's the coaster? Oh! There it is."

Turn your hand over and the coaster will automatically slide over to cover the palmed coin (**3**). Place the coaster over the mouth of the glass (**4**). In so doing, it is an easy matter to trap the coin between it and the lip of the glass (**5**)! Let go. The coin will stay in position, hidden from view (**6**), leaving your hands empty. Pick up the paper packet and place it on top of the coaster (**7**).

"Now watch closely everyone. I will show you some really penetrating magic!"

Show that your hands are empty and then give the packet a sharp tap with your finger (**8**). This will dislodge the trapped coin. It will drop visibly into the glass with a very satisfying clatter (**9**). It looks for all the world as if it has penetrated right through the paper packet and the coaster! *Don't touch anything!* Let the spectator remove the coaster and his coin from the glass. He checks his identification marks. There is no doubt about it. It is the same coin! If there is any justice in life, he will now buy you a drink!

9

♣ AFTERTHOUGHTS ♣

If you cannot find a coaster for this trick, a pack of cards or a small book will do just as well as the "cover" for the glass.

HEADS YOU LOSE!

The simplest tricks are always the best – and this one is simplicity personified! Please, please *practice* until you can do the trick smoothly. If you do, you will have an absolute stunner that you will be able to perform anywhere and at any time. Get the timing right and you will be able to fool even quite knowledgeable magicians with it!

◆ EFFECT ◆

You put a coin in a spectator's hand and it completely vanishes! Then it falls out of the sky and appears in her hand again.

REQUIREMENTS
Just a coin – the larger the better

➤ WHAT YOU DO ◄

Stand facing the spectator with the coin in your right hand. Ask her to hold her hand out, palm upward (**1**). Tell her that you are going to count "One" – "Two" – "Three" and on the count of "Three" she must grab the coin. If she manages to get it, she can keep it! But she must wait until you say "Three."

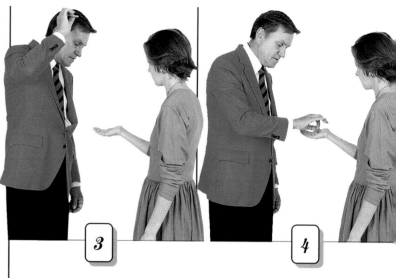

Raise your hand above your head and then bring it down again, pressing the coin on to her palm (**2**), as you count "One." Again raise your hand above your head (**3**) and bring it down, pressing the coin on to her palm (**4**), as you count "Two." Once again raise your hand (**5**), only this time *place the coin on top of your head* (**6**) . . . before bringing your hand down again as if it still contained the coin! Press your *fingers* into her palm as you count "Three." Practice this until it looks exactly like the first two times. Get a nice flowing rhythm going and she will never notice that the coin has already gone.

As soon as she hears you say "Three," she will instantly close her fingers over your fingers as she makes a grab for the coin (**7**). She may even believe that she has got it! You extract your fingers from her grip and ask her to open her fingers (**8**).

The coin has vanished!

To make the coin come back, ask her to hold her hand out again and keep staring at her empty palm. She must say to herself, "Magic Money Come Back!" *Slowly* bow your head forward. The coin will slide off the top of your head and land with a plop on her palm (**9**)! The moment it arrives on her palm, you must suddenly look upward toward the sky as if you think that the coin must have come from somewhere up there (**10**). Open your mouth in amazement as if you can hardly believe it yourself!

A magician is really an actor playing the part of a magician – so remember to give an Oscar-winning performance!

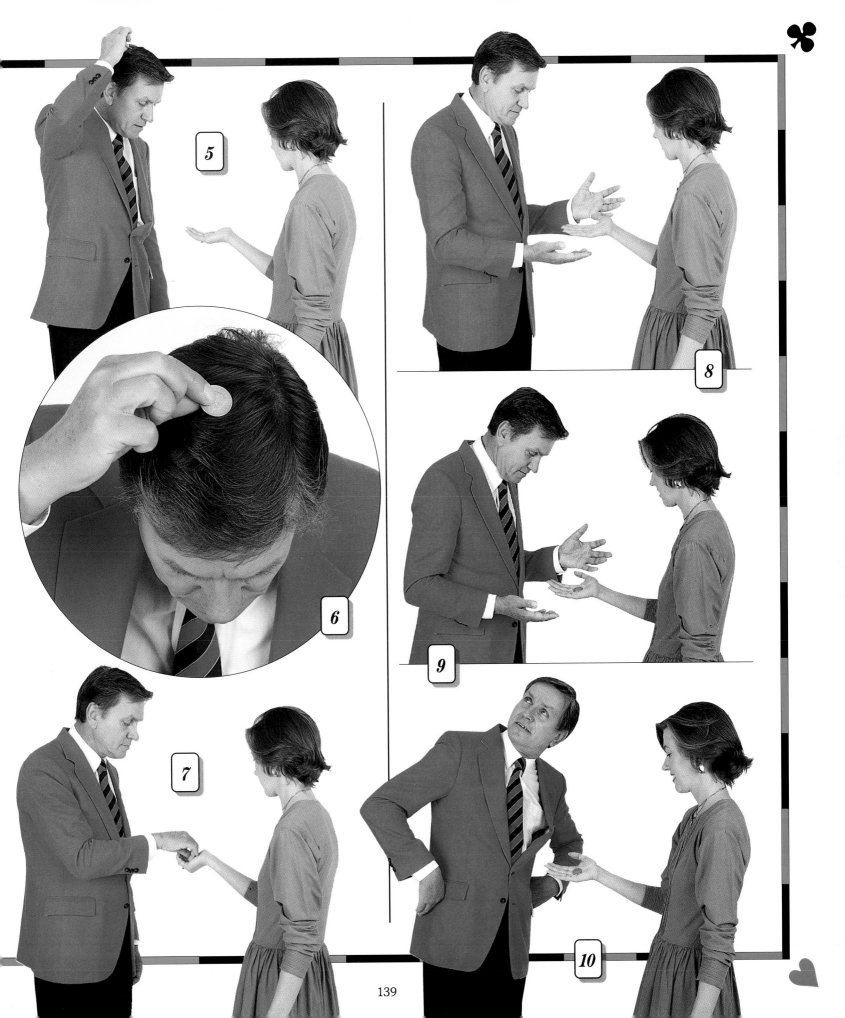

IN POCKET

Y̶ou will certainly be "in pocket" if you learn to do this clever trick. It is very simple in execution but utterly bewildering to your spectators. You will need to wear a jacket or a shirt with a breast pocket to perform it, though.

◀ EFFECT ▶

An inexplicable vanish of a coin! It disappears when you cover it with a handkerchief.

REQUIREMENTS
A coin (which may be borrowed)
A handkerchief or napkin

♣ WHAT YOU DO ♣

Display the coin held in the fingertips of your left hand at chest level, and about 20in in front of your body (**1**). Drape the handkerchief up and over the coin (**2, 3**). Keep pulling the handkerchief over your left hand by drawing your right hand toward your body. This hand comes to rest in line with your jacket pocket as the coin comes into view again (**4**).

Now repeat the above actions (**5**) *but* this time, as soon as your two hands come together (**6**), just grip the coin between your right finger and thumb and steal it away under cover of the handkerchief (**7**). Your right hand continues toward your top pocket as before (**8**). As soon as it reaches it, let the coin drop into your top pocket (**9**)! The handkerchief has now cleared your left hand, and the coin has vanished (**10**). Show that both hands are empty and hand the handkerchief out for examination (**11**). It's mystifying!

5

6

7

8

9

10

11

THE MAGIC PEN

I consider this very pretty coin trick to be worth more than the price of this book!

◆ EFFECT ◆

You hold a borrowed coin in your right fist which you tap with your "magic pen." When you open your fist, the coin has disappeared! You close your empty hand into a fist again and once more tap it with the magic pen. The coin suddenly reappears!

> **REQUIREMENTS**
> A borrowed coin
> A pen with a clip top. Put the pen into your inside jacket pocket

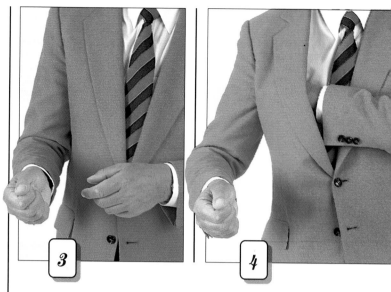

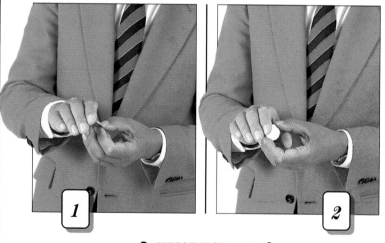

➤ WHAT YOU DO ◄

Borrow a coin and display it between your left thumb and forefinger (**1**). Perform the "Voodoo Coin Vanish" (**2**), apparently taking the coin away in your right fist, but actually retaining it in a left hand finger palm (**3**). Reach inside your jacket with your left hand (**4**) and secretly drop the coin down your sleeve opening. In the same action bring out the pen (**5**).

Practice until the movements are smooth and it looks as if you have merely reached into your pocket to bring out the pen (**6**).

Tap your right fist with the pen (**7**). Open the fist to show that your hand is completely empty – the coin has vanished (**8**)! Display your "magic pen" proudly and at the same time lower your right hand to your side, cupping the fingers (**9**). The coin that you placed in the top of your sleeve will now slide down and drop into your cupped fingers (**10**). Close your right hand into a fist again and tap it with the magic pen (**11**). Open your hand – the coin has magically reappeared (**12**)!

6

7

8

9

10

11

12

SNAPPY COIN TRICK

Coin tricks are always fun to do. This is probably the fastest one that I know. Be careful not to fool yourself.

◀ EFFECT ▶

You openly drop a coin into your sleeve and then magically pluck it through the cloth at your elbow.

◆ WHAT YOU DO ◆

First you must learn and practice the "Snap Vanish" of a coin. It is really an optical illusion – very easy to do – but most deceptive! Hold the coin between your right index finger and thumb (**1**). Force the finger and thumb together with a "snap." The coin apparently

vanishes (**2**). The reveal photograph (**3**) shows what actually happens. The bottom edge of the coin slides away across your thumb and the top edge drops and, as you grip it, it becomes hidden by the fleshy parts of your finger and thumb. You will soon get the hang of it. Once you feel confident that you can do the Snap Vanish, proceed as described.

Sit with your *right* side turned toward the spectators. Bend your left arm and rest your left elbow on the table. Hold the coin over the opening of your left sleeve (**4**) and perform the Snap Vanish. It will appear that you have dropped the coin down your sleeve (**5**).

Don't move your right hand.

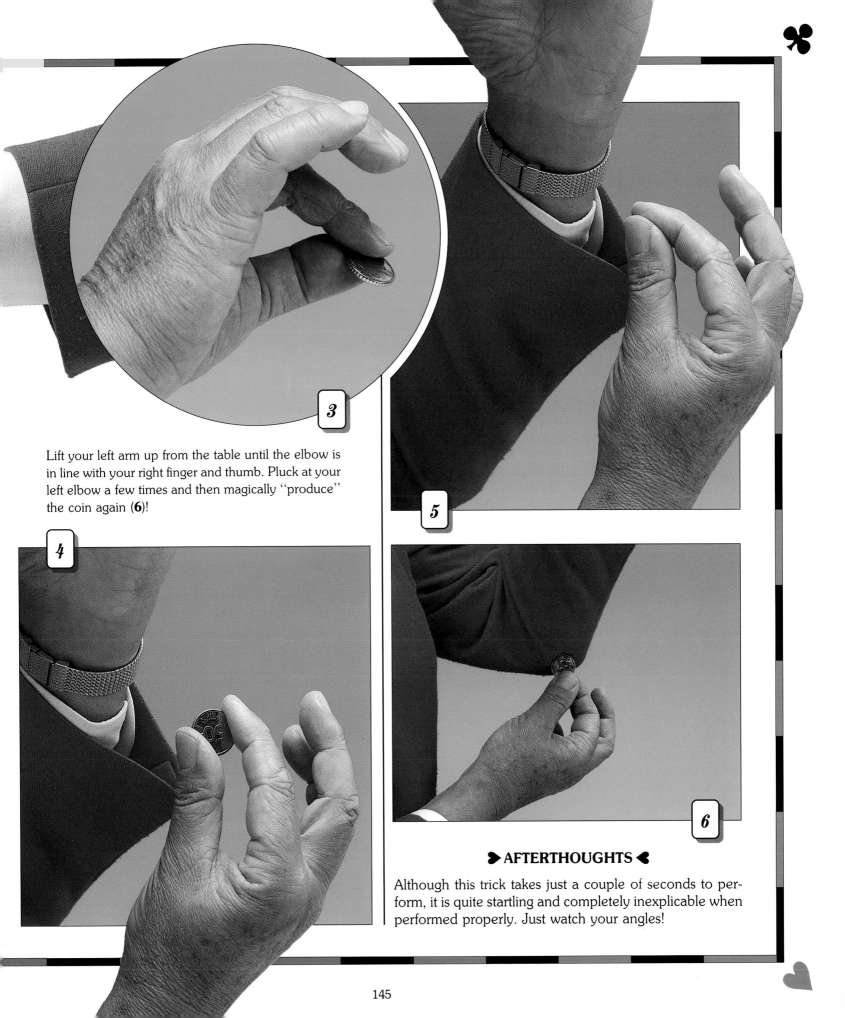

Lift your left arm up from the table until the elbow is in line with your right finger and thumb. Pluck at your left elbow a few times and then magically "produce" the coin again (**6**)!

3

5

4

6

➤ AFTERTHOUGHTS ➤

Although this trick takes just a couple of seconds to perform, it is quite startling and completely inexplicable when performed properly. Just watch your angles!

"GONE!"

This classic of close-up magic is as delightful to perform as it is to watch – a real object lesson in presentation, misdirection, and timing.

◀ EFFECT ▶

A borrowed, marked coin is placed beneath an upturned glass. Not only does the coin vanish but the glass vanishes too!

♣ WHAT YOU DO ♣

Sit at a table with your legs tucked well under it. Borrow a large coin. Give the coin's owner the adhesive label and have him stick it on to his coin anyway that he wishes – front, back, even on its edge – it is up to him. Give him the pen and have him write his initials on the label. When he has done this (**1**), you turn the tumbler upside down (**2**) and fashion a paper cover around it with the paper (**3**). It should be folded loosely enough to slide easily off and yet firm enough to retain the shape of the glass (**4**).

"I'm going to show you a trick called 'Gone'."

Place the coin, marked side up, on the table about 12in in front of you. Put the covered glass over it (**5**).

"Anything that I place under the glass will disappear when I say the magic word 'Go.' I just have to say 'Go' and the coin will disappear, because that's what happens when I say 'Go.' The coin vanishes. In a moment I will say 'Go' and it will be gone."

"Right, the coin will now disappear! 'Go!' "

Lift up the cover and tumbler together (**10**) and swing your hand inward as before. Keep it low. As soon as it is over your lap area (**11**), ease your grip a little and let the glass drop silently into your lap (**12**). You keep hold of the paper cover which, of course, still retains the shape of the glass. Nobody will notice because they are all looking at the coin on the table, which *has not* vanished, and you have already acclimatized them to the movement of the glass and its cover.

While you are spouting the above "garbage" you perform the following actions *at least three times*. With your right hand slide the paper cover about half-way up the tumbler showing the coin (**6**). Lower the cover again. Lift up the cover *and* glass together by gripping them firmly. Then swing your arm back so that the glass and cover are just hovering above the edge of the table – over your lap (**7**). Move your right hand forward again and replace the glass and cover back over the coin (**8**). These actions must accompany the "patter" and the combination of words and actions are designed to draw the onlookers' attention to the *coin*. To increase their attention on it, you can even turn it face-side down at one point in the routine (**9**). Why is this important? *Because we are now going to vanish the glass instead*!

"Oh dear! It didn't work. Perhaps it would be better turned over the other way. I'll try."

Turn over the coin (**13**) and put the *cover* back over it (**14**). The spectators will subconsciously assume that the tumbler is there too.

"O.K. I'm ready . . . 'Go'."

Lift the cover up to expose the coin again (**15**) but *do not swing it toward you this time*. Look at the coin with apparent dismay and desperation. Then, as if light was suddenly dawning, say:

"I'm sorry! I got a little confused. This is the trick where the *glass* vanishes!!!"

Open up the paper cover to show that the glass really has gone (**16**). The effect is astonishing! Crumple the paper cover up into a ball and throw it into the audience. This causes more mayhem. Take advantage of the uproar. Reach into your lap with your *left* hand. Grab the tumbler and push it up on the outside of your jacket. Grip it under your armpit (**17**). You must be very quick about this. Once it is safely in place, just *relax*. After a few seconds the spectators will turn back to you.

"If you look carefully you will see where the glass went."

Somebody will eventually spot it and point it out to the rest. Place it on the table with a flourish (**18**).

"This is the vanishing glass . . . and *this* . . ."

Reach forward with your right hand toward the coin (**19**), pulling it back toward you and execute the "Sitting-Down Coin Vanish" (**20**). Lean forward with your right fist closed (**21**), then slowly open your fingers (**22**) . . .

". . . is the vanishing coin . . . which has completely disappeared!"

➤ AFTERTHOUGHTS ◄

There is quite a lot to learn here. However, the sequences are all logical and easy to perform. Needless to say, you *must* practice until you can perform all the actions smoothly. Set a table up in front of a mirror. See what it looks like from the audience's point of view. Be careful not to fool yourself!

MONEY TO BURN

For some reason we all tend to laugh when somebody slips up on a banana skin. The humor in this next classic trick is derived from watching the reactions of your unsuspecting volunteer to the bizarre situation in which he finds himself.

♣ EFFECT ♣

You borrow the highest denomination bill that you can persuade the spectator to part with. Having sealed it in an envelope, you proceed to set fire to it! Everything is reduced to ashes! You resurrect it from the ashes in a most amusing way and return it to the relieved spectator.

> **REQUIREMENTS**
> A borrowed bill
> A standard letter envelope
> Box of matches and ashtray
> A deck of cards
> A pen or pencil

◆ PREPARATION ◆

Cut a 2in slit in the envelope on the *address* side (**1**). If the envelope is shown flap side up, the slit should be hidden from view by the back pouch. Set up by putting the envelope and the pencil in your inside jacket pocket. Put the matches and the deck of cards in your left jacket pocket. We will call the idiot (sorry, volunteer!) who lends you the money Neil.

← WHAT YOU DO →

Talk to Neil:

"Lend me a bill, Neil, and I will show you a fantastic trick!"

Neil obliges and lends you a bill. You might be lucky and get a really high-value bill; gratefully accept whatever he offers you. Take the pencil out of your pocket and hand it to Neil.

"In case you are fortunate enough to see your money again, I would like you to sign your name across it."

While he does this you remove the envelope from your pocket and place it (address side down) on the table.

"Did you know that paper money is virtually indestructible? Let me show you . . ."

Take the signed bill from Neil (**2**) and fold it in half *three times* so that you end up with a little packet

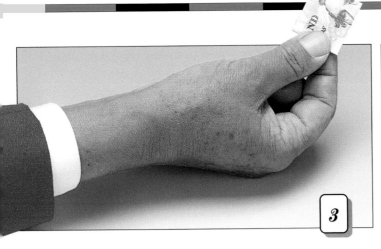

approximately 2in square (**3**). Put the folded bill on the table. Hold the envelope in your left hand, fingers covering the secret slit, thumb on top (**4**). Pull back the flap with your right hand, pick up the bill and push it into the envelope (**5**). The leading edge of the folded bill goes through the slit on to the *outside* of the envelope (**6**) and is hidden by your left fingers. Neil can still see part of his bill on the inside of the envelope.

Lift the flap up to your mouth by raising your left hand, and lick the sticky flap. Lower your hand again so that Neil gets one last flash of his money, then fold the flap over and press it down to seal the envelope (**7**). Your right hand takes the envelope away and places it on the table. *At the same time* your left fingers hang on to his folded bill and, without hesitation, you thrust your hand into your left jacket pocket. When your left hand is out of sight, push the folded bill into the middle of the deck of cards.

Leave it there and bring out the box of matches. Your two hands have moved in opposite directions simultaneously. The actions are very natural and because of this will not cause suspicion. Practice until you can synchronize the two actions smoothly.

"You will enjoy this Neil! I'm going to set fire to your money! Please don't worry about it – I've done this trick before! Once!"

the secret slit area – thus you destroy the evidence (**9**)! You must now give an Oscar-winning performance . . . Smilingly you say:

"The amazing thing, Neil, is that your money will have withstood the heat and flames and will be completely unharmed! Let me show you . . ."

9

8

10

Pull the ashtray toward you. Strike a match and then, holding the envelope by one corner, apply the flame to the diagonally opposite corner (**8**). Be careful; don't burn your fingers! Just make sure that you destroy as much of the envelope as possible – especially

Start to poke around among the ashes looking for his money (**10**). Slowly your smile and confident attitude change to embarrassment and an air of doom.

"Oh dear!" You look shocked. Poke around some more (**11**). **"It seems to have gone slightly wrong. I just can't understand it. It worked fine last time..."** You give up your forlorn search for his money. **"Look, Neil, I'm terribly sorry ... Let me show you a card trick instead!"**

Bring the deck out of your pocket and place it face down on the table. The bill, you will remember, is sandwiched in the middle of the deck.

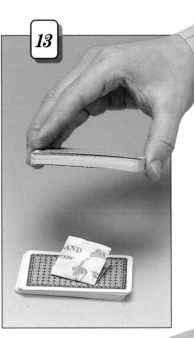

"I want you to cut the deck somewhere near the middle."

He will automatically lift off all the cards above the folded bill (**12**), bringing it into view in a surprising way (**13**).

"Oh! Now I remember how to do the trick! Pick up the bill, Neil. Open it up. Check your signature carefully. Is it your bill? The one that we burned?"

Neil will breathe a sigh of relief at getting his money back (**14**). You can now remind him that it is his turn to buy the drinks!

PART FIVE

SAFETY PIN MAGIC

SPOOKY PINS

Tricks that use ordinary household objects are always effective because the spectators can "relate" to them easily. Our association with safety pins often began on the day that we wore our first diapers!

♣ EFFECT ♣

Two perfectly ordinary safety pins are firmly linked together. You hold one in each hand and pull in opposite directions. They become magically unlinked without opening!

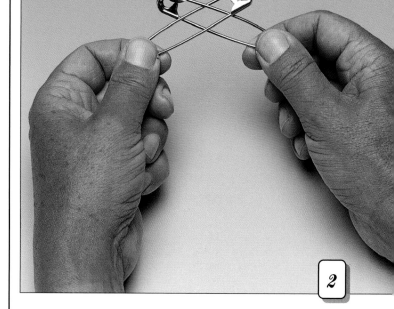

REQUIREMENTS
Two ordinary safety pins. Try to find quite large ones – they will make the trick look more impressive

◆ WHAT YOU DO ◆

The trick is self-working provided that you link and hold the pins exactly as shown (**1**). Note particularly the position of the *opening* and *non-opening* bars of the two safety pins (**2**). Once you are sure that you have the correct position, hold them firmly and pull your hands *sharply* in opposite directions. The pins will separate automatically (**3**). Practice until you can unlink them smoothly. It is a little knack that you will very soon acquire.

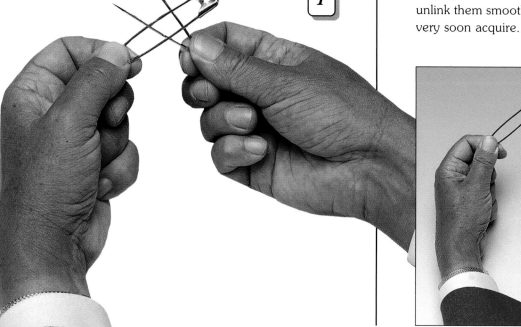

HANKY PANKY

Another little safety pin gem. It looks quite impossible, while, in fact, it is entirely self-working.

➤ EFFECT ◀

A safety pin is fastened to a handkerchief. You remove it without opening it!

REQUIREMENTS
One good-sized safety pin
A linen handkerchief, which is best borrowed

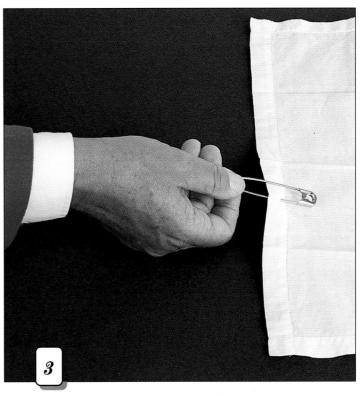

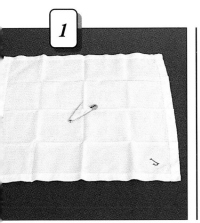

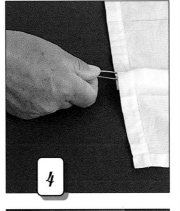

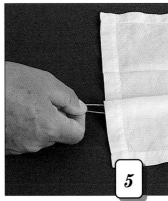

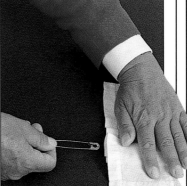

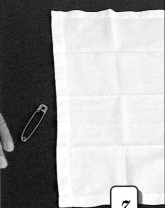

◀ WHAT YOU DO ➤

Follow the instructions and you will find the trick self-working. Spread the handkerchief out on the table (**1**). Fasten the safety pin on to the handkerchief near its edge (**2**). Turn the pin over to the left – *three times*. The handkerchief will, of course, roll over too (**3**, **4**, **5**). Press firmly down on the handkerchief with your left hand to hold it firmly in place. Grip the protruding end of the pin between your right forefinger and thumb and *pull down sharply*. The pin comes off cleanly and yet is still closed (**6**)! Return the un-damaged handkerchief (**7**) to the amazed spectator.

A RIPPING YARN!

Don't do this trick in front of people of a nervous disposition! It is hard on their nerves!

♣ EFFECT ♣

A spectator holds up her handkerchief before her. You fasten a safety pin in the hem at one end, give it a sharp pull and the pin ends up at the *other* end, still fastened! Although a resounding ripping sound is heard, the handkerchief remains undamaged.

REQUIREMENTS
A good-sized safety pin
A linen handkerchief, borrowed if possible

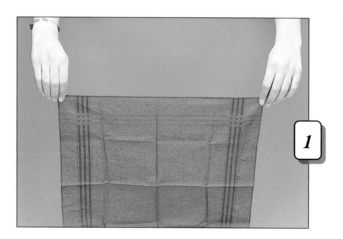

◆ WHAT YOU DO ◆

The spectator should hold the handkerchief tautly as shown in picture (**1**). You should insert the safety pin at the point in the hem shown (**2**). Note that the solid (non-opening) bar of the pin is to your *left* (**3**). *This is very important.* Grip the end of the pin firmly (**4**) and pull the pin sharply to the *right* (**5**) for about 8in (**6**) and then push in. The pin will still be fastened but is

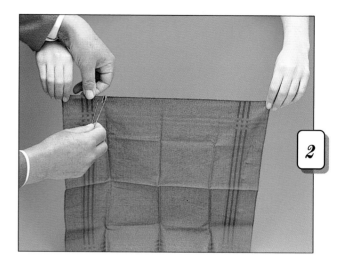

now at the other end of the handkerchief. And despite the sound of tearing, the handkerchief will be intact (**7**).

I suggest that you try this on your own handkerchief until you get the hang of it. It is an easily acquired knack. Picture (**5**) shows what happens when you pull the pin to the right. The bar disengages slightly from the clasp, allowing the point of the pin to slide along the cloth without damaging it. You must push in at the end of your "run" to make the pin penetrate the handkerchief again, and so complete the illusion.

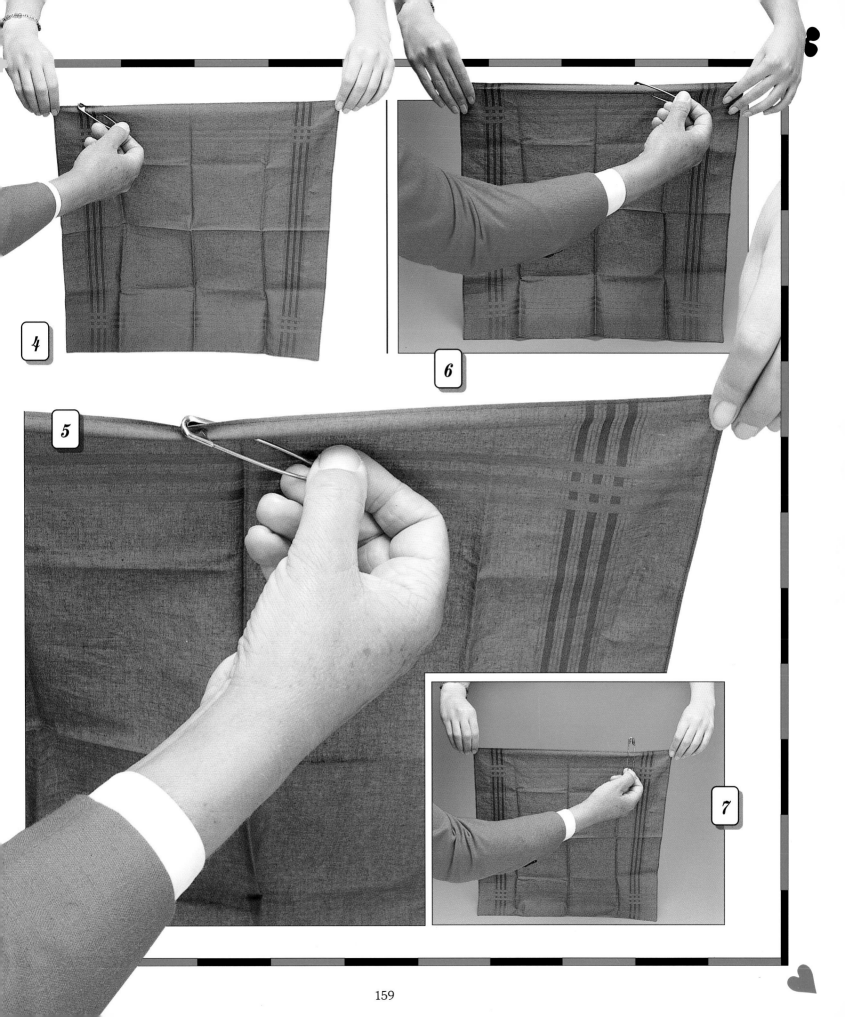

4

6

5

7

DROP OUT

This unusual "quick trick" is really an optical illusion. It should fool most people.

♣ EFFECT ♣

Two *closed* safety pins are shown. You just drop them gently on to the table and both spring open as if by magic!

◀ PREPARATION ▶

The pins are *never* closed! Look at picture (**1**) carefully. It shows two opened safety pins with their *pins* resting in each other's *shields*. If you now hold the safety pins with your thumb covering the loops (**2**) it will appear that you are holding two closed safety pins! The illusion is perfect.

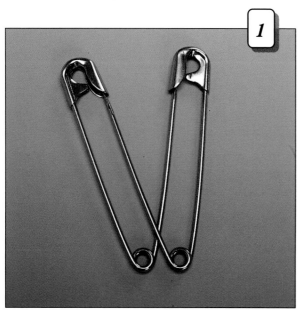

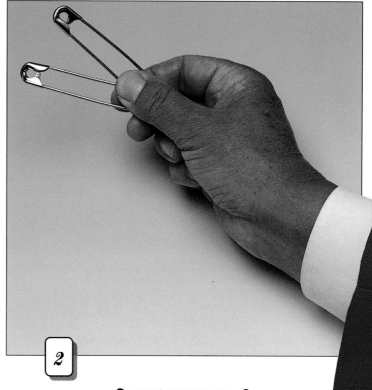

➤ WHAT YOU DO ◀

Display the two safety pins in your hand as shown (**2**). Point out to the spectator that they are securely fastened. Hold them about 12in above the center of your table. Drop the safety pins. They will naturally come to rest in the open position (**3**). Now close each safety pin properly and give them to the spectator to try and duplicate your feat!

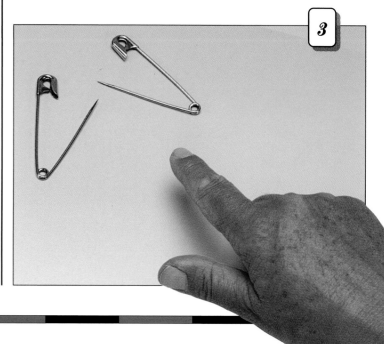

PIN IN A SPIN

This mini-miracle is a superb optical illusion. It will baffle even the most eagle-eyed of spectators.

◆ EFFECT ◆

A matchstick repeatedly penetrates through the bar of a safety pin.

REQUIREMENTS
A safety pin
A matchstick

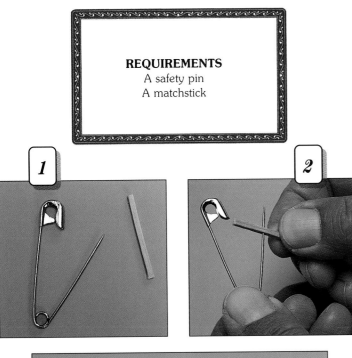

➤ PREPARATION ◄

First cut off the head of the matchstick so that both ends look the same (**1**). Then carefully impale this matchstick on the safety pin (**2**). Make sure that the safety pin passes through the center of the matchstick. At first you may find that the matchstick splits. Try again until you find one that does not. Twist the matchstick backward and forward until it revolves easily and freely on the bar.

◄ WHAT YOU DO ➤

Hold the pin between your left finger and thumb (**3**). Make sure that the matchstick is impaled by the bar *nearest* you and rests under the bar *furthest* away from you.

To create the illusion that the matchstick penetrates the solid bar of the safety pin, just flick down sharply on the end nearest to you (**4**). The far end of the match (B) will appear to penetrate the bar that it was resting under. It is now seen to be on the upper side of the bar (**5**)! What actually happens is this: if you flick hard enough, the matchstick will rebound and spin around in the opposite direction. It is really end "A" that now rests on the bar and *not* end "B!" The matchstick has turned full circle but too quickly to be followed by the naked eye.

You will have to try this out in your own hands to appreciate the effect. It is very deceptive and can be repeated as often as you wish.

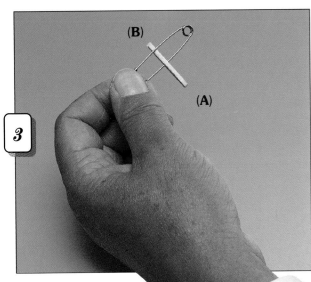

(B)

(A)

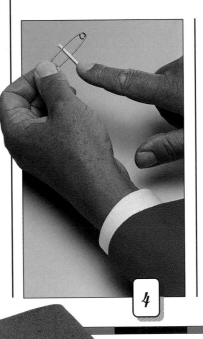

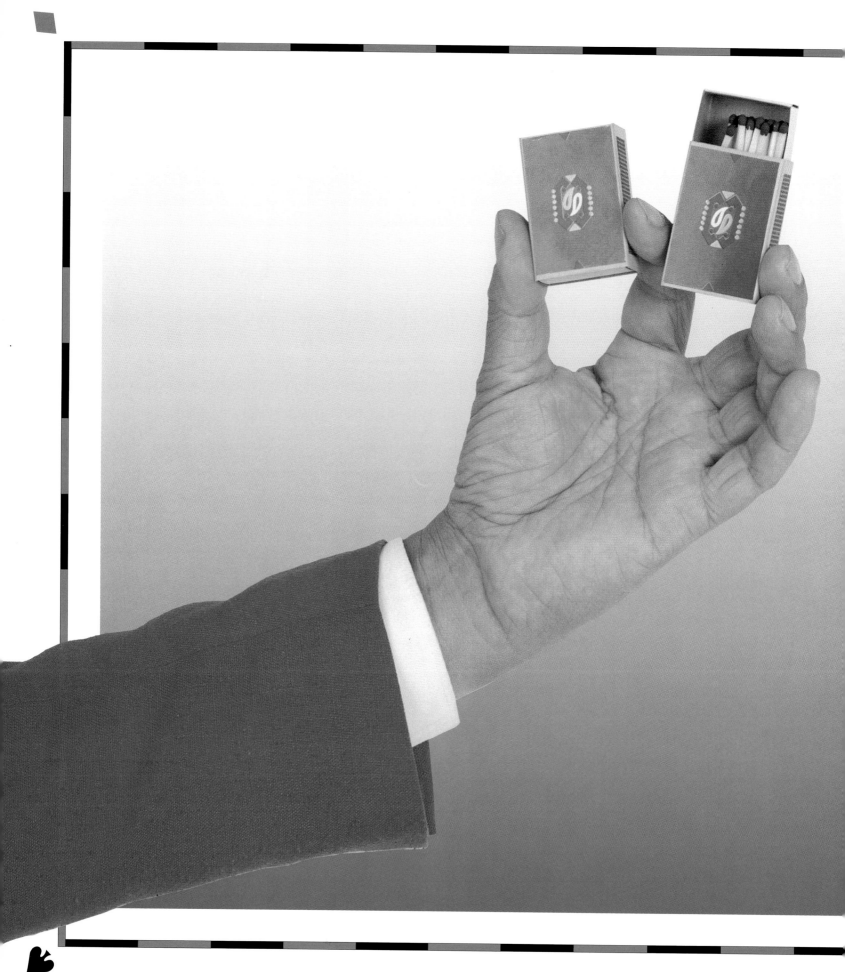

MATCHBOX MAGIC

SOUNDS EASY

Tricks that rely on *sound* are very rare in magic. This is a good one and the method employed is very subtle.

♣ EFFECT ♣

Three empty matchboxes are shown and a borrowed coin dropped into one of them. The spectator is asked to remember which matchbox the coin is in. Slowly and deliberately you mix the boxes around. No matter how carefully she looks, the spectator is never able to pick out the correct box! Finally the coin completely disappears and is produced from your jacket pocket!

REQUIREMENTS
Four identical empty matchboxes

Two coins (one of which must be borrowed)
Elastic band
Small sticky labels
A pen
A spectator. We will call her Louise.

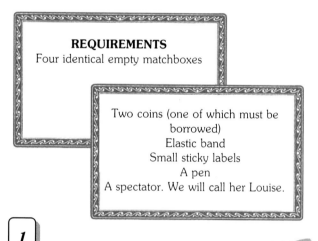

◆ PREPARATION ◆

Put *your* coin in a matchbox and strap it to the underside of your left wrist. It should rest just out of sight up your jacket sleeve (**1**). If you now shake your left hand you will hear a rattling sound. Put the three empty matchboxes in your right jacket pocket with the labels and the pen. You are all set.

➤ WHAT YOU DO ◀

Start by saying:

"Lend me a coin, Louise, and I will show you a famous circus trick."

Louise lends you the coin although she secretly wonders if she will ever see it again! Bring out the pen, sticky labels and one matchbox. Have the coin labeled and marked as in previous tricks (**2**). Remove the drawer from the matchbox to show that it is empty. Place the marked coin in the matchbox and shut the drawer (**3**). You are now going secretly to remove her coin from the box.

Hold the box upside down in the rattling position (**4**) and give the sides a little squeeze (**5**). The coin will slide out on to your palm (**6**). Place the box on the table keeping the coin palmed in your right hand. This move should be practiced until you can do it smoothly. It should seem that you merely rattled the box, then placed it on the table.

Now put your hand in your pocket – leave the coin there – bring out the other two empty matchboxes. Show these to be absolutely empty, reassemble them and place them on the table to the *right* of the other one (**7**).

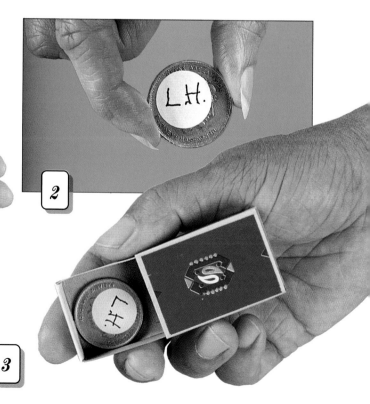

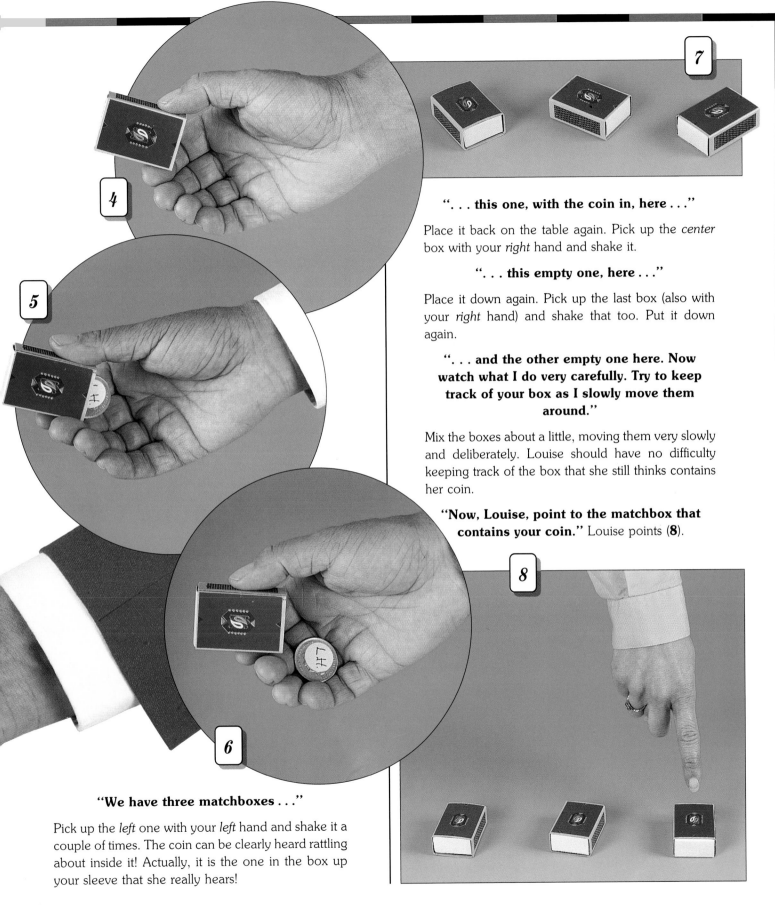

"...this one, with the coin in, here..."

Place it back on the table again. Pick up the *center* box with your *right* hand and shake it.

"...this empty one, here..."

Place it down again. Pick up the last box (also with your *right* hand) and shake that too. Put it down again.

"...and the other empty one here. Now watch what I do very carefully. Try to keep track of your box as I slowly move them around."

Mix the boxes about a little, moving them very slowly and deliberately. Louise should have no difficulty keeping track of the box that she still thinks contains her coin.

"Now, Louise, point to the matchbox that contains your coin." Louise points (**8**).

"We have three matchboxes..."

Pick up the *left* one with your *left* hand and shake it a couple of times. The coin can be clearly heard rattling about inside it! Actually, it is the one in the box up your sleeve that she really hears!

We will let her win the first round! Pick up the one that she indicates with your *left* hand and shake it (**9**). It rattles – so this time she is correct. Shuffle the boxes around on the table again. Ask Louise to point again (**10**). Notice that we always say *"point"* and not *"choose."* That is because we do not want Louise to pick up the box that she selects. This time pick up the selected box with your *right* hand and shake it (**11**). It will not rattle. Pick up one of the other boxes with your *left* hand and shake it (**12**).

"No Louise. I caught you that time. *This* is the one – over here!"

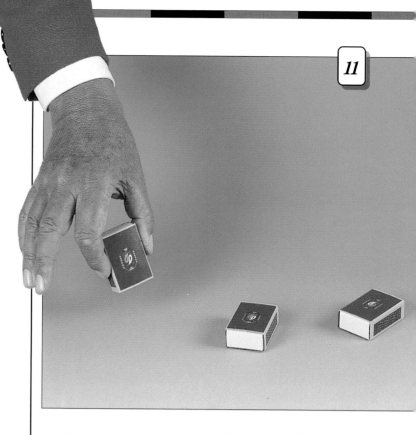

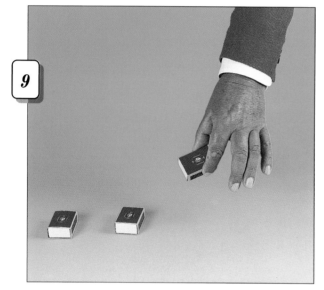

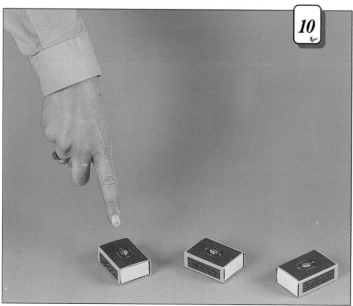

Place the box that apparently contains the coin between the other two and slowly mix them around again. Louise points to a box once more. Again prove that she is wrong by shaking her selected box with your *right* hand and one of the others with your *left*! By this time Louise will be thinking of having her eyes tested at the earliest opportunity!

Now we "kick her when she is down." Place the box that she thinks contains the coin a little apart from the other two. Give it a shake with your left hand so that she can hear the "rattle." Gesture with both your hands to show that they are empty as you say:

"Now, Louise, I will attempt the impossible. I will make your coin completely disappear! Watch!"

Wave your right hand mysteriously over the box and then count . . .

"One . . . Two . . . Three! Now I shall open the box."

You open the box and show that the coin has gone (**13**). Louise will immediately grab for the other two boxes in a vain search for her coin. Too late! Bring the trick to a stunning conclusion by producing the marked coin from your pocket (**14**).

◆ AFTERTHOUGHTS ➤

On occasions I have been able secretly to slip the spectator's coin into *her own jacket pocket!* The mixing about of the boxes provides the misdirection that makes this possible. The trick then becomes a little miracle because you state that you will make the coin jump from the matchbox into her own pocket! You then ask Louise to produce her marked coin herself! The effect is stunning! If you think that you can get away with it, without spoiling the trick, then *go for it!* He who dares – wins!

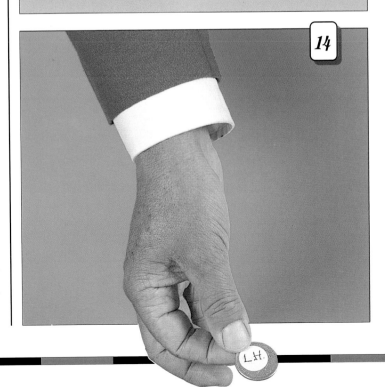

THE ACROBATIC MATCHBOX

This little gem has been my favorite "pocket trick" for more than 35 years. I pass the routine on to you with pride and the wish that you practice it until you can perform it perfectly. Do not be put off because the effect is achieved by using a secret thread. If you perform it correctly, *no one will ever know!*

♣ EFFECT ♣

A matchbox is placed on the back of your hand. It suddenly "comes to life" and performs some staggering acrobatic feats. It stands up on its end. The drawer suddenly rises. It then runs down your wrist, does a twirl and stands on its side. For a finale, it does a complete somersault, stands up and then opens all by itself! In explanation, you state that this is all made possible by using an invisible hair. You pretend to pluck a hair from a spectator's head and attach it to an invisible hook on the end of the matchbox. When you "pull" the hair, the drawer of the matchbox is seen to open as if being pulled by the hair!

REQUIREMENTS
A matchbox
A length of thin nylon fishing line or
dressmaker's invisible thread
A small safety pin
A needle

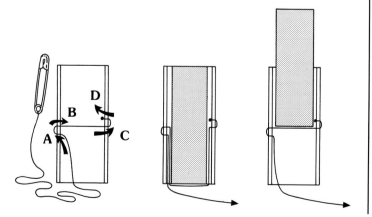

➤ PREPARATION ◄

You will have to "gimmick up" the matchbox. *N.B.* I have used black thread in the photographs, so that you can see how the tricks work. For performance you should use colorless fishing line. First make sure that the drawer slides in and out smoothly and does not jam. Thread about 20in of nylon fishing line on to your needle. Now thread it through the matchbox as shown in the diagram. First remove the drawer. Then, from the inside, push the needle through the outer cover so that it comes out on the outside of the box about half way up (**A**). Move the needle up about ¼in, and thread it back through the box again (**B**), across, and out through the middle of the other side (**C**). Go up another ¼in and push the needle through again from the outside (**D**), only this time do not thread it right across – just pass the needle up through the sleeve and out at the top. Remove the needle and tie about three knots in the end of the thread, all on top of one another. This knot will now be too fat to unthread through the holes in the matchbox case that you have made.

Put the drawer back in the case from the top. It will take up some of the slack thread. Place a light pencil dot on the underside of the box at the end furthest from where the thread runs under the drawer. This will not be noticed by the spectators. It is there so that you can tell at a glance which side is which. Tie a safety pin on the other end of the thread. Fasten the safety pin to the inside of your left jacket pocket and after putting a few matches in the box, place it in the same pocket. Your simple preparation having been completed, you are now ready to perform.

1

◆ WHAT YOU DO ◆

Take the box out with your left hand and hold it by its long edges about half way down. Your right hand comes over and holds the box by its free end, between your right thumb and index finger. Push open the drawer with your left thumb and remove it completely between your right index finger and thumb in the usual manner (**1**). The fingers of your *left* hand retain hold of the cover, and the thread is completely hidden by your left hand and coat sleeve. Both hands should be held across the body and the two sections of the box displayed by moving your wrists, *not* your arms. Be content to show the box for a second very casually but not carelessly, and then assemble the box as before.

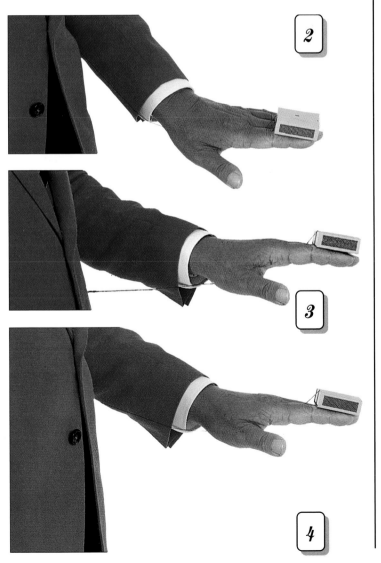

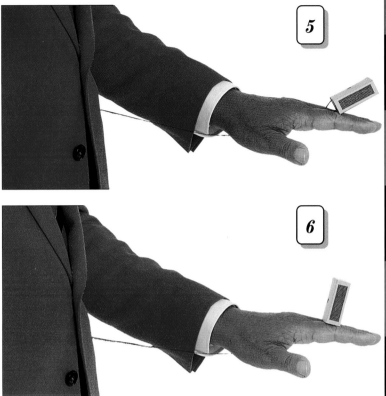

The box should now be held in your left hand between your index finger and thumb. Take the box in you right hand (index finger and thumb), straighten the fingers of your left hand and, holding this hand in a horizontal position, place the matchbox on the back of this hand with the pencil dot uppermost and nearest the finger-tips (**2**). The thread must be arranged so that it passes from the top of the end nearest your body, between the first and second fingers, under the palm and from there to your jacket pocket (**3**). You will discover that this is easily accomplished during the action of placing the box on the back of your hand. When the right fingers take the box, slightly part the first and second fingers of your left hand. By dropping this hand a little, you will engage the thread and it will pass between the required fingers. Then place the box on the hand as described. The end of the box nearest you should be resting on or near the middle joints of the fingers (**4**). *This is very important.*

If, with the box still on the back of your hand, you push your hand *gently* forward a little, you will find that the box will be levered up into a standing position (**5, 6**). This is caused by the pull on the thread originating from the forward movement of the hand.

By pushing your hand still further forward, you will find that the drawer will rise up from its cover (**7**). If this does not happen, it means that your thread is too long and you will have to shorten it. The thread will be of the correct length if, when you stand with your hand and arm held at waist level with the box as in picture (**4**), there is no slackness in the thread. Check also that your pencil dot is uppermost.

The big drawback with moving your hand forward in this way is that a fairly observant spectator may notice it. I have only described it in order that you may readily grasp the working principle of the matchbox. I work my matchbox by moving my body and not my hand. This is by far the best method because the hand stays motionless throughout the routine. This pretty routine is in six parts and we are now ready to start.

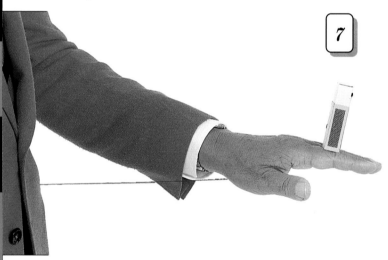

➤EFFECT NO 1◀

Place the box on the back of your left hand, as shown in picture (**4**). Keep your hand stationary but bend your body at the waist, apparently bowing over the box. At the same time give a waving gesture, simulating a magic pass, with the free right hand. These are perfectly natural actions but necessary from our point of view. You will find that the slight bending movement of the body will bring pull to bear on the thread and the box will lever itself into a standing position (**5, 6**). By bending the body a little more or, alternatively, pulling your left side backward a little, you will find that the drawer of the box will slowly rise (**7**).

Remember to keep the hand motionless.

◆ EFFECT NO 2 ◆

Close the box and place it, once again, on the back of your left hand. With your right hand slide the box straight back over your left hand until the end nearest you rests on, or very near, your wrist (**8**). The thread, as the photograph shows, now runs beneath the box, along the back of the hand, between the first and second fingers, under your hand, and from there to your pocket. Although about 2in of thread is actually running across the back of your hand it will *never* be noticed. It is only on view for a second in any case, and the spectator does not have time to focus on it, as the box is the object of attention.

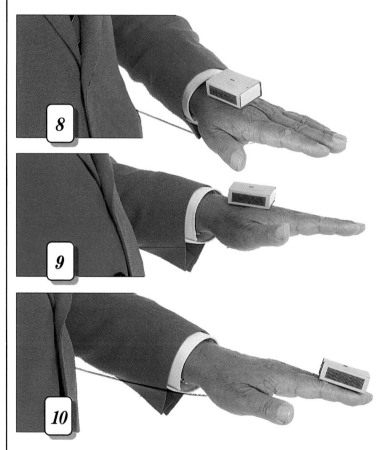

You will find now that by creating tension on the thread (i.e. by bending your body), the box will slowly crawl along the back of your hand (**9**) and finally come to rest at your finger tips (**10**). By pointing your fingers in a *slightly* downward direction, this movement of the box can be assisted. This matchbox move, like all the others, should be executed slowly and gracefully, avoiding all jerky actions.

♣ EFFECT NO 3 ♣

For this effect, turn the box so that the end where the thread makes its entry is *facing* the spectators (i.e. the pencil dot is nearest to you) and place the box at the extreme tips of the *second and third* fingers (**11**). Hold your hand perfectly relaxed and you will find that by bringing a slight but steady pressure to bear on the thread, the box will swing right around to occupy its former position (**12**), stand on end (**13, 14**), and finally raise its own drawer (**15**)! You will find it easier to perform the "swing around" movement if, once again, you point your fingers in a *slightly* downward direction. Remember, only slightly downward – do not try to defy the law of gravity!

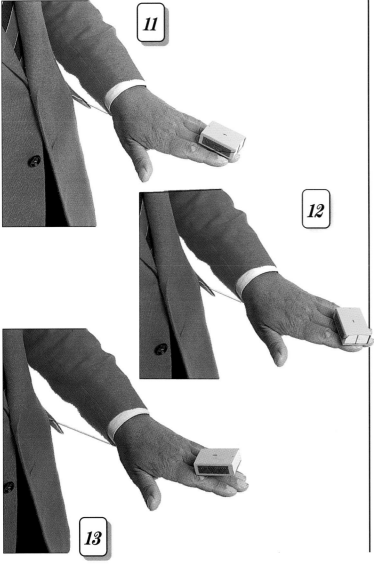

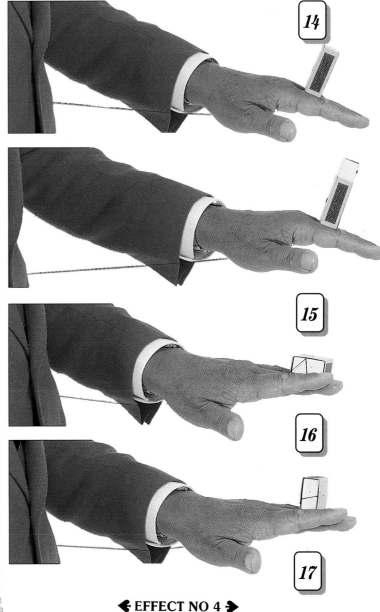

◀ EFFECT NO 4 ▶

Close the box and place it sideways across your second, third and fourth fingers, with the long edge resting on the far side of the middle joints. Raise your index finger very slightly until it rests alongside, but does not grip, the end of the box (**16**). Pulling on the thread now will cause the box to lever itself into an upright position standing on its *long edge* (**17**)! The position of the index finger is important because it prevents the box from pivoting around. The rough bumpy skin of the middle joints of the fingers also helps to keep the box crosswise on your hand, and so makes this effect possible.

♣ EFFECT NO 5 ♣

Now place the box on the back of your hand as in picture (**4**) once again. Pick up the box in your right hand by its near (attached) end. Draw the box toward yourself (**18**) and at the same time turn the box completely over (**19**) and lay it back on your hand again, quite close to your wrist (**20**). In this position the attached end of the box is toward the audience and a single strand of thread runs along the top of the box, down between your first and second fingers and from there to your pocket. If you bend your body again to pull the thread, the box will run down your hand (**21, 22**), turn a complete somersault (**23, 24, 25**), run down your hand again toward your fingertips (**26**), stand up on end (**27, 28**) and, finally, raise its own drawer once more (**29**)!

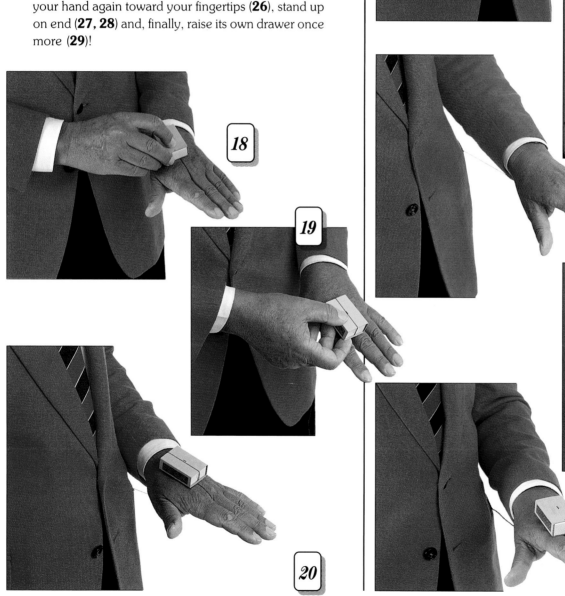

26

27

28

29

➤ EFFECT NO 6 ◄

Finally the box is reassembled and held by the left index finger and thumb as before. Tell your audience that, "The trick is made possible by using a hair." So saying, you pluck an *imaginary hair* from the head of a nearby spectator and wind the imaginary hair around an *imaginary hook* at the unattached end of the box. Pretend to pull on the end of this imaginary hair and, at the same time, bend your body to bring pressure to bear on the thread. This will cause the drawer to open (**30**). When these two actions are properly synchronized it will appear that the drawer of the matchbox is actually being pulled open by an invisible hair!

You have finished the sequence of six effects so turn your left side slightly, but not furtively, away from the audience and casually replace the matchbox into your left jacket pocket.

30

◄ AFTERTHOUGHTS ➤

Well, that's it! I have gone into great detail with the explanation so that you will be able to master the whole routine. You do not always have to perform it in its entirety. Practice with the first effect until you have mastered it – then have fun learning the other gymnastics! Remember, you should, of course, use nylon fishing line, which is colorless. It does not show up very well in photographs, so we have gimmicked our matchbox with *black thread* for the sake of clarity.

THE WALKING DEAD

This is a wonderfully impossible looking trick that uses just a book of paper matches. The final effect really packs a punch!

➤ EFFECT ◀

You let a spectator count the matches in a book of paper matches. Let us say there are thirteen. You tear out one match – strike it – then extinguish the flame. The match then *disappears*! The spectator recounts the matches in the book. There are *still* thirteen matches in the book even though you tore one out just a few seconds ago! To make matters worse, on closer inspection the spectator discovers that one of the matches is *dead – yet still firmly attached to the book*! Who said that the dead do not walk?!

```
REQUIREMENTS
Just a book of paper matches
```

◆ PREPARATION ◆

Bend back one match, light it and then quickly blow it out (**1**). Close the flap of the book and, in so doing, slide it between the spent match and the rest (**2**). Put the book away in your left pocket and you are ready to begin.

◀ WHAT YOU DO ➤

Remove the book of matches from your pocket. Before you actually bring it into view, fold back the spent match and cover it with your thumb (**3**). Open the flap with your right hand (**4**), and, still maintaining your left hand grip, ask the spectator to count how many matches there are in the book. He says "Thirteen."

"You counted them very well. Education is a wonderful thing – you must have gone to a *private* school!"

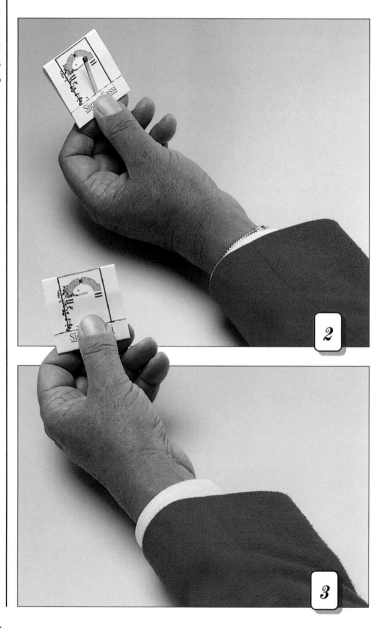

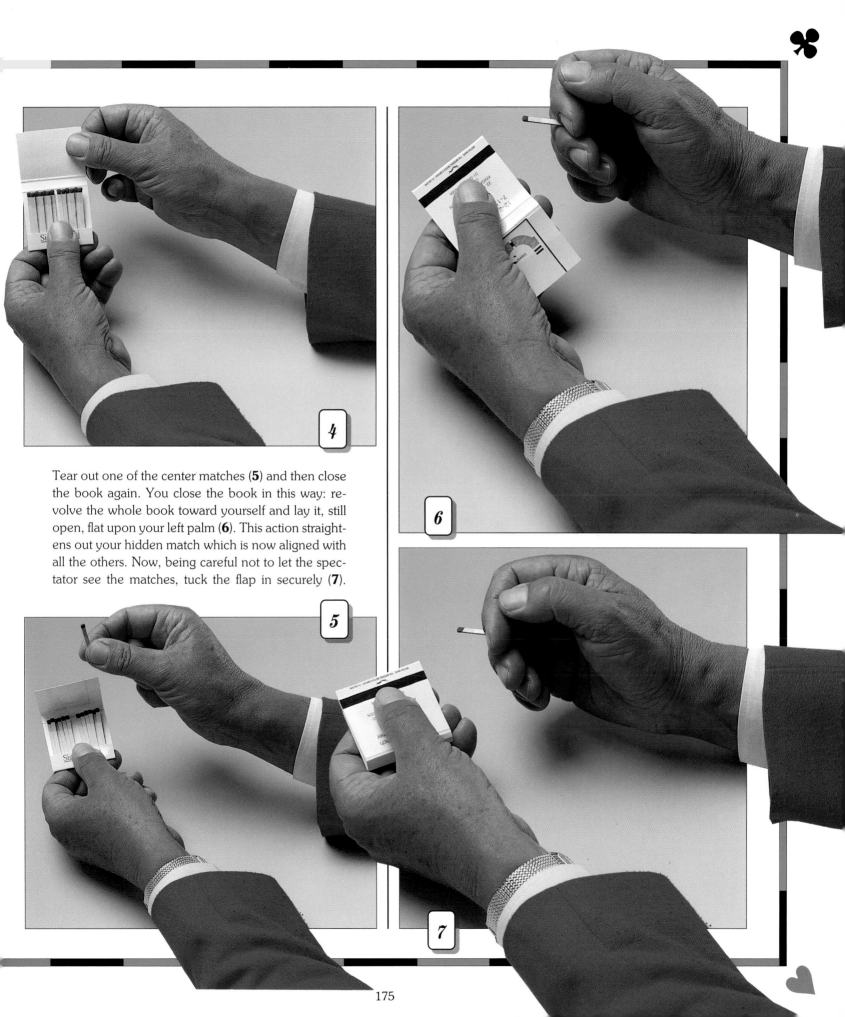

Tear out one of the center matches (**5**) and then close the book again. You close the book in this way: revolve the whole book toward yourself and lay it, still open, flat upon your left palm (**6**). This action straightens out your hidden match which is now aligned with all the others. Now, being careful not to let the spectator see the matches, tuck the flap in securely (**7**).

Strike the match that you have torn out on the striking plate (**8**). As it starts to burn (**9**), put the book down on the table or bar.

Shake out the flame after a couple of seconds. This is the moment that you vanish the match! It will take a bit of practice but it is quite easy really. Just get your *timing* right. Shake the match diagonally upward (**10**) and downward across your body (**11**). On about the second or third shake the flame should go out. Keep shaking and on the downward stroke of about the fifth or sixth shake *let the match go*! Continue shaking as if you were still holding the match. Do not look down – look *up* throughout. Fix your eyes on the spot where your hand ends up when it reaches the top of its upswing.

If you are seated at a table when you perform this trick, the match will end up harmlessly in your lap. If you are standing at a bar, the match will end up on the floor somewhere. Either way it will not be noticed! Diabolical, isn't it! Methods in magic are really immaterial – it is the overall effect that counts. If the effect is the same, but there is an easy and a difficult way to achieve it, then it is only common sense to take the easy way out! Just *practice* until you can vanish the match smoothly.

Stop shaking your hand and look at your hand in amazement – the match has disappeared (**12**)! Where has it gone? Maybe it has gone back in the book of matches.

Do not touch them yourself!

Ask a spectator to pick up the book and count the matches. He does so. There are still thirteen matches even though you tore out one after he last counted them!

*Even more amazing is the fact that one of them appears to be the dead match that just vanished, and it is still affixed to the book (**13**).*

➤ AFTERTHOUGHTS ◄

If you do not feel confident enough to use the "Shake Vanish" that I have just described, use the "Voodoo Vanish" or "Sitting-Down Vanish" explained earlier in this book. They are basically coin vanishes but are just as suitable for any small object.

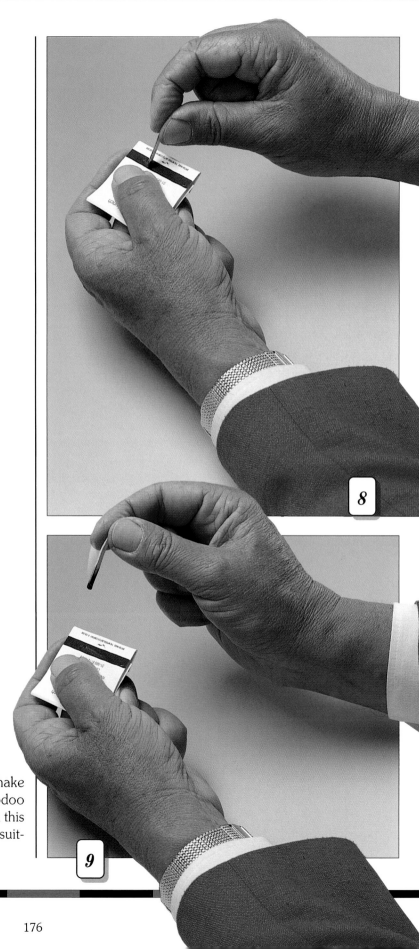

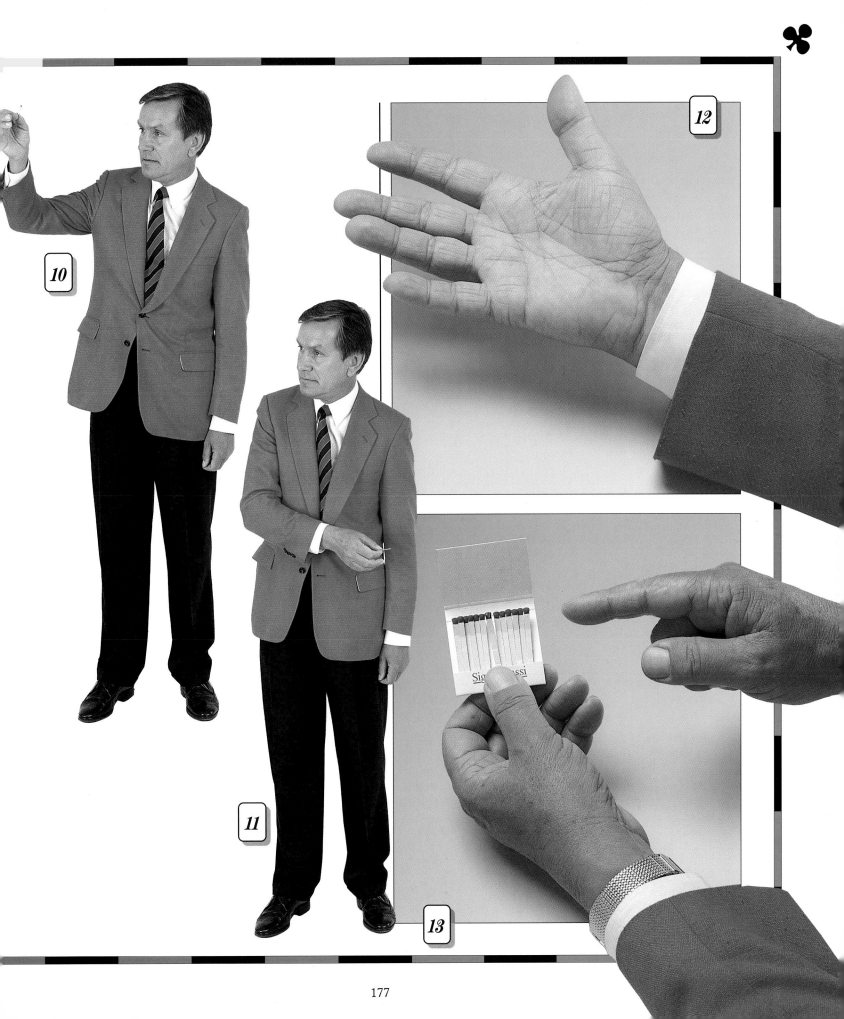

PART SEVEN

ROPE MAGIC

THE KNOT THAT IS NOT!

There is an old saying that goes, "Give him enough rope and he will hang himself." Well, with enough rope or string you need not fear hanging yourself – rather you will be able to do this inexplicable trick.

♣ EFFECT ♣

You form a "figure-eight" with a length of rope or piece of string and finish it off securely with three or four knots at the top. The spectator is given the figure-eight. You explain that the problem is to undo the loop in the center so that you end up with a plain circle of rope. This feat must be accomplished *without undoing the knots at the top*! However much he plays with and manipulates the rope, he fails to remove the middle loop. You (oh wise one) take back the figure-eight and succeed in removing the loop in a fraction of a second.

REQUIREMENTS
A length of rope or string about
6ft long

❦ WHAT YOU DO ❧

Take the rope and tie a simple loop in it (**1**). Tie a couple of knots in the ends of the rope to form the figure-eight (**2**). Leave the ends long enough so that you can now offer them to the spectator to tie a few more knots himself (**3**). Now explain the "problem" to him. His task is to remove the center loop without undoing the knots at the top. He will fail dismally. Why? Because it is impossible!

Well our motto is "The *impossible* we do at once – *miracles* take a little longer!" So, as this is only "impossible," we can do it at once. How! We cheat! After his vain attempt to remove the loop, you take back the rope (**4**) and turn your back on him for a second.

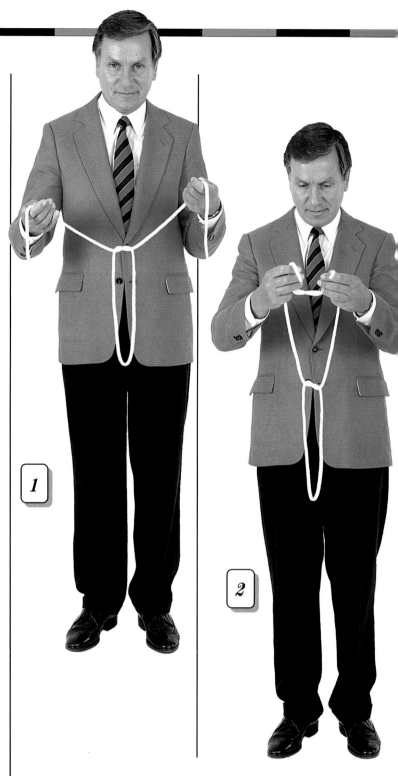

All you have to do is work the center loop down (**5**) until it joins the knots at the bottom (**6**). One more knot there will never be noticed, believe me (**7**)!

Do not be too quick about it. Make it look as if the feat requires considerable skill. At the end, undo all the knots, reform the figure-eight again and leave the rope with him!

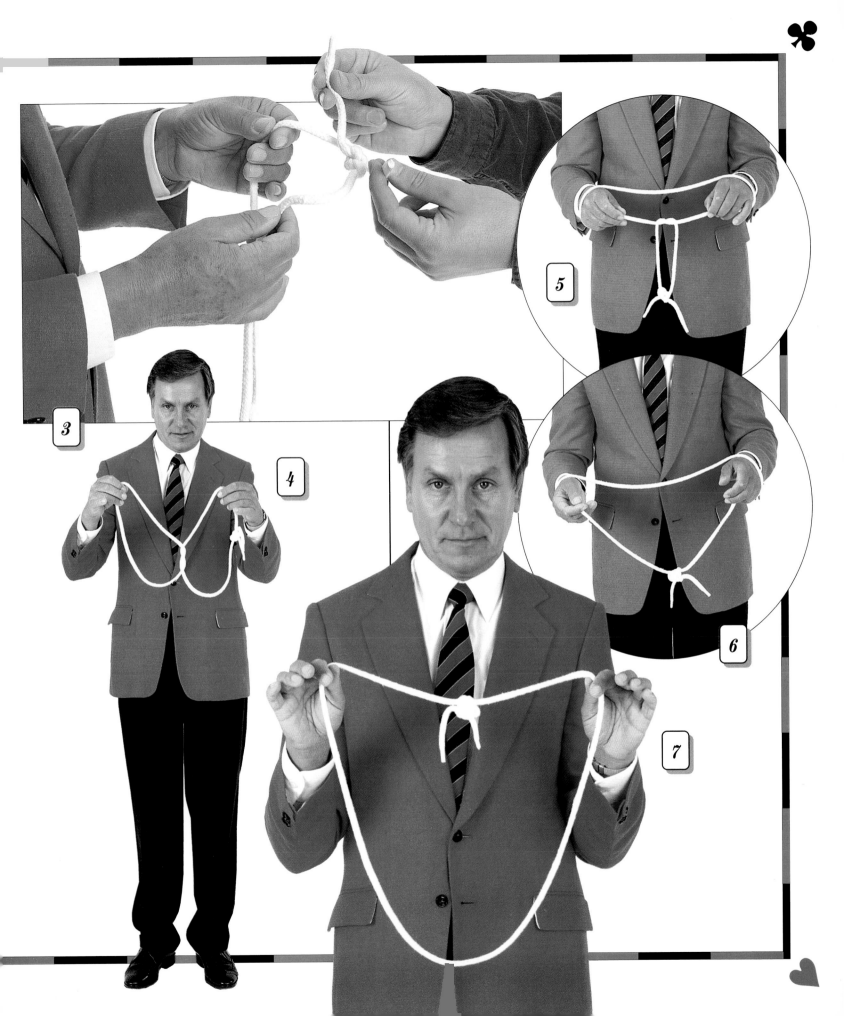

3

4

5

6

7

THE SNIP

The cut and restored rope trick has long been a favorite among magicians. Some beautiful routines have been created. Here is a simple but very effective method of performing this classic trick.

◆ EFFECT ◆

A rope that you have clearly cut in half is magically made whole again.

> **REQUIREMENTS**
> A length of rope (or string) about
> 6ft long
> A pair of sharp scissors

♣ PREPARATION ♣

Put the scissors in your right pocket.

◆ WHAT YOU DO ◆

Display the rope between your hands (**1**). Transfer the right end into your left hand alongside the other end (**2, 3**). You are now apparently going to lift up the center of the rope and place it alongside these two ends – I did say *apparently*! What actually happens is you lift up the center, letting it drape over your right index finger and thumb (**4**) and raise it toward your left hand. As soon as it is hidden from the spectators' view by the back of your left hand, grip the right hand rope between your index finger and thumb (**5**) and pull some of that into view instead (**6**). The *true* center is now hidden by your left hand but it looks as if you have lain it beside the other two ends (**7**).

Take the scissors out of your right jacket pocket and snip through the center of the visible loop (**8, 9**).

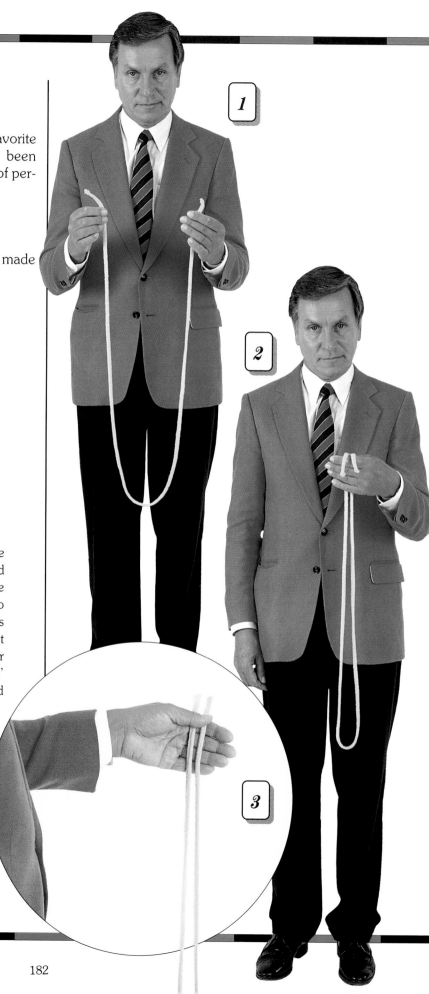

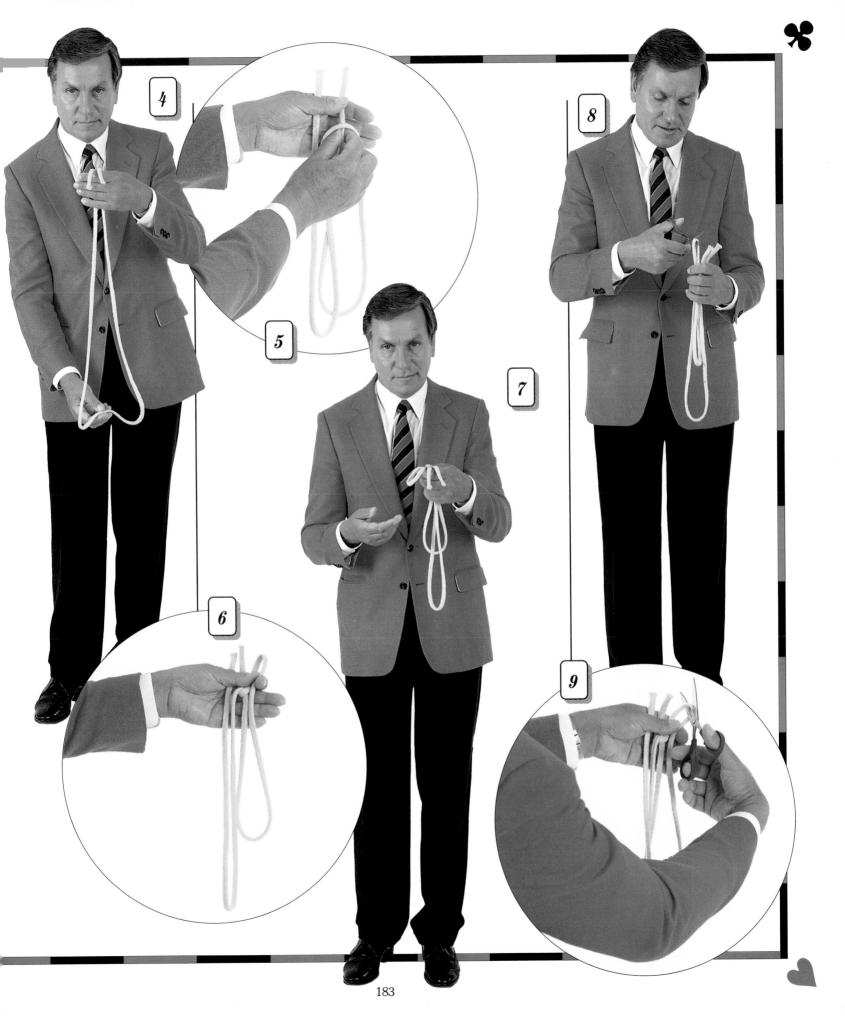

4

5

6

7

8

9

Four ends now show (**10**). Hang on to the two centre ends and let the other two drop (**11**). It looks as if you are holding two equal lengths of rope when, in fact, you are holding one long piece linked to a very short piece (**12**). Put the scissors away in your pocket. *This is important* – you will see why later.

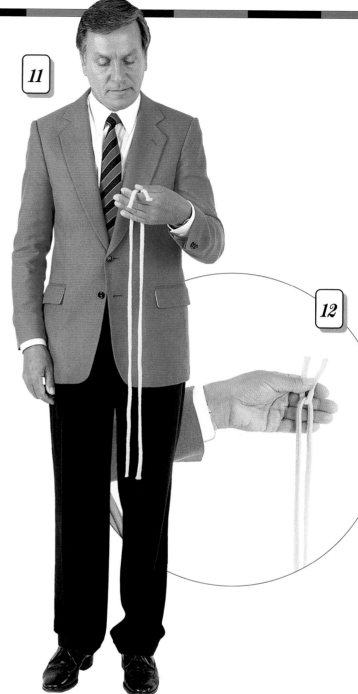

You must now tie the top visible ends together in a double knot. The back of your hand still conceals the hidden loop. What you actually do is tie the little rope on to the centre of the long one (**13**). The appearance is now of two equal lengths of rope tied together. Let the complete set up dangle from your left hand (**14**). Remove the scissors from your pocket and trim off most of the protruding ends of the knot (**15, 16, 17**).

Hang on with your left hand and with your right hand, still holding the scissors, start to wind the rope around your left hand (**18**). Keep winding (**19**), until the complete rope is now wound around your left hand (**20**). You will have found that the small piece of rope that was forming the "knot" (**21**) will have slid right off the rope (**22**) and is now concealed in your right fingers and is further hidden by the scissors! This hand immediately goes to your right pocket, where it drops the scissors, and, of course, the knot. That gets rid of the "evidence"! Apparently you have wound the knot into your left hand. Slowly unravel the rope from your left hand (**23**) to show that it has somehow been magically restored (**24**)!

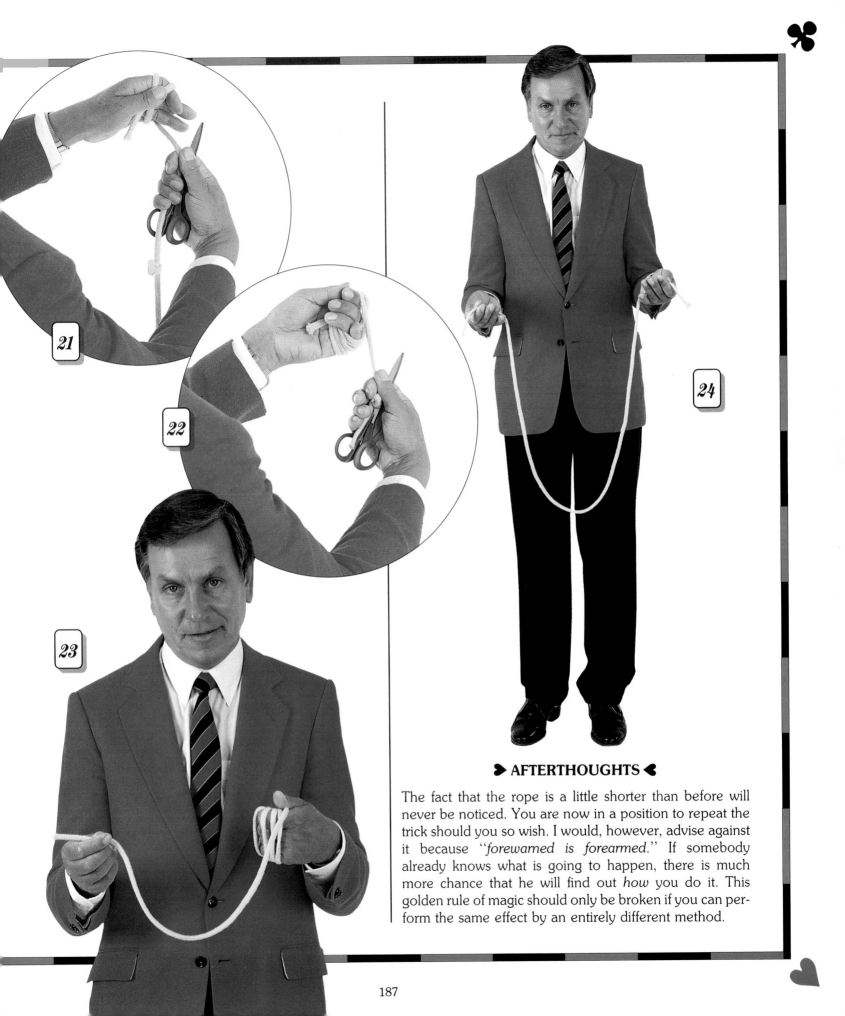

21

22

23

24

➤ AFTERTHOUGHTS ◄

The fact that the rope is a little shorter than before will never be noticed. You are now in a position to repeat the trick should you so wish. I would, however, advise against it because "*forewarned is forearmed.*" If somebody already knows what is going to happen, there is much more chance that he will find out *how* you do it. This golden rule of magic should only be broken if you can perform the same effect by an entirely different method.

HOW LONG IS A PIECE OF ROPE?

This is a real "gem." It never ceases to amaze me that such a simple principle can have such a devastating effect on an audience. They will literally gawp at this one!

♣ EFFECT ♣

Three ropes of dramatically different lengths are shown to, and examined by, the audience. Suddenly, they become all the same length and are clearly seen to be so. In an instant they change back to their original unequal lengths. No trace of the "method" can be found.

REQUIREMENTS
3 pieces of rope (or string)
A spectator – let us call him Clive

◄ PREPARATION ►

You need to cut the ropes to specific lengths. The first piece (**A**) should be about as long as the distance between your outstretched arms. The second piece (**B**) should be about 10in long. The third piece (**C**) should be *half* as long as the long piece (**A**) plus *half* the length of the short piece (**B**). Photograph (**1**) should make this clear. Link the long and short ones

together so that you get the exact measurement for the third rope. The correct proportions are *vital*!

Please note that we have used ropes of different colors for the reveal shots in this routine. This is simply so that you can see exactly what happens. Obviously, in performance, all the ropes should be of the same color.

◆ WHAT YOU DO ◆

Hold the three ropes out toward Clive as if offering them to him.

"If you would like to examine these three ropes Clive . . . (Pause) . . . I would be much obliged if you would mind your own business!"

This gets a laugh – but relent anyway and have Clive examine them carefully. Take the ropes back and hold them in your left hand.

"A question that has puzzled people for centuries is . . . 'How long is a piece of rope?'"

Take the longest one away in your right hand (**2**).

"Some people say that a piece of rope is about *this* long . . ."

Take the second one across (**3**).

"Other people say it is *this* long."

Take the smallest one across (**4**).

"Still other people swear that a piece of rope is only *this* long! I think that Confucius had it right. He said that 'how long' was a Chinese person! To a magician, however, all ropes are the same length . . . which is the distance between its opposite ends! Let me show you . . ."

Put the ropes back in your left hand again (**5**, **6**, **7**).

Reach across – *behind* the long one and *in front of* the middle one – to grip the short rope by its lower end (**8, 9**). Lift it up and deposit it in the hollow of your left thumb so that it lies next to its other end (**10**). This secretly links the smallest rope around the longest rope (**11**). Bring up the other two bottom ends and lay them to the *right* (**12, 13, 14, 15**).

"If all the ends are equal – the ropes must be equal too!"

Grasp the first three ends in your right hand and keep hold of the last three ends with your left hand (**16, 17**).

Now pull *slowly* in opposite directions (**18, 19**). The three ropes appear visibly to change to the same length (**20**). The effect is very magical! Drop the ends that you are holding in your right hand and display the ropes in your left hand. Photograph (**21**) shows the spectators' view.

"The three ropes have changed back to their original size again. We have a long one – a medium one – and a very small one!"

Count them back into your right hand (**24, 25, 26**). Drop the ropes on the table so that they may be examined if the spectators so wish. They will wish!

"That's how long a magician's piece of rope is! But then we can do the impossible! Possibly your eyes have been deceiving you because..."

Push your right index finger and thumb through the loops as shown (**22, 23**), and pull downward. The short rope will now come clear as you take the long rope away. Quickly replace the long rope back in your left hand with the other two before Clive has a chance to focus upon it.

➤ AFTERTHOUGHTS ◀

Practice until you can execute the simple moves smoothly. Use a mirror to see how everything looks from the audience's point of view. Do not rush anything. The beauty of this trick lies in the slow, deliberate way that you perform it. And I stress, to make this description clear, we have used three different colored ropes in some of the photographs. It goes without saying that in actual performance the ropes *must* be all the same color!

RING OFF

A ring, a piece of string and a handkerchief are all you require to perform this simple but effective trick.

◀ EFFECT ▶

A ring is borrowed from a spectator. You thread and knot it on to a piece of string. You magically remove the ring even though both ends of the string are being held by the spectator!

REQUIREMENTS
A finger ring, which should be
borrowed for best effect
A piece of string about 3ft long
A linen handkerchief

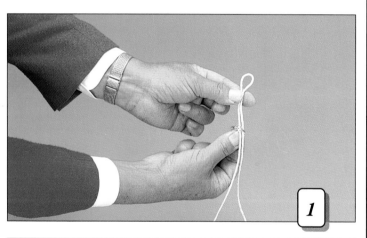

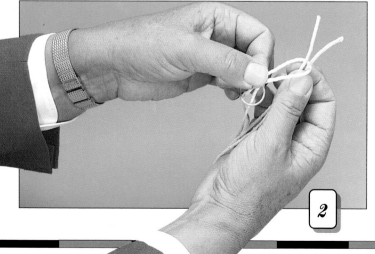

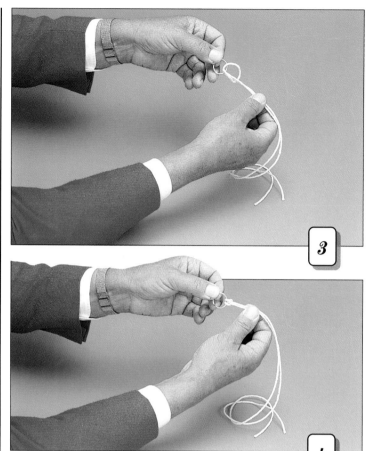

♣ WHAT YOU DO ♣

Having borrowed a substantial looking ring, you thread and tie it onto the string. The "special knot" is our secret because it is not a knot at all! This false knot can be tied in front of the spectator provided that you are very casual about it and do not let her look too closely! Push the *center* of the string through the ring (**1**) and then feed the loose ends through the loop (**2**), tighten (**3**) and work the knot down to the bottom (**4**). Hold an end of the string in each hand and display the ring, apparently securely tied to its center. Hand the set-up to the spectator to hold in the same way (**5**).

"While you are holding both ends of the string, it is obviously impossible for me to remove your ring from the string – unless I saw it off!"

Drape the handkerchief over the ring and string (**6**).

"I promise not to do that – instead I will perform a little magic!"

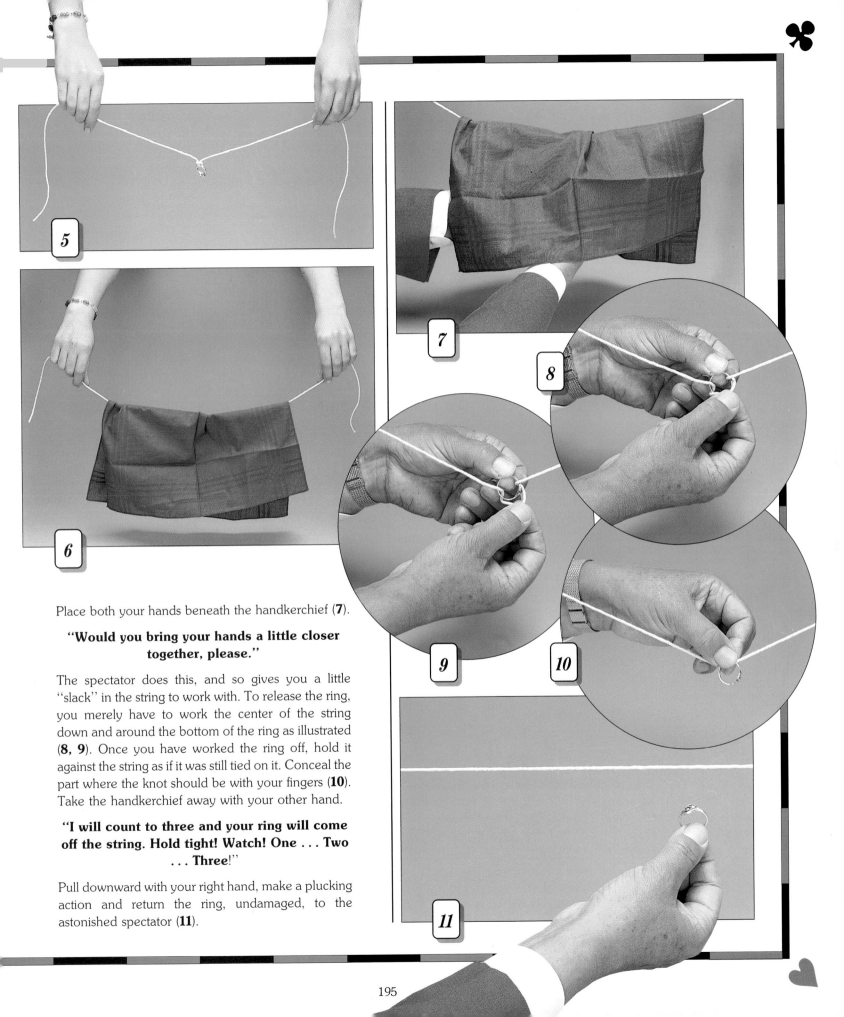

Place both your hands beneath the handkerchief (**7**).

"Would you bring your hands a little closer together, please."

The spectator does this, and so gives you a little "slack" in the string to work with. To release the ring, you merely have to work the center of the string down and around the bottom of the ring as illustrated (**8, 9**). Once you have worked the ring off, hold it against the string as if it was still tied on it. Conceal the part where the knot should be with your fingers (**10**). Take the handkerchief away with your other hand.

"I will count to three and your ring will come off the string. Hold tight! Watch! One . . . Two . . . Three!"

Pull downward with your right hand, make a plucking action and return the ring, undamaged, to the astonished spectator (**11**).

MINT OFF

When you are an experienced magician, you often find that your mind works in a peculiar way. You start to think laterally. Only a magician would be crazy enough to think of this next trick!

➤ EFFECT ◀

The effect is exactly the same as in the last "Ring Off" trick, but the method is completely different. This time you use a mint candy (the type with a hole in the middle) and the spectator threads it on himself!

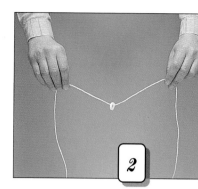

```
REQUIREMENTS
A packet of mint candies with holes
in the middle
A length of string
A linen handkerchief or napkin
```

◆ PREPARATION ◆

Snap a mint candy in two. Keep trying until you get one with a nice break (**1**). Now moisten the ends and push the two halves together again and allow the mint to dry. If the join still shows, try rubbing a little powdered sugar over the cracks. Place another unprepared mint in your right jacket pocket together with a clean handkerchief. Put your "special" mint back in its packet and you are ready to begin.

◀ WHAT YOU DO ➤

Give the string to the spectator. Carefully prise the mint out of the package and let the spectator thread it on the string. As soon as it is done, have him hold the ends of the string as before. This prevents him from examining the mint too closely (**2**)! Remove the handkerchief from your pocket and at the same time palm the unprepared mint and bring that out too, secretly concealed in your curled fingers.

Drape the handkerchief over the string and the visible mint (**3**). Place both your hands beneath the handkerchief (**4**) and snap the threaded mint in two.

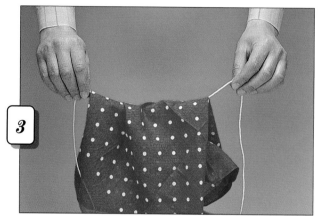

Because of your secret preparation it will break *silently*! Place the pieces in your *left* hand (**5**). Hold the unprepared mint against the string with your *right* hand (**6**). Take the handkerchief away with your left hand and put it away in your left pocket (together with the broken pieces)! Finish by apparently plucking the visible mint off the center of the string (**7**) and immediately handing it to the spectator to examine! He will be baffled!

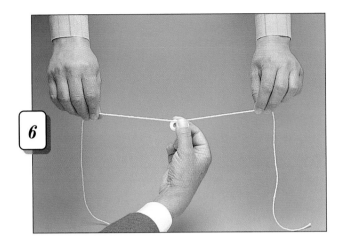

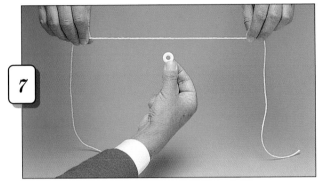

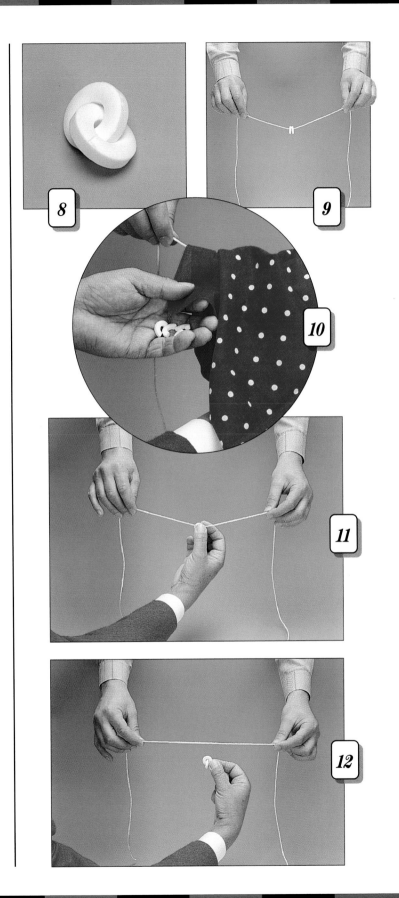

♣ A NICE VARIATION ♣

Once you have learned to snap a mint in two and re-assemble it undetectably, you can perform this super, quite zany, variation of the Mint Off trick. Snap a mint and stick it together again, linking it through an un-prepared mint (**8**)! Snap and reassemble two more mints. Keep them separate this time and, when they are dry, put them both back in the package again. Place the linked mints in your *right* jacket pocket to-gether with the handkerchief.

Remove the two mints from the package and let the spectator thread them on the string and then hold the ends (**9**). Now proceed exactly as before. Break *both* the threaded mints. Take the pieces secretly away with the handkerchief (**10**), which you dump in your left pocket. Now pluck the two mints off the string (**11**) and give them to the spectator (**12**). His face should be a picture because, not only have you removed the two mints, but in the process you have somehow linked them together. Grab the mints back after a while and eat the evidence!

Stunning magic!

PART EIGHT

MAGIC MISCELLANY

THE HAUNTED KEY

I love weird tricks. This one is extremely weird and I have had a lot of fun with it over the years! Eat your heart out, Uri Geller!

◆ EFFECT ◆

A large, heavy key is laid across your palm. Merely by "concentration" you cause it to come alive and turn itself right over! The key is immediately handed out for examination. No trace of the method can be found. It must be haunted!

REQUIREMENTS
The largest, heaviest key that you can find (**1**). Strangely enough, the larger and heavier the key, the easier and yet more spectacular the trick actually is.

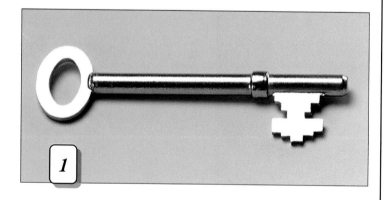

◆ WHAT YOU DO ◆

This is a "knack" really. It will take a little practice but just like riding a bicycle, it will suddenly come to you. Lay the key across your right palm. The exact position is very important (**2**). Notice that the flat part that is normally inserted into the lock is pointing back toward your wrist. The other end of the key that has the ring on it must be "free" and not resting on your hand at all. Look down on your hand.

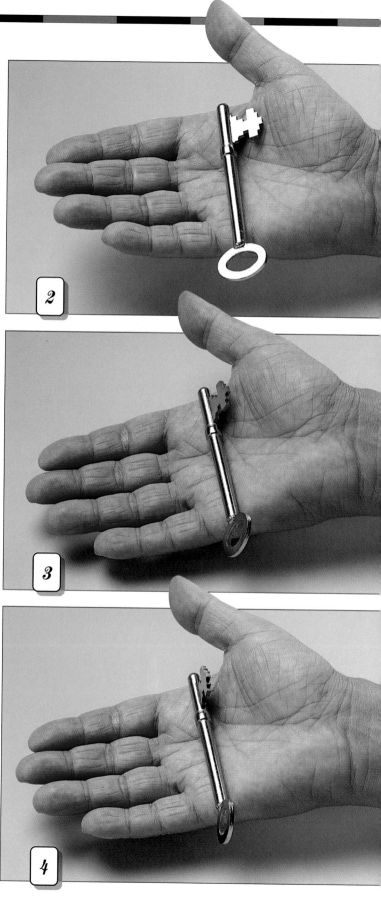

Very, very slightly dip your fingers toward the floor and, at the same time, *will* the key to turn over! I know that sounds crazy but it really helps! Slowly and mysteriously the key turns itself over (**3, 4, 5, 6**)! At first you will probably find that the key will roll over very quickly and probably end up on the floor! However, with a little practice, and by varying the degree that you tip your fingers, you will be able to control the movement of the key completely so that it turns over very slowly, spookily and inexplicably! Try it! You'll have fun!

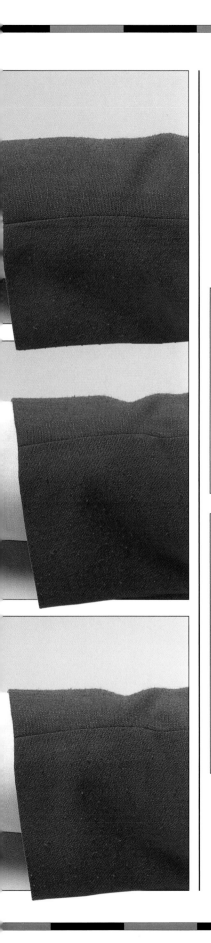

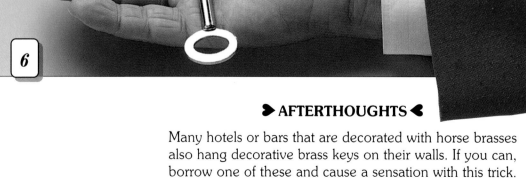

5

6

➤ AFTERTHOUGHTS ◄

Many hotels or bars that are decorated with horse brasses also hang decorative brass keys on their walls. If you can, borrow one of these and cause a sensation with this trick. Uri Geller did!

SHORT AND SWEET!

Y ou will not always be able to perform this trick. However, when the conditions are right, it is an absolute stunner and well worth remembering!

♣ EFFECT ♣

Somebody hands you a wrapped sugar cube from the bowl on the table. You place the packet on the back of your hand and tap it smartly with the other hand. The sugar cubes penetrate through your palm and plop into the coffee cup – leaving the crumpled wrapper still on top of your hand!

REQUIREMENTS
Just two packets of wrapped sugar cubes

◆ PREPARATION ◆

When you find yourself in a restaurant that leaves wrapped sugar cubes on the table, secretly pocket one. Then excuse yourself to the lavatory. Once in private there, carefully unwrap the sugar cubes (**1**). Put them in your pocket and then carefully reassemble the wrapper again. Moisten the adhesive flap and you will find that very likely it will stick down again, and the package will resume its former shape even though it is now empty. Keep this empty parcel secretly cupped in your fingers as you return to the table. Be careful not to crush it.

➤ WHAT YOU DO ◄

Palm the sugar cubes in your left hand. The empty package is carefully palmed in your right fingers. As soon as coffee has been served and before anyone can reach for the sugar you say, apparently on the spur of the moment (**2**),

"I've just had an idea for a trick – let's see if it works – does anyone take sugar?" Jane says that she does. **"O.K. Jane. Hand me some sugar, please."**

She hands you a package of sugar. Take it with your right hand and place it about 4in from the edge of the table and in line with your lap (**3**). With your right fingers draw the sugar package toward yourself with a sweeping action (**4**). Let the wrapped sugar cubes secretly fall into your lap (**5, 6**) and simultaneously bring the *empty* package into view, placing it on the back of your closed left fist (**7**). Practice this "switch" until you have got it down pat. It should look as if you have just picked up the sugar that she has chosen and placed it on the back of your left fist.

Position your left hand above the coffee cup (**8**). Now synchronize these two actions. Tap the wrapper smartly with your right fingers and *at the same time* spring open your left fingers. The two sugar lumps "splash down" into the coffee and the crumpled wrapper is left for examination (**9**). The illusion of the sugar lumps penetrating your hand is perfect. Pocket the lapped sugar cubes at your leisure. Short and sweet!

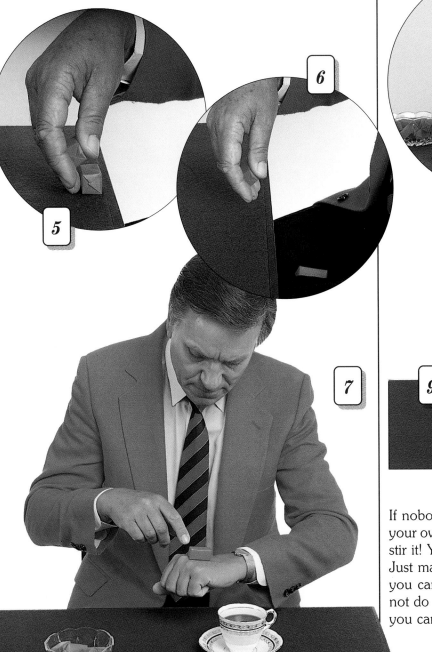

❧ AFTERTHOUGHTS ❧

If nobody in your party takes sugar, perform the trick on your own coffee cup. If *you* do not take sugar either, don't stir it! You will be amazed how effective this little trick is. Just make sure that you do your preparation properly. If you cannot pocket a sugar cube without being seen, do not do the trick. Remember to practice the "switch" until you can do it in your sleep.

OVER THE TOP

With just a few bottle caps you give a demonstration of incredible sleight-of-hand, and it is easier than you think!

✣ EFFECT ✣

Four bottle caps are laid out on the table. One is covered for a split second by your left hand. It instantly disappears, only to be found under your right hand. You cover another. That, too, disappears and reappears instantly beneath your right hand. The last two bottle caps go the way of the first two – until all four bottle caps invisibly travel across.

REQUIREMENTS
Five identical bottle caps – the type that have scalloped edges. The audience only ever sees four!

❦ PREPARATION ❦

You will have to learn to palm a bottle cap. The scalloped edges make this a very simple task. Lay a bottle cap on the table with its scalloped edges facing upward. Place your right hand over it so that the bottle cap is positioned in the direct center of your palm (**1**). Press down. Squeeze the sides of your hand inward. See how little you have to squeeze before the flesh of your palm is able to get a grip on the bottle cap. Still keeping your hand flat, lift your hand off the table. (**2**). The bottle cap stays palmed (**3**). The scalloped edges make this a very easy palm to execute. Practice until you can "palm" with either hand. When you can do that, you are ready to learn this classic routine.

◀ WHAT YOU DO ▶

Sit at a table with your legs tucked well under it. Lay four bottle caps out as shown (**4**). You start with the secret extra cap palmed in your *right* hand.

"This is a trick called 'Over The Top.' What's it called?"

Your audience replies . . . "Over The Top."

"That's right. O.T.T. for short! O.T.T. goes like this . . ."

Cover "A" with your left hand and "B" with your right hand (**5**). Wiggle the fingers of both hands up and down a few times. Release the palmed cap from your right palm to join "B" which it is covering, and at the same time palm "A" in your left hand. Move both hands away to show that "A" has apparently jumped across to join "B" (**6**). Move one of the caps at "B" back to position "A" again (**7**).

". . . or, sometimes, like this . . ."

Cover "A" and "B" with your hands again (**8**).

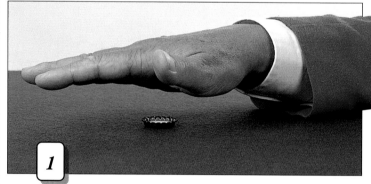

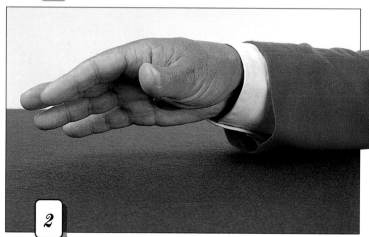

204

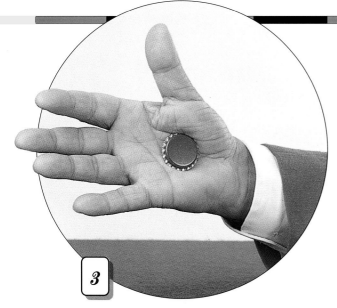

3

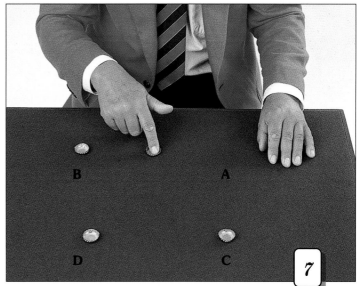

6

B   A

D   C

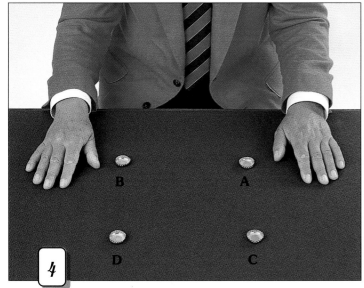

4

B   A

D   C

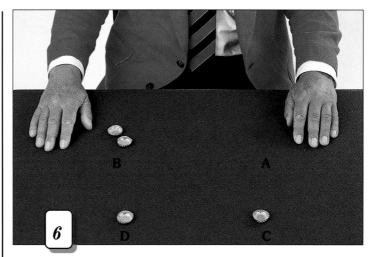

7

B   A

D   C

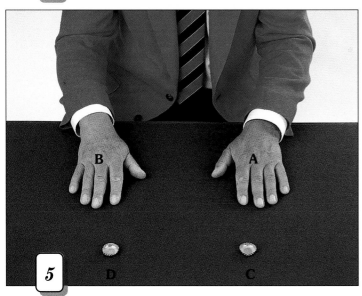

5

B   A

D   C

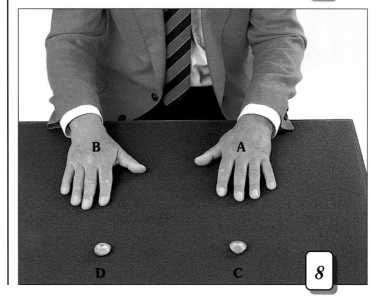

8

B   A

D   C

Drop the palmed cap to join "A" and at the same time palm "B." Wiggle your fingers a little, then move your hands to the sides again. Apparently "B" has jumped over to join "A" (**9**). Move one of the caps at "A" back to position "B" (**10**), once more forming the square.

". . . although it is usually like this . . ."

Cover "A" and "B" again (**11**). Palm "A" and drop at "B." "A" seems to have jumped to "B" again (**12**)

"Sometimes, however, O.T.T. is like this . . ."

Cover position "B" with your *left* hand and reach across to cover position "C" with your *right* hand (**13**). Palm at "C" and drop at "B." Move your hands away (**14**).

"Once in a blue moon, it looks like this . . ."

Cover "D" with your *left* hand and "B" with your *right* (**15**). Palm at "D," drop at "B." Lift your left hand off the table and bring it back to rest on the edge of the table above your lap (**16**). Lift up your right hand and turn it, slowly, face upward. At the same time let the cap that is palmed in your left hand drop secretly on to your lap! Then, slowly, turn your left hand face up too! (**17**) You are, as we say, "clean!"

"That's 'Over The Top'!"

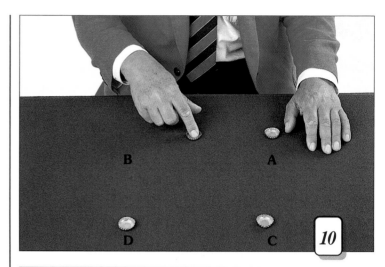

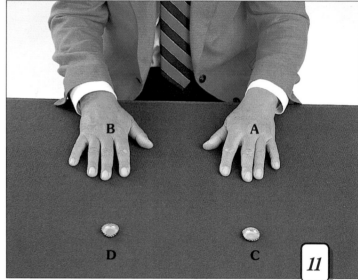

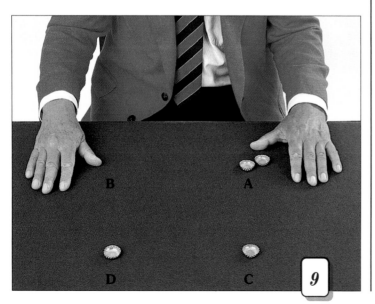

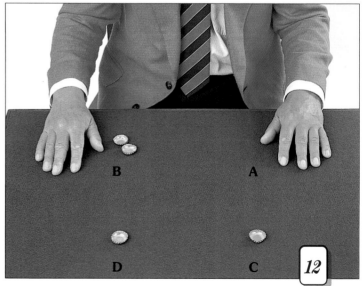

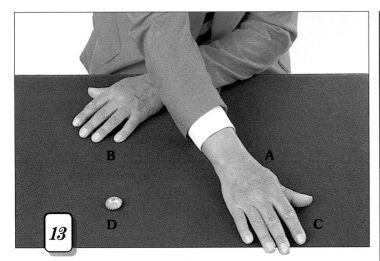

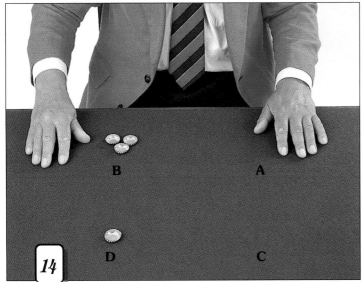

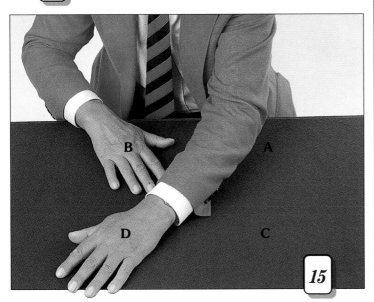

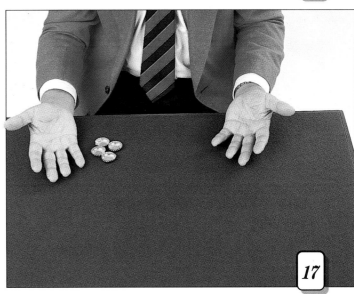

◆ AFTERTHOUGHTS ◆

Once you have taught yourself this routine, and you can perform it smoothly and palm with equal dexterity with either hand, I suggest that you throw the bottle caps away! Try using sugar cubes instead. The "palm" is slightly more difficult but once you have the hang of it, you should be able to palm sugar cubes. Bottle caps are great to practice with, but, unfortunately, the scalloped edges that make them so easy to palm can also give the game away. Nobody imagines that you could possibly palm a flat-sided cube!

PENCIL PUSHER

This trick takes only three seconds to perform, yet is most effective given the right conditions.

♣ EFFECT ♣

A pencil vanishes from your bare hands!

REQUIREMENTS
A pencil, which may be borrowed

◆ WHAT YOU DO ◆

This trick is best performed to just one person. It is 99 per cent *presentation*. Although it is a small trick, you must make a big show of it! Have a pencil ready – borrowed if possible. Stand with the spectator on your *left* (**1**). Hold your left hand palm upward in front of you. Hold the pencil in the "writing" position in your right hand (**2**). The following moves must be performed in a smooth, rhythmic sequence to the count of "three."

"Watch closely! I will make this pencil pass right through my palm!"

Bending your right arm at the elbow, swing your hand up in an arc until the pencil is level with the top of your right ear (**3**). Bring your hand down again, reversing the arc and press the point of the pencil into the palm of your left hand (**4**). You count "One." Do it again, lift the hand and pencil up to ear level then bring it down again, pressing the pencil into your palm, and counting "Two." Do it again, but this time slide the pencil *behind your ear*. Leave it there and swing the hand down again as if it was still holding the pencil (**6**). Press your fingers into your palms (**7**), and count "Three!" Display both hands empty (**8**). The pencil has disappeared! Try this out. You will be amazed how deceptive it is.

➤ AFTERTHOUGHTS ◀

This trick works because the spectator's attention is misdirected toward your left palm. The wide arc described by your right hand is too wide for her angle of vision. The pencil is, therefore, out of sight for a fraction of a second.

You can reverse the procedure and make the pencil reappear. Just retrieve the pencil from behind your ear *after* the count of two. Any long object can be vanished in this way. I have seen it done with a cigarette – unlit of course!

SUPERMAN!

Alex Natus, a businessman from South Africa, only knows two tricks. He showed me this one in 1950! He claimed that he was taught the trick by his father who in turn learned it from his father before him. In his hands it is a "miracle." If you practice, it will be a "miracle" in your hands too!

♣ EFFECT ♣

Three silver balls are manufactured on the spot from silver paper . . . then one ball is pushed into the corner of your eye! Another is pushed into your ear! The third is "massaged" into the back of your neck! The three balls are now magically reproduced one at a time from your mouth. They are all placed in your left hand and then completely disappear!

REQUIREMENTS
A sheet of tin foil paper from a cigarette paper or chocolate bar, which should be borrowed whenever possible.

➤ WHAT YOU DO ➤

All the moves of this routine must be performed *slowly* and gracefully – thus enhancing the truly magical qualities of this trick. Openly and unmistakably tear the foil into three equal-size pieces (**1, 2**). Roll them into three tight little balls (**3**) and display them on your left palm (**4**).

"I have three little silver balls, which is unusual, even in New York . . ." (Change this according to where you live.)

Now close both hands into fists, keeping them about 18in apart (**5**).

"I am going to try to make the three balls travel from my left hand over here into my right hand! Would you like them to go visibly or invisibly?"

If the spectator says, "Visibly," open both hands palms up and simply tip the three balls from your left on to your right palm!

"That's 'visibly!' *Invisibly* looks like this . . ."

Tip the balls back on to your left palm. Close both hands into fists again. Make a "throwing" action with your left hand and a "catching" action with your right *but at all times keep your fists tightly closed*. "They are now over here" you say, looking at your right fist but not opening it.

"That was easy, but to make them go back again — that takes a lot more practice!"

Repeat the "throwing" and "catching" actions as before and open both hands (**6, 7**) to show that the three balls have "returned" to the left hand! This preliminary bit of nonsense may sound like a waste of time to you. I assure you that it is not! It impresses on your audience that you are only using *three* balls and that you do not have any more concealed anywhere. Now for the trick proper.

The three balls are displayed on your left palm. Reach over with your right hand with the action of picking up a ball between your fingers (**8**). Actually you secretly pick up *two* balls, one on top of the other. Your left fingers close back into a fist at the same time as your right hand is removed. Hold the right hand up in front of you for a moment. The spectator should only see the top ball (**9**). Place it between your lips (**10**).

Now . . . we are holding *two* balls remember . . . so this is what *actually* happens: one ball is dropped secretly into your mouth and the second one is left between your lips, openly displayed. Let the ball in your mouth drop beneath your tongue. Do not worry about it. Try to forget that it is there. With a little practice you will be able to leave it there and yet talk unimpaired, drink quite freely, etc. Needless to say, it is imperative that your audience remains unaware of its presence. Now back to the visible ball. With your right index finger roll the ball backward and forward along your lips a couple of times and then remove it openly between your index finger and thumb (**11**) and place it, for display, on the top of your closed left fist (**12**).

"It is easier to manipulate the silver balls if I moisten them a little."

Reach across and apparently remove the ball from the top of your left fist (**13**) but, as soon as your fingers shield the ball from view, let it drop back inside your left fist by relaxing the fingers slightly. Immediately remove your right hand as if grasping the ball. Hold the hand in the display position for a second, then "push" your fingers into the corner of your right eye as if you were actually pushing the ball into it (**14**). Lower your right hand and show it to be empty (**15**). Blink a few times!

"It hurts at first – but you get used to it!"

Open your left hand and show that it only contains *two* balls (**16**)! One really has gone! Now watch *them* blink! Two balls are now displayed on your left palm.

Reach over, as before, apparently removing one but actually removing *two* balls, closing the left fingers as before (**17**). Display your right hand, and once more secretly load a ball into your mouth while apparently only placing a ball between your lips for moistening (**18**). Remove the visible ball and place it on your left fist as before (**19**). Drop it secretly back into your closed left fist in the action of picking it up (**20**). Display your right hand again for a moment and then ''push'' it into your right ear (**21**)!

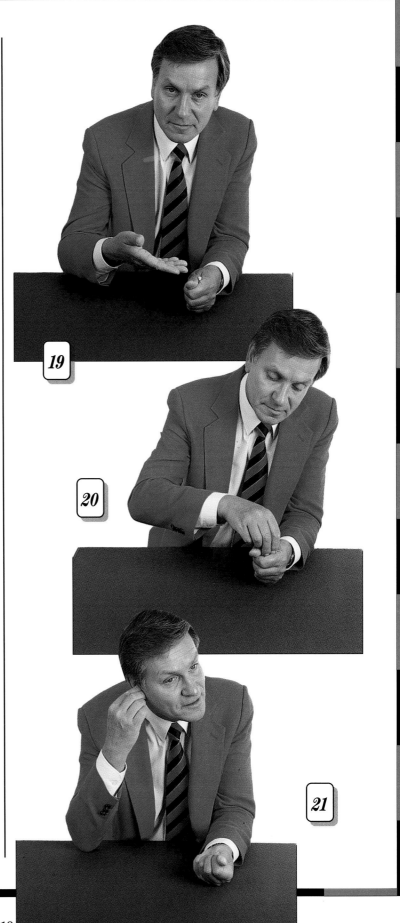

The routine now varies a little. Remove the remaining silver ball with your right hand, duplicating your previous actions when you were secretly removing two balls (**23**). Hold it in the display position. Place it between your lips, moisten it (**24**), then remove it and place it on the top of your left fist exactly as before (**25**). When you reach across for the ball, this time you actually do pick it up! Hold it in the display position for a moment, making sure that the ball is clearly seen (**26**). Now "massage" this ball into the back of your neck (**27**). Actually you quickly push the ball down the back of your shirt collar (**28**) and then continue rhythmically rubbing the back of your neck. After three or four rubs, remove your hand and then show both hands completely empty back and front (**29**).

Pause and smile. Apparently the trick is over. This is the impression that you must give. The position at this stage is that you have two balls concealed in your mouth and one down the back of your collar. You can forget about this last one – you will not be needing it again. Your "pause" should last about six seconds.

"Of course if you want the balls to return, you just rub a little under your chin."

As you do this you push one of the balls forward with your tongue so that it appears between your lips. Your right thumb and index finger rise to remove it (**30**) but, as soon as the ball is masked by your fingers, let it secretly drop back into your mouth again. Remove your right hand as if actually holding the ball and push the ball into your closed left fist (**31**). Rub under your chin again and "regurgitate" another ball so that it is displayed between your lips. Follow the actions exactly as before, apparently removing the ball and pushing it into your fist, when in actual fact you let it drop back into your mouth again. Repeat all these actions for a third time.

Now pause again for a few seconds. Again your audience will think that the trick is over. Take advantage of this. Be "off beat." Apparently you are now holding three balls in your closed left fist. Speak to the nearest spectator:

"Look after the balls for me, please."

As he extends his hand, slowly open your left hand as if to dump the balls on to his palm. Too late! The balls have flown (**32**)!

26

27

28

29

30

31

32

◆ AFTERTHOUGHTS ◆

Well – that's it. Three great "climaxes" plus an absorbing and extremely mystifying, close-up, *impromptu* trick. I consider it to be one of the best in my repertoire. What about the two balls still in your mouth? Relax! Nobody knows they are there. Keep them under your tongue until you can dispose of them without being seen.

THE FADE-AWAY PEN

In this trick we use a very old principle to create a very modern mystery. Tricks that use "ordinary" everyday objects are always effective because the spectator is familiar with the object and will not expect it suddenly to develop magical properties.

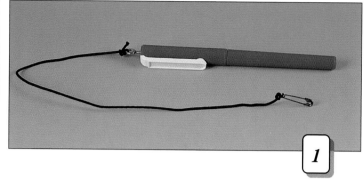

♣ EFFECT ♣

A pen is removed from your inside jacket pocket and shown quite openly. You cover it for a split second with a linen handkerchief and in the space of this split second, it *completely vanishes!* The pen is then reproduced from the jacket pocket from which you originally took it!

REQUIREMENTS
Two identical pens with tops that
screw or clip on firmly
One small screw-eye
A foot of elastic cord
A small safety pin
A linen handkerchief

◆ PREPARATION ◆

One of the pens must be gimmicked beforehand by inserting the small screw-eye in the top of the cap. Onto this you tie 12in of good quality elastic cord at the end of which you attach the small safety pin (**1**). Place the ungimmicked duplicate pen in your inside left jacket pocket. The gimmicked pen is hung inside your right sleeve. The safety pin fixes inside the jacket near the arm pit. The elastic runs along the inside of the sleeve. The end of the pen should come to rest midway between your elbow and your wrist. If you have allowed too much elastic, adjust it until it hangs correctly. The handkerchief goes over your left arm.

Just before you intend to perform this trick, place your hand casually behind your back. Reach inside your right sleeve with your left fingers. Grasp the end of the pen and pull it down so that you can grip it against your right palm with your right fingers (**2**). You are now ready to perform.

◀ WHAT YOU DO ▶

Reach inside your jacket with your right hand (pen concealed). As soon as your fingers are out of sight gradually work the pen forward until it is held, by the fixed end, between the thumb and fingers. Remove your hand from inside your jacket with the pen openly displayed (**3**). Unscrew the pen with your left fingers and show both parts (backs of hands toward the spectators, (**4**). Screw the pen back into the cap.

Take the handkerchief and hold it, spread out, in your left hand (**5**). Place the end of the pen in about the center of the handkerchief and then throw the folds over it so that the pen is held by the right hand as in (**6**). With your left hand, grasp the *handkerchief* at the top, *not the pen*, although it should appear that you are holding it too. As soon as your left hand has a grip on the handkerchief, release your hold on the pen and it will fly up (down!) your left sleeve! Now comes a beautiful subtlety! Remove your right hand from beneath the handkerchief and grip it on the outside at about where the bottom of the pen would be if it were still there (**7**). Remove your left hand from the top. Due to the natural stiffness of the handkerchief it looks as if the pen is still there (**8**)! Finally grasp a corner of the handkerchief in each hand, and slowly let the handkerchief open out to show that the pen has completely vanished (**9**)!

This looks very pretty, especially if you hold both hands so that your palms are toward the audience, showing that they are both unmistakably empty. Now, after showing your right hand empty, reach inside your jacket and remove the duplicate pen (**10**). Hold it by the ends exactly as you did the gimmicked one. Unscrew the cap and display the two parts separately. Reassemble the pen (**11**) and hand it and the handkerchief out for examination by the audience.

2

3

8

9

4

5

10

11

6

7

❥ AFTERTHOUGHTS ❧

Please practice this series of moves in front of a mirror until you can perform them smoothly and rhythmically. Let's face it, the trick is a simple one to perform, technically speaking. Therefore the bulk of your efforts should be directed toward a clean and graceful *presentation*. Maybe you will have the opportunity to use the genuine pen earlier. You could lend it to somebody to write something down, mark a coin, etc. He will then remember, when you are performing this trick, that he actually wrote with the pen earlier on.

MIGHTIER THAN THE SWORD

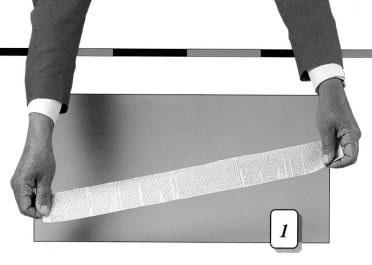

Have you ever wondered what to do with your old newspapers? Here is one answer...

♣ EFFECT ♣

A long strip of newspaper is shown on both sides. Boldly and deliberately the strip is cut in half and the two parts displayed separately. They are then placed together, given another snip and then a shake... Lo and behold, the two pieces have joined together into one long strip again!

REQUIREMENTS
A newspaper
A pair of sharp, scissors
Rubber cement
Talcum powder

◆ PREPARATION ◆

Cut a long strip of newspaper from the classified section. Avoid a strip with any distinctive photographs or other bold features. The strip should be at least 18in long and 2in wide (**1**). Paint a spread of rubber cement across the center of the newspaper strip in a band about 2in wide (**2**). Allow it to dry and then sprinkle talcum powder over the treated area. Blow off any surplus. As I am sure you know, when two surfaces that have been treated with rubber cement come into contact with one another they stick. This is the principle behind self-sealing envelopes. The talcum treatment prevents this from happening prematurely.

❥ WHAT YOU DO ❥

Hold the strip of newspaper up by one end. Fold the strip in half so that the "treated" side goes to the *outside*. Cut the strip in half, through the center loop (**3**). Display the two halves, one in each hand (**4**). Place both halves together – this time with the treated sections on the *inside* (**5**).

Keeping the two halves aligned, just snip off a fraction of an inch from the ends (**6**). This cutting action has the effect of forcing the rubber cement from each section to weld together along the complete length of the cut edge (**7**). The talcum powder prevents a more widespread adhesion that would spoil the effect. Let one end of the newspaper drop. The newspaper is restored (**8**)!

4

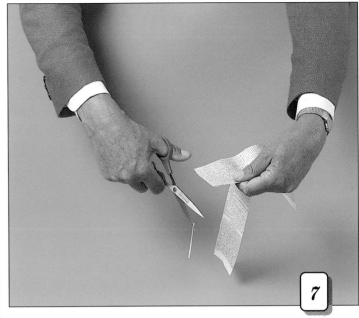

7

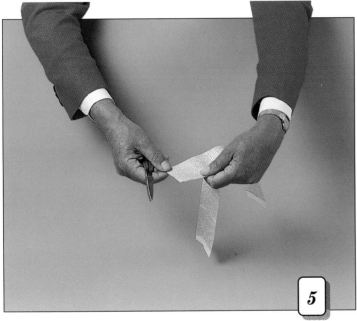

5

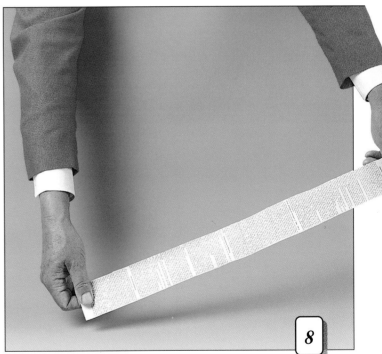

8

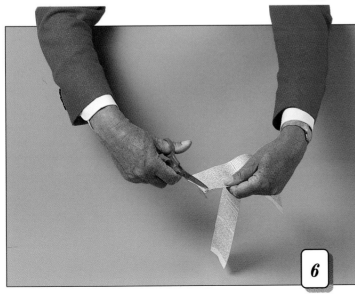

6

❧ AFTERTHOUGHTS ❧

I sometimes use this as a "Continuity Gag," picking up the strip between my other tricks and attempting to "do a trick with two pieces of paper." However, the paper keeps joining up again, much to my apparent frustration. After about three attempts at the trick, I finally give up, crumple the newspaper into a ball and throw it away in disgust!

FINAL AFTERTHOUGHTS

There are a few general do's and don't's for a magician that I would briefly like to touch upon.

1. Do not overdo it! It is always a mistake to do too many tricks. Four or five knockout tricks should be quite enough for one session. Leave them wanting more.

2. Never divulge your secrets! If someone asks you ". . . how do you do it?" . . . just answer: "Very well!!!" or "It's magic!".

3. Never repeat a trick unless you can create the same effect by using a totally different method. Forewarned is forearmed – if an audience knows *what* is about to happen, there is much more chance that they will discover *how* it happens.

4. People will be watching your hands so make sure that they are clean and well manicured.

5. Practice until you know the trick backwards – until you can perform it in your sleep. The more you practice, the slicker you will become. Practice in front of a mirror so you can see how it looks from the spectator's point of view.

6. Know what you are going to say before you say it. Your patter has to be practiced as much as your technique. There is nothing worse than a waffling magician. You could write yourself a script or record it on tape to help you develop a smooth flow.

7. These tricks are described and photographed from a **right-handed** person's point of view. If you are left-handed, just reverse the instructions.

8. Do not try to make your audience look foolish. Some people get annoyed if they cannot work out a trick. Explain beforehand that your object is to *entertain* them. If they knew how you did your tricks, it would not be worth doing them in the first place, would it?!

9. Tricks do sometimes go wrong. It happens to the best of us. Sometimes you will be able to disguise your embarrassment because you very seldom tell an audience what you are going to do until you have done it! If it is not possible, the best policy is to laugh it off and go on to your next trick. Try not to be thrown off your stride by the problem. Find out what went wrong and, at your first opportunity, get in some more practice so that you do not make the same mistake again.

10. Smile! Do not take your newly found skill as a wonderworker too seriously. You will not be entertaining if you do. Nobody likes a smart alec.

My sincere wish in writing these books is to encourage new talent so if, after reading this book, you feel that you would like to progress further, the following notes will be most helpful.

MAGIC CLUBS AND SOCIETIES

Unlike other branches of the entertainment world, magicians seek one another's company and revel in the exchange of ideas. You would do well to join a club (most large towns have one). Space prevents me from mentioning all of them here. These are the main ones:

International Brotherhood of Magicians
Headquarters
P.O. Box 192090
St. Louis
MO 63119-9998
U.S.A.

The Magic Circle
The Players Theatre
Villiers Street
The Strand
London, U.K.
WC2 6NG

For details write to:
Christopher Pratt, Secretary of The Magic Circle,
13 Calder Avenue, Brookmans Park, Herts, U.K.,
AL9 7AH

The Society of American Magicians
Write to:
John Apperson
S.A.M. Membership Development
2812 Idaho
Granite City
Illinois 62040
U.S.A.

Society of Young Magicians
P.O. Box 375
Nashua
NH 03061
U.S.A.

MAGIC MAGAZINES

These keep you up-to-date with the latest news from the world of magic and are essential reading for serious magicians.

Abracadabra (weekly)
Goodliffe Publications Ltd
150 New Road
Bromsgrove
Worcestershire, U.K.
B60 2LG

Magic (monthly)
Stan Allen & Associates
7380 South Eastern Avenue
Suite 124-179,
Las Vegas
NV 89123
U.S.A.

Genii (monthly)
P.O. Box 36068
Los Angeles
CA 90036
U.S.A.

MAGIC SUPPLIERS

There are many specialist shops around the world which supply the magical fraternity with apparatus and books that are not otherwise available. They all produce catalogues. I list a few below.

Magic, Inc.
5082 North Lincoln Avenue
Chicago
IL 60625
U.S.A.

Magic Center
739 Eighth Avenue
New York
NY 10036
U.S.A.

Stevens Magic Emporium
3238 E. Douglas
Wichita
KS 67208
U.S.A.

Louis Tannen, Inc.
6 West 32nd Street
4th Floor
New York
N.Y. 10001
U.S.A.

Jeff Busby Magic, Inc.
The Barnard Building
612 Cedar Street
Wallace
Idaho 83873-2233
U.S.A.

If you have enjoyed reading and performing the tricks in this book, you will like its companion volume – *The Amazing Book of Card Tricks* too. It starts by teaching you some simple principles using just an ordinary deck of cards. Then *The Amazing Book of Card Tricks* presents you with two dozen superb tricks that will astound your friends. Each trick has been chosen to enable you, with a little practice, to build up a reputation as somebody not to play cards with!